The Civil War in Pennsylvania

To my children Dylan and Madison,
without whom there would be no future.
~M.K.

In memory of my parents, Bernard and Evelyn Neville.
~D.N.

To my Dad, a highly decorated WWII Marine who taught me
my love of country, and my Mom who had the Civil War
ancestors, and to my son Kasey and his wife Erica, who mean
everything to me; and to my wife and best friend Pam,
who was always behind me; and my other best friend CCI
assistance dog Aragon, who was always at my foot.
~K.T.

THE CIVIL WAR IN PENNSYLVANIA

★★★

A PHOTOGRAPHIC HISTORY

Michael G. Kraus, David M. Neville, and Kenneth C. Turner

Copyright © 2012 Pennsylvania Heritage Foundation

PUBLISHED BY THE SENATOR JOHN HEINZ HISTORY CENTER FOR PENNSYLVANIA CIVIL WAR 150,
a collaboration with the Pennsylvania Historical and Museum Commission

1212 Smallman Street
Pittsburgh, PA 15222
www.heinzhistorycenter.org

All rights reserved, including the right to reproduce this book or portions thereof in any form or by any means, electronic or mechanical, including photocopying, recording, or by any information storage and retrieval system, without permission in writing from the publisher.

Printed in USA

10 9 8 7 6 5 4 3 2 1

FIRST EDITION

Project Manager and Editor: Brian Butko
Assistant Editor: Kelly Anderson Gregg
Designer: Pammy Pieretti, PARK Creative Design

PREVIOUS PAGE
Unknown Drummer A drummer of the 6th Pennsylvania Heavy Artillery poses in an idealized camp scene. The large cannonball was appropriated as a prop to enhance the image. *Kraus/Messick Collection.*

Library of Congress Cataloging-in-Publication Data

Kraus, Michael G.

The Civil War in Pennsylvania : a photographic history / Michael G. Kraus, David M. Neville, and Kenneth C. Turner.

 p. cm.

Includes bibliographical references and index.

ISBN 978-0-936340-19-7

1. Pennsylvania–History–Civil War, 1861-1865–Pictorial works. 2. Pennsylvania–History–Civil War, 1861-1865–Social aspects–Pictorial works. 3. United States–History–Civil War, 1861-1865–Pictorial works. 4. United States–History–Civil War, 1861-1865—Social aspects–Pictorial works. I. Neville, David M. II. Turner, Kenneth C. III. Title.

E527.K73 2012

974.8'030222–dc23

 2012022116

Contents

Foreword **7**

Introduction **9**

1 — **From Frontier colony to the Threshold of War**................... **12**
A Resourceful Colony
Pennsylvania Confronts Slavery
Politics
Pennsylvania Militia
Call for Volunteers

2 — **1862: War** **54**
Photography of the 19th Century
Uniforms
Camp
Immigrants Fighting for Their Adopted Country
Chaplains
Music
Pennsylvania's Battle Flags
Arsenals/Technology
The United States Marine Corps
The United States Navy
Campaigns of 1862

3 — **1863: Defending the State**.. **142**
Prelude to Gettysburg
Battle of Gettysburg: July 1, 1863
Battle of Gettysburg: July 2, 1863
Gettysburg: July 3, 1863
Kentucky Cavalrymen Incite Panic
Military Hospitals
Western Theater of Operations
Chattanooga Campaign: October 1863
Badges of Circles, Clovers, Diamonds, and More

4 — 1864: Emancipation 208
Rise of the United States Colored Troops
Help from the Home Front – United States Sanitary Commission
United States Christian Commission
Money and Politics
Veteran Volunteers
Keystone Men for Dixie
Fighting On
Hell on Earth for Prisoners of War

5 — Aftermath 250
Industrial Might
Last to Be Counted
Medal of Honor
Medals from Within
Lincoln Assassination
Fraternity Among Veterans
Medals of the Grand Army of the Republic
The Women's Relief Corps
Battlefield as Monument
1913: 50th Anniversary
1938: 75th Anniversary

Bibliography 294

About Pennsylvania Civil War 150 298

Acknowledgments 302

Index 304

FOREWORD

The 150th anniversaries of the American Civil War and Emancipation offer us a great opportunity and a great challenge. More than at any time since those momentous events, we have a chance to see them fully and clearly.

When veterans first met to commemorate the war in the decades following the conflict, they bore the physical and mental scars from their many battles along with the medals they wore with such pride. The 50th reunion at Gettysburg in 1913, in particular, demonstrated the country's desire to remember the war without opening old wounds. Slavery, the fundamental cause of the war, was glossed over in the nation's memory. Most African Americans present at the reunion were there as laborers, even though some 200,000 had served alongside whites on land and at sea. Woodrow Wilson, the first Southern president since the Confederacy's surrender, promoted the mythology embodied in works such as *Birth of a Nation*.

National memory at the 100th anniversary celebrations was just as impaired. While blacks now served as commissioners on various commemoration boards in 1963, they were not allowed to sleep in the same Charleston, South Carolina, hotels as their white counterparts. Jim Crow laws, racial prejudice, and a desire to present a united front in the Cold War meant that slavery was again downplayed as the main reason that America went to war with itself. Although the wounded and widowed were no longer living a century after the war's end, the scars on the nation's consciousness still ran deep. Many Americans continued to be divided along geographic and racial lines, and violence still flared along those boundaries.

As we look to the 150th anniversary of the Civil War and the freedom it brought, we must redraw the historical picture once more, more fully and more accurately. Divorced from the strong emotions which influenced previous commemorations, we now include the many voices that have been silent for so long. Generals and soldiers, African American troops and freedom seekers, volunteer nurses and enterprising women—on the following pages, all now are given the chance to tell their stories. Seeing and listening to them, we can gain a better understanding of our history and thus of our future as well.

~ Edward L. Ayers
Author of *In the Presence of Mine Enemies: Civil War in the Heart of America*
President, University of Richmond

Death on Pennsylvanian Soil Alexander Gardner, whose photographic wagon can be seen in back, recorded views at Gettysburg starting on July 5. These Confederate soldiers fell near the Rose Farm on July 2. Due to the extreme heat, battle dead from both sides were hastily interred. Samuel Weaver supervised the exhumation of 3,512 Union bodies from the battlefield, much of the labor performed by local African American men. Weaver carefully examined the remains of bodies for identification before they were reburied in the Soldiers National Cemetery. Union soldiers were laid to rest by state in graves arranged in a semi-circle; Confederate soldiers usually remained in shallow graves near where they fell. *Library of Congress, cwpb-00882.*

INTRODUCTION

by Andrew E. Masich

CHAIRMAN, PENNSYLVANIA HISTORICAL AND MUSEUM COMMISSION,
PRESIDENT AND CHIEF EXECUTIVE OFFICER OF THE
SENATOR JOHN HEINZ HISTORY CENTER

On October 20, 1862, just a month after the Battle of Antietam—the deadliest single day in American history—*The New York Times* reported on the new photographic images that at once captivated and horrified civilians on the Civil War's home front:

> Mr. Brady has done something to bring home to us the terrible reality and earnestness of war. If he has not brought bodies and laid them in our dooryards and along the streets, he has done something very like it.

Then, as now, photographic images as well as paintings, engravings, and artifacts connect us with people and events we yearn to know better. They have the power to engage our visual sense and provide understanding in ways that escape even the most gifted writer. This photographic and pictorial history of the Civil War in Pennsylvania is intended to offer new insights into a war that changed our nation and a way of life that is now gone, save for the memories imprinted in silvered glass, collodian-coated iron, and nitrated paper. Many of these rare images have never been published. Authors Michael Kraus, David Neville, and Ken Turner have combed archives, museums, and most of all, private collections to find pictures, both famous and forgotten, that help us piece together the visual history of Civil War Pennsylvania. Turner's personal collection can be found on most every page of this book, showing a level of devotion to the subject unmatched in the commonwealth.

The "Keystone State" shared the Mason-Dixon line with the Southern Confederacy and so served as the bulwark of the Union, bearing the brunt of Robert E. Lee's 1863 invasion that resulted in the Gettysburg campaign and the greatest battle ever fought in the Americas. Pennsylvania was also the breadbasket and arsenal of the Union, its farms and industrial might sustaining the largest armies the continent had ever seen. The Union's armies and navy comprised hundreds of thousands of Pennsylvania men, forming regiments of infantry, cavalry, and artillery as well as sailors and merchant seamen—supplying more manpower, in fact, than any state except for New York, the most populous state in the Union. African American men sprang to the call early in the war but not until 1863 did their numbers and passion for the cause of freedom—their freedom—make a significant difference on the muster rolls of Union regiments. Women and children also served, in arsenals, workshops, hospitals, farms, schools, and Sanitary Commission fairs. Wives and mothers carried on the work of the farm, home, and family that did not stop or wait for war.

It is appropriate that on the occasion of the 150th anniversary of the Civil War, a visual record of Pennsylvania's people be compiled and offered in a single, readable, and accessible volume. It is for this reason that a consortium of Pennsylvania's historical organizations collaborated on this effort, pooling staff and resources, and commissioning diligent researchers and scholars to ferret out the most compelling (yet, in some cases, the least-known) images that could tell the story of the Civil War in Pennsylvania.

This book is organized chronologically and thematically, beginning with pre-war Pennsylvania. The colony, then commonwealth, grappled with slavery—the root cause of the Civil War—and became a hub of the Underground Railroad. Photography came of age in the decade preceding the conflict, and the new art form was transformed into a communication tool of the first order as the war progressed. While the military photographed maps, uniforms, and equipage, news services used photos as the basis for woodcuts and newspaper illustrations. Soldiers sent photographic keepsakes home and families reciprocated with images cherished by their men in the field or at sea.

The Civil War in Pennsylvania also attempts to represent the war in art and artifacts—paintings, broadsides, sketches, weapons, uniforms, medals, and personal effects—as well as photographs. Rare photographic images of United States Colored Troops (U.S.C.T.) are seen as are photographs of Pennsylvania men who fought for the Confederacy. The home front is pictured too, from the work of the volunteer Christian Commission to factory workers manufacturing war materiel. Images of the war's aftermath document attempts to memorialize, and remember—or, in some cases, forget—the war. In all, nearly 500 images help tell the story of the conflict and the people who were part of it, at home, at work, or in battle.

This book is intended to complement other publications and programs initiated by the Pennsylvania Civil War 150 consortium including museum exhibitions, a comprehensive digital database of photographs and archival materials, and a collaborative website that allows for sharing Civil War genealogical information, book reviews, and a calendar of events hosted by nearly 100 museums, educational institutions, and cultural organizations across the state.

First Defenders This rare image is the earliest known photograph of Pennsylvania troops deployed during the Civil War. Pennsylvania's First Defenders led the Union in rushing troops to Washington, D.C., in the wake of the firing on Fort Sumter, April 12, 1861. On April 21, the Ringgold Light Artillery of Reading, Berks County, posed for this photo at the Washington Navy Yard. Commanding the yard was Philadelphia born Captain John A. Dahlgren (USN) who was appointed by President Lincoln. By 1863 Dahlgren had become an admiral, renowned for his tactical ability and innovative advancements in cannon design (see page 125).
Ken Turner Collection.

Gettysburg will almost certainly be the place that millions of Americans seek out during the sesquicentennial observances. The passage of 150 years has not extinguished the memory of the struggle of July 1–3, 1863, that resulted in more than 50,000 casualties, including nearly 8,000 killed in combat or who later died from wounds received in action. These men of the North and South, representing very different ideologies—Union and Confederate—were Americans all. It was on Pennsylvania soil, too, that Abraham Lincoln memorialized those "brave men, living and dead, who struggled here." In his November 19, 1863, dedication speech for the new national cemetery, he articulated most clearly the meaning and importance of the conflict and the great sacrifice. The Gettysburg Address, considered by many historians to be the greatest speech ever uttered by an American president, succinctly reaffirmed the principle upon which the democratic republic of the United States was founded: "All men are created equal." The battle and the war, he said, provided the United States with "a new birth of freedom."

Lincoln's words reminded the people of the nation that the war was about freedom for all Americans. It is altogether fitting and proper that, on this the 150th anniversary of the Civil War that forever changed and reunited our nation, we commemorate the occasion with *The Civil War in Pennsylvania: A Photographic History* so that future generations may *see* their forebears, take inspiration from those who have gone before, and endeavor to build the nation "of the people, by the people, and for the people" for which they, with devotion and sacrifice, laid the foundation.

An Engineering Marvel The Allegheny Mountains had long been a barrier to settling the interior of North America. Canals created a transportation revolution, breaching the ridges and connecting east and west. Pennsylvanians dug 1,356 miles of canals, the most of any state, though railroads would supplant canals within a few decades. Here, canal boats on the Erie Extension Canal near Sharon, Mercer County, await their cargo of coal. *Albumen Print, Ken Turner Collection.*

Ch. 1

FROM FRONTIER COLONY TO THE THRESHOLD *of* WAR

In the 1680s, Pennsylvania—"Penn's Woods"—was a land of natural abundance. Forests and fertile soil blanketed stores of rich minerals. Rivers traversed the land, supporting wildlife and nations of indigenous peoples. William Penn's followers arrived to astonishing potential, a new home offering religious freedom and opportunity.

Over the next century, Pennsylvanians joined the fight for independence from Britain and lent great minds to the formation of a new nation. Their colony molded its own statehood and provided the first home for the nation's capitol. After the Revolution, the commonwealth's eastern region blossomed with centers of education, business, and culture; its western territory became a jumping off point to the frontier.

PENNSYLVANIA SENT SOME 337,963 MEN TO
PRESERVE THE UNION
33,183 WOULD PERISH IN THIS CONFLICT

FROM FRONTIER COLONY TO THE THRESHOLD OF WAR

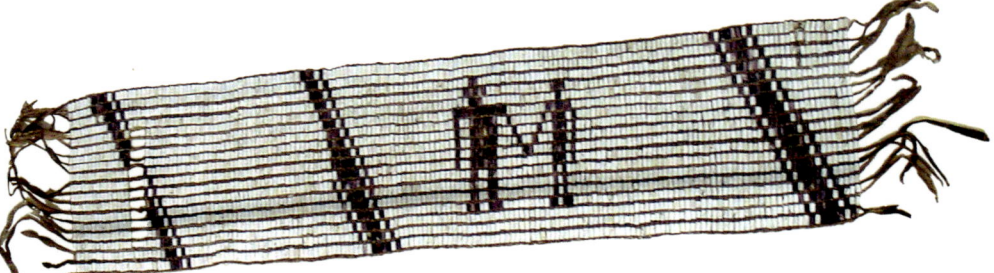

Farms, waterways, coal, and oil launched industries and drew workers. Bustling cities also became home to free-born and formerly enslaved blacks who pursued education, unskilled work, and occasional apprenticeships. Waves of immigrants arrived to work in coal mines, textile mills, shipbuilding yards, and ironworks that, before long, would furnish half the nation's iron.

ABOVE
William Penn A royal charter in 1681 granted land in British America to William Penn as settlement for a loan his father had made to King Charles II. As a Quaker, he encouraged fellow believers to settle the colony, which promised religious freedom. Penn, for whom Pennsylvania was named, was an early proponent of uniting the colonies.
Carte-de-visite, Kraus/Messick Collection.

ABOVE RIGHT
Wampum Belt of Peace Unity between the Lenni-Lenape people (also called the Delaware) and the colonists of Pennsylvania is symbolized by the clasped hands of a Delaware chief and a Quaker man, woven into this shell-bead belt. Although no copy of the 1682 agreement survives, the Treaty Wampum serves as evidence of William Penn's goodwill to the natives of the Delaware Valley.
Atwater Kent Museum of Philadelphia, Historical Society of Pennsylvania Collection, HSP.1857.3.

CHAPTER 1

PITTSBURG, FROM THE NORTHWEST.

This view was taken from the hill behind Sligo. In the foreground are seen a glass-house and dwellings of manufacturers. On the right is the Monongahela bridge, the Steamboat landing, and the Monongahela House, near the end of the bridge. To the left of that is the cupola of the University, and farther to the left, on high ground, the new Court House and Cathedral, with the spire of the Presbyterian Church between them. On the left is the Allegheny river, with several bridges leading to Allegheny town: the second bridge sustains the acqueduct of the canal. Beyond these bridges are seen Bayard's town and Lawrenceville.

ABOVE
Steamboats Open the Frontier With the inaugural voyage of the steamboat *New Orleans*, which departed Pittsburgh in 1811, Lancaster County native Robert Fulton launched commercial steamboat travel on western rivers. Capable of powering against the current, steamboats enabled swift travel up and down the Ohio and Mississippi rivers. Many Pittsburgh-built vessels would serve as troop transport and gunboats during the Civil War, providing a strategic advantage to the Union. In this 1843 wood engraving, steamboats line Pittsburgh's Monongahela River wharf.
Historical Collections of the State of Pennsylvania, 1843, Kraus/Messick Collection.

OPPOSITE
Chestnut Street, Philadelphia Shop owners pose in their doorways for one of the earliest known outdoor photographs taken in Pennsylvania. On June 17, 1843, Philadelphia amateur daguerreotypist William Mason recorded this image of houses 46–52 on the south side of Chestnut Street, just west of Second Street. *Library of Congress, USZC4-9389.*

RIGHT

Philadelphia Ladies These well-to-do women of the early 1860s pose with personal items from a narrowly defined lifestyle in which women were typically engaged in domestic and artistic endeavors.
Carte-de-visite, Kraus/Messick Collection.

BELOW

Memorial Daguerreotype Early childhood mortality was a grim fact of life in 19th-century America. Photography provided a means to memorialize dead children. This c. 1855 image captures four generations of a Pennsylvania family posing reflectively as the grandmother displays the deceased infant.
1/6th plate Daguerreotype, Kraus/Messick Collection.

CHAPTER 1

Small Town Life Mercer, the county seat of Mercer County, c. 1860. *Ken Turner Collection.*

Pennsylvania provided the first home for the nation's capital.

— 17 —

FROM FRONTIER COLONY TO THE THRESHOLD OF WAR

ABOVE

***View Along the Allegheny Near Aspinwall Pa.* by William Coventry Wall, 1867.** Agriculture was and is the leading industry of Pennsylvania. This painting from just after the war looks across the verdant Allegheny River Valley from Sharpsburg to Aspinwall, about three miles upriver from the Allegheny Arsenal in Lawrenceville. Today this vista is crossed by the Highland Park Bridge. *Westmoreland Museum of American Art, gift of Jack and Suzanne Shilling and family.*

RIGHT

Liquid Asset On August 28, 1859, Edwin Drake struck oil in Venango County near Titusville, launching a "black gold" boom in northwest Pennsylvania. This group, most likely investors, pose on a storage tank of the Leroy Well while two men stand atop its derrick. *Library of Congress, 1s01748.*

Oil Skimmers Barefoot children rest while working along the bank of Oil Creek, named for the percolating oil springs beneath its surface. Although the practice of skimming oil was known early in the century, the success of the 1859 Titusville Well created a boom market for petroleum and kerosene. The grimy, tedious work performed by these children provided meager revenue to their impoverished families.

Pennsylvania State Archives, MG-219 Philadelphia Commercial Museum Collection, Industry, Petroleum, #3792.

CHAPTER 1

As war loomed, Keystone State businessmen with ties to cotton, raw materials, and transportation hesitated to break commercial relations with the South. With the Confederate firing on Fort Sumter in April 1861, however, sympathies for the South largely evaporated. Though some citizens remained ambivalent to enlistment, Pennsylvanians from diverse backgrounds rushed to join the Northern army that would punish the South for dissolving the Union. Recent immigrants from Ireland and Germany would march alongside one another, commanded by men whose ancestors had arrived on the Mayflower. Two years later, they would be joined by black men in blue uniforms.

ABOVE
Mule Boys Good horses and mules were appropriated for the war, leaving substandard animals for everyday use. These boys are leading their mule through Schuylkill Haven, Schuylkill County, about 90 miles west of Philadelphia. *Carte-de-visite, Kraus/Messick Collection.*

ABOVE
A Shared Look Two young women from Myerstown, Lebanon County, wear identical dresses for their portraits. Identified only as Sarah and Malinda, they are typical of residents who patronized small town photography studios throughout the commonwealth. *Carte-de-visite, Kraus/Messick Collection.*

ABOVE
Quaker Girl This Frankford, Philadelphia County, girl's distinctive shawl and bonnet identify her as a member of the Religious Society of Friends, or Quakers. The Friends' charitable contributions include the establishment of Frankford's Asylum for Persons Deprived of the Use of Their Reason—the country's first hospital for the treatment of mental illness, founded in 1813.

Carte-de-visite, Kraus/Messick Collection.

ABOVE
Market Day in Carlisle, 1860 Carlisle, Cumberland County, was the scene of an 1847 riot involving runaway slaves, but on this day, a year before the War of the Rebellion broke out, the outdoor market is quiet. The photo was snapped by Carlisle photographer Charles Lochman. *Library of Congress, 1s01540.*

CHAPTER 1

ABOVE

Working Children Children in the 19th century often worked dangerous, unskilled jobs. The Myers boys labored at the Sligo Iron Works (also known as Lyon, Shorb & Company) across the Monongahela River from downtown Pittsburgh. Martin Myers, Jr., was a "pull-up boy" whose job was to raise the puddling furnace door. P. Myers, an assistant "bundler" or "shearer," may have trimmed iron sheets to size. Most of the 282 carte-de-visite photographs in this company album from the mid-1860s were made by Robert M. Cargo, Pittsburgh's best-known early photographer.

HHC L&A, Lyon, Shorb & Company Photographs, PSS 6.

ABOVE

Knife Sharpeners A portable grinding stone and ragged aprons tell of the strenuous itinerant lifestyle endured by these boys, who are smoking clay pipes.

Carte-de-visite, Kraus/Messick Collection.

Steam Engines, Iron Rails Steam-powered trains played a major role in the Civil War, moving troops and supplies to battle. By 1860, some 2,400 miles of track covered Pennsylvania. Manufacturers like Norris and Sons and Baldwin Locomotive Works of Philadelphia built hundreds of engines. This view shows Locomotive Number 146, which ran on the Pennsylvania Railroad during the Civil War. *Library of Congress, 1s01565.*

CHAPTER 1

Pennsylvania Confronts Slavery

For the past 150 years, Americans have associated ownership of slaves with the South, and opposition to human bondage with the North. In truth, slaves were owned in every colony and state, including Pennsylvania, where the arrival of slaves in the Delaware River Valley began as early as 1639. By the 1680s, Philadelphia was the state's chief entry point for the importation of slaves.

Pennsylvania utilized slave labor not only for construction, field work, and domestic service, but also for assistance in the skilled trades of its rapidly growing economy. African Americans worked alongside whites in industries as diverse as sail-making and iron-forging.

The 1860 census enumerated the white and free colored populations in Pennsylvania. Most blacks were in urban areas, as can be seen by the numbers from Pittsburgh, Harrisburg, and Philadelphia (county and city were counted as the same). Added here is the percent of free colored in the total population.

	White Population	Free Colored Population	%
Philadelphia	543,344	22,185	3.9
Pittsburgh	48,063	1,154	2.3
Allegheny County	176,106	2,725	1.5
Harrisburg	12,084	1,321	9.9
Dauphin County	45,047	1,709	3.6
Erie	9,318	101	1.1
Erie County	49,251	181	.36
Potter County	11,455	15	.13

An Act for the Gradual Abolition of Slavery, 1780 Pennsylvania's 1780 Act of Gradual Abolition prohibited the importation of slaves and required that children of slaves born after March 1, 1780, be freed once they reached age 28. Those enslaved before the law went into effect remained enslaved for life. (A subsequent act of the Pennsylvania legislature in 1847 freed all slaves.)
Pennsylvania State Archives, RG-26 Records of the Dept. of State, Engrossed Laws.

FROM FRONTIER COLONY TO THE THRESHOLD OF WAR

RESCUE OF JANE JOHNSON AND HER CHILDREN.

JANE JOHNSON.

ABOVE AND LEFT

Abduction or rescue? In 1855, the assisted escape of Jane Johnson in Philadelphia precipitated a national debate of the Fugitive Slave Law of 1850. Accompanying her master, diplomat John Hill Wheeler, on a trip that included a stop in Pennsylvania, Johnson sent out word of her wish to flee. Members of the Underground Railroad daringly took Johnson from her owner, escorting the enslaved woman and her two sons to freedom. *Both John L. Ford Collection.*

RIGHT

Freed by the Woman He Rescued Unlike the black participants, who were denied due process, Passmore Williamson, a leader of the Pennsylvania Anti-Slavery Society, stood trial for kidnapping Jane Johnson. Emerging from hiding, Johnson risked capture to testify she had left her master voluntarily. *Chester County Historical Society, West Chester, Pa.*

CHAPTER 1

CHAPTER 1

Resistance to slavery emerged early in Pennsylvania's history among Quakers and enslaved Africans. The Germantown Quaker Petition against Slavery appeared as early as 1688. Slave importation was banned in 1767. In the following decade, many slaves earned their freedom fighting alongside colonists in the Revolutionary War. In 1780, the state legislature passed An Act for the Gradual Abolition of Slavery, limiting bondage of slave children born after 1780 to 28 years. In opposition to the federal Fugitive Slave Act of 1850, Pennsylvania would write its own legislation extending freedom and protection to escaped slaves from the South.

ABOVE

Abolitionist Jane Swisshelm Born in Pittsburgh, Jane Grey Cannon married James Swisshelm and moved to Kentucky where she witnessed the unforgettable conditions of human slavery. Upon returning to Pittsburgh, Swisshelm penned anti-slavery articles for several abolitionist newspapers and founded the *Pittsburgh Saturday Visiter*, the most widely circulated reform paper in the country. Swisshelm, photographed c. 1880, also became an early proponent of women's rights. *HHC L&A, GPC Individuals.*

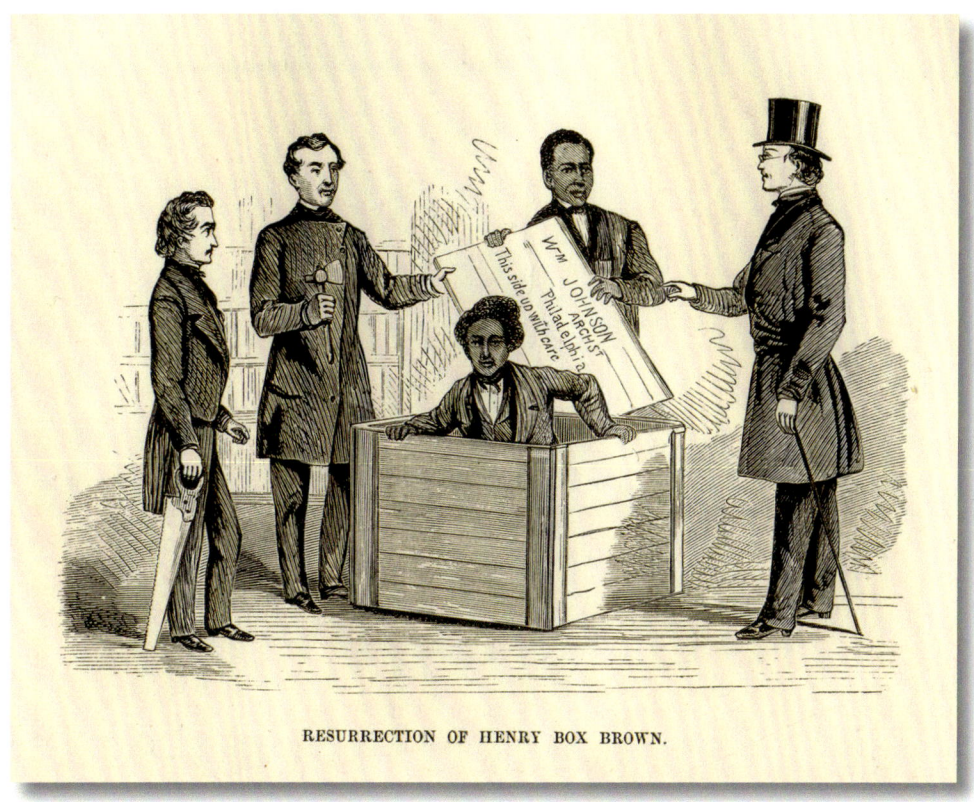

LEFT

Henry "Box" Brown Of the hundreds of documented escapes from slavery, the one achieved by Henry Brown was simple and ingenious. After his wife and children were sold to a slave trader, Brown devised a plan to reunite his family. With the aid of two sympathetic white shopkeepers, Brown was concealed inside a crate and shipped to a Philadelphia abolitionist. After a journey of 27 hours, Brown's first words upon emerging from the crate were, "How do you do, gentlemen?" *John L. Ford Collection.*

OPPOSITE

A Free Black Man This c. 1860 portrait was obtained from one of Beaver County's first African American families, but the identity of the subject remains unknown. *Kraus/Messick Collection.*

FROM FRONTIER COLONY TO THE THRESHOLD OF WAR

As a result of the growing free black population centered in Philadelphia in the late 1700s and early 1800s, black abolition organizations sprang up, among them the Free African Society and the Philadelphia Colored Female Free Produce Society, which boycotted items produced by slave labor.

Between 1863 and 1865, Pennsylvania raised several regiments of black soldiers who picked up arms in defense of the Union. Although sharply divided views and conflicting political interests existed in Pennsylvania during the war and for decades afterward, white and black leaders continued to exert pressure on state and national government to procure equal rights for blacks.

ABOVE
Servant Girl This African American girl, who worked for a white family in Pittsburgh, poses with her employer's child, for whom she was likely the primary caretaker.
Ken Turner Collection.

RIGHT
Henry A timely irony exists in this 1862 photo of Henry, a janitor at Dickinson College in Carlisle. Henry poses beside a globe and a flame-illuminated projector known as a Magic Lantern, but his work tools (a coal bucket, broom, and key ring) remind us that Henry's entrance into classrooms was permitted only for the purposes of cleaning and maintenance.
Library of Congress, 2s01462.

CHAPTER 1

Outspoken Opponent In 1824, nine-year-old Henry Highland Garnet and his slave family escaped from Maryland for Pennsylvania. After obtaining a higher education in New York, Garnet dedicated himself to the abolitionist movement, giving inflammatory speeches that called for black resistance at any cost. This image of Garnet comes from *Distinguished Colored Men*, a c. 1883 chromolithograph. *Library of Congress, pga-02252.*

A DARING ESCAPE

Although she could pass for white, Ellen Craft was raised in bondage, the illegitimate daughter of a slave mother and white master. The intrepid woman and her slave husband, William Craft, escaped in disguise as a Southern gentleman (despite being a woman) traveling with a black male servant. Their dangerous eight-day journey ended successfully with the couple's safe arrival in Philadelphia on Christmas Day, 1848.

John L. Ford Collection.

FROM FRONTIER COLONY TO THE THRESHOLD OF WAR

"His zeal in the cause of freedom was infinitely superior to mine.... I could live for the slave; John Brown could die for him."

~ Frederick Douglass

ABOVE
Frederick Douglass On August 30, 1859, two of America's leading abolitionists, Frederick Douglass and John Brown, met in a stone quarry near Chambersburg, Franklin County. Brown revealed his plan to attack the U.S. armory in Harpers Ferry, Virginia, in order to seize firearms for a slave uprising. He asked Douglass to accompany him and his followers on the raid, but the prominent African American leader declined. *Ken Turner Collection.*

FAR RIGHT
John Brown From 1826 to 1835, Brown lived at New Richmond near Meadville in Crawford County where he operated a tannery. Familiar with the state, the radical abolitionist chose the rural community of Chambersburg, just north of the Mason-Dixon line, as a staging point for his Harpers Ferry raid. On October 16, 1859, Brown and his followers attacked the U.S. armory. The mission ended in disaster—all of Brown's men were killed, wounded, or captured by federal troops. Brown was convicted of treason and hanged at Charlestown, Virginia, on December 2, 1859, making him a martyr in the cause for ending slavery. Brown is pictured here c. 1856, before growing his trademark beard.
Ken Turner Collection.

LEFT
Brown's Pike This pike, ordered by John Brown to arm slaves during his planned revolt at Harper's Ferry, was numbered "149" and reputedly taken from the house in Chambersburg where Brown stayed prior to the 1859 raid.
The State Museum of Pennsylvania, Pennsylvania Historical and Museum Commission, 21.7.

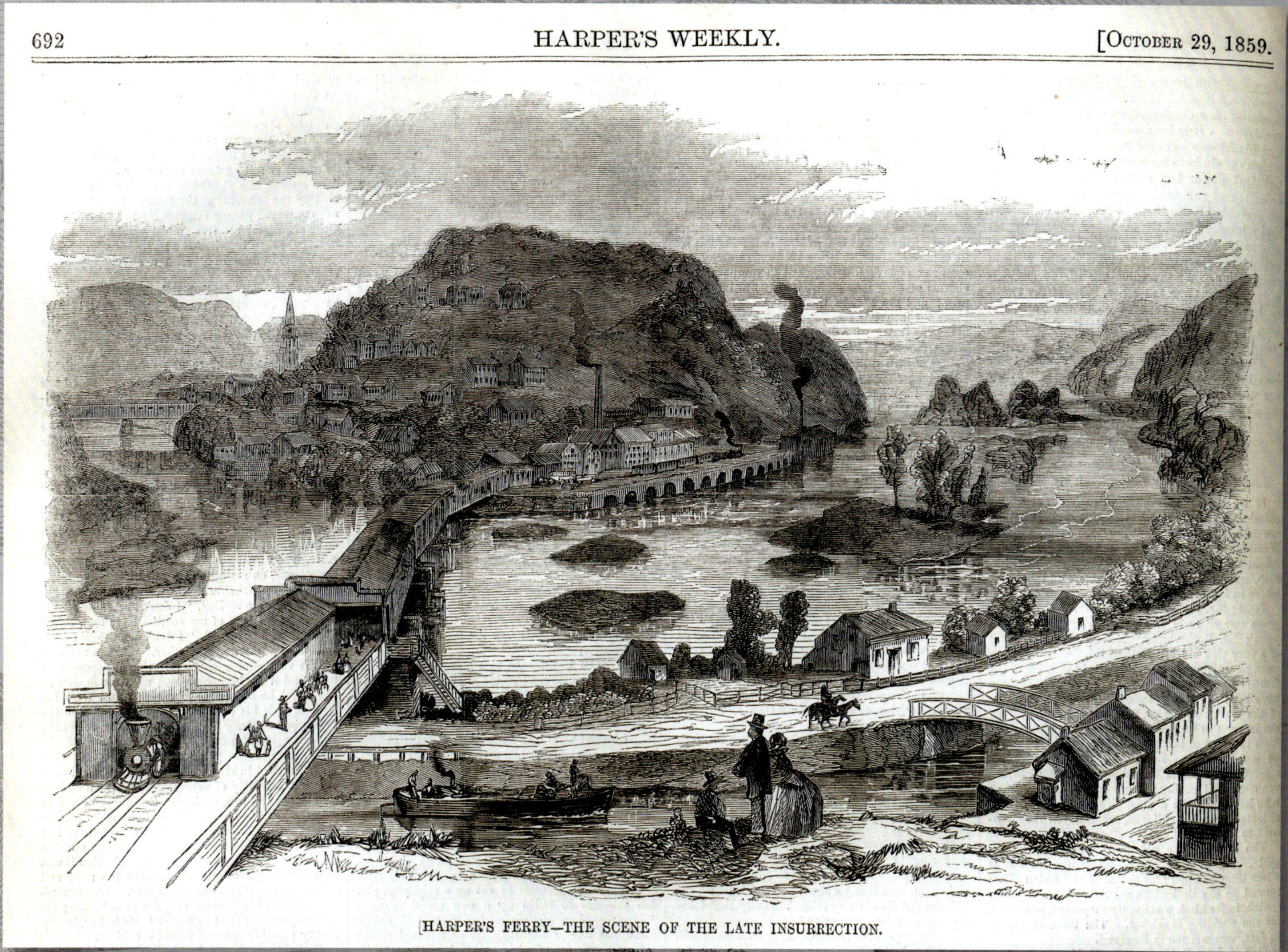

692 HARPER'S WEEKLY. [OCTOBER 29, 1859.

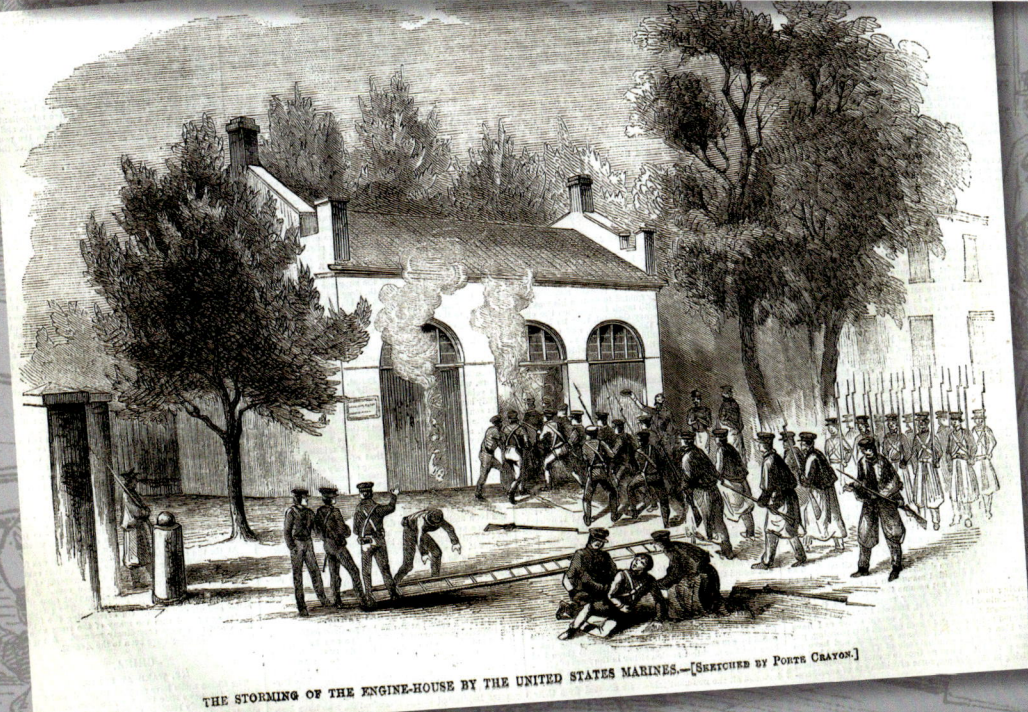

[HARPER'S FERRY—THE SCENE OF THE LATE INSURRECTION.

THE STORMING OF THE ENGINE-HOUSE BY THE UNITED STATES MARINES.—[SKETCHED BY PORTE CRAYON.]

Harper's Weekly Readers of *Harper's Weekly* were hungry for news of John Brown's raid on Harpers Ferry. The news magazine responded with reports and numerous images, including the panorama above and, a week later, a depiction of the military response.
Both Heinz History Center, Library & Archives.

FROM FRONTIER COLONY TO THE THRESHOLD OF WAR

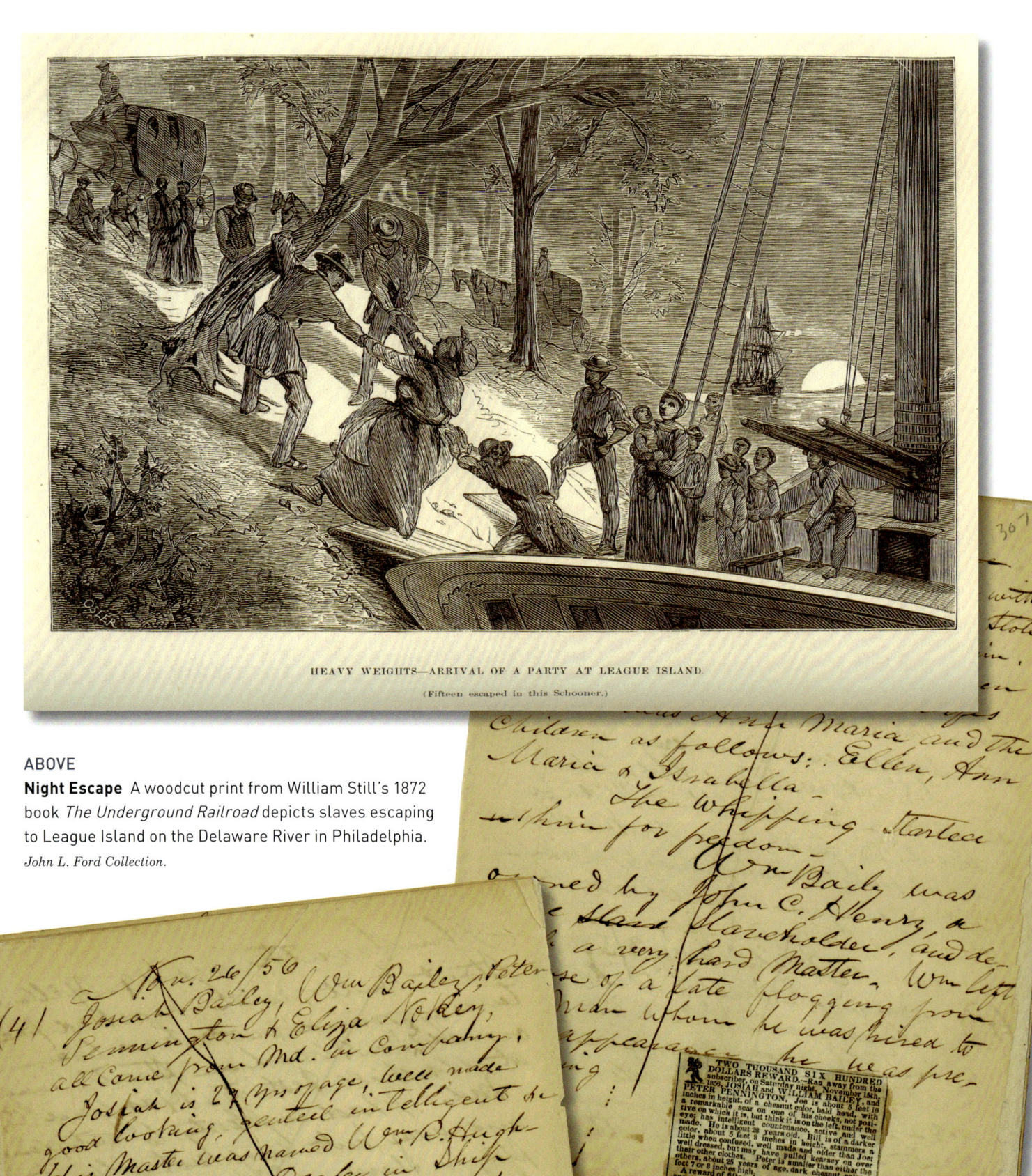

HEAVY WEIGHTS—ARRIVAL OF A PARTY AT LEAGUE ISLAND.
(Fifteen escaped in this Schooner.)

ABOVE
Night Escape A woodcut print from William Still's 1872 book *The Underground Railroad* depicts slaves escaping to League Island on the Delaware River in Philadelphia.
John L. Ford Collection.

CHAPTER 1

William Still and his Book Without William Still's work, hundreds of escaped slaves may never have reached freedom. And if not for his book, *The Underground Railroad*, the authentic voices of those escapees may never have been heard. Still worked diligently as a clerk for the Philadelphia Anti-Slavery Society, recording every interview he conducted with runaways. Of the fugitives Still aided, one revealed himself to be Still's long-lost brother, Peter, who had escaped from Alabama.
Both John L. Ford Collection.

OPPOSITE

William Still Notebooks William Still, known as the Father of the Underground Railroad, kept extensive handwritten notes on each of the 649 escaped slaves that he aided. Pages 306 and 307 for November 26, 1856, are typical, describing the escaped slaves of William Hugh, and include a newspaper ad offering a reward for their return.
Historical Society of Pennsylvania, DAMS 2030, file# 0060_0001_162, 0060_0001_163.

WILLIAM STILL WAS KNOWN AS THE
FATHER *of* THE
UNDERGROUND RAILROAD

Heroine In 1849, young slave Harriet Tubman, born Araminta Ross, walked from her Maryland plantation to freedom in Philadelphia. From her adopted city, Tubman returned to Maryland to rescue her family, one group at a time. Tubman played a strategic role on the Underground Railroad, escorting many groups of slaves to freedom. In addition, the abolitionist provided information about Confederate troop movement to the Union and assisted Colonel James Montgomery's raid at Combahee Ferry, South Carolina, freeing a total of more than 750 slaves. Reporting on the raid to Secretary of War Stanton, Brigadier General Rufus Saxton wrote, "This is the only military command in American history wherein a woman, black or white, led the raid, and under whose inspiration it was originated and conducted."
Library of Congress, 3a10453.

CHAPTER 1

LEFT
Military School This school at 1210 Chestnut Street in Philadelphia offered to teach white soldiers how to command colored troops. From *Philadelphia in the Civil War, 1913.* *Kraus-Messick Collection.*

BELOW
Forgotten Hero Octavius Catto was born free and was educated at the Colored Youth Institute in Philadelphia, where he became a teacher. In the course of his work with Frederick Douglass, Catto fought for the recruitment of black army regiments and became one of the most influential and articulate activists in the country. In October 1871, a year after passage of the 15th Amendment (which guaranteed blacks the right to vote), Catto was shot and killed while walking to his polling place. He was memorialized later that month with this illustration in *Harper's Weekly.*
Library of Congress, 2008677286.

Christiana Riot The 1850 federal Fugitive Slave Act legalized the apprehension of escaped slaves on Northern soil and called for the prosecution of Northerners who blocked their capture. In 1851, Marylander Edward Gorsuch, his adult son, and a U.S. Marshall pursued four escaped slaves to Christiana, Lancaster County, tracking them to the home (above) of a free black, William Parker. The riot that broke out between the fugitives' supporters and the slave owner resulted in Gorsuch's death; Parker and the escapees fled to Canada. Arrests were made but no convictions were ever handed down, fueling widespread anger among slave owners.
Friends Historical Library of Swarthmore College.

Lincoln was so impressed by Delany that he granted him a commission as major.

Staunch Abolitionist Born in Virginia of a slave father and free mother, Martin Delany moved with his family to Pennsylvania to be educated. In 1850, he was one of the first three blacks enrolled at Harvard Medical School, but resigned within a few weeks when white students protested. As an adult, Delany worked tirelessly to free slaves and repatriate blacks to Africa, authoring numerous articles on the subject for his Pittsburgh newspaper, *The Mystery*, and, later, for William Lloyd Garrison's *The Liberator* and Frederick Douglass's *The North Star*.

Most notably, Delany endorsed the recruitment of black soldiers and petitioned Secretary of War Edwin M. Stanton for command of a black regiment. His request ignored, Delany secured a meeting with President Lincoln, who was so impressed that he granted Delany a commission as major in the 104th United States Colored Troops. After the war, Delany worked for blacks' rights as a politician and author.

RG98S-CWP-145.96, The Bill Gladstone Collection at the U.S. Army Military History Institute, Carlisle, Pa.

Pennsylvania's President In March 1861, James Buchanan, the 15th president of the United States and the only national executive from Pennsylvania, left office in disgrace after the secession of seven Southern states. *Library of Congress, 2004664487.*

Politics

In 1856, with its first national meeting convened in Pittsburgh and the national convention assembled in Philadelphia, the newly established Republican Party put down firm roots in Pennsylvania. By 1860, two of the most influential figures in national politics were Republicans from the Keystone State: Senator Simon Cameron from Lancaster and Congressman Thaddeus Stevens from Gettysburg, Adams County. That year, the state elected Republican (and Bellefonte native) Andrew Gregg Curtin as governor. Curtin's support of the party's nominee for president, Abraham Lincoln, was invaluable in assisting the relatively unknown lawyer to carry the state in the national election.

BY 1860 TWO OF THE MOST INFLUENTIAL FIGURES IN POLITICS WERE FROM THE KEYSTONE STATE

During Lincoln's administration, Pennsylvanians continued to wield clout in both houses of Congress—Edgar Cowan and David Wilmot in the Senate, and Galusha Grow and John Covode in the House of Representatives. Simon Cameron was appointed Lincoln's first secretary of war and Thaddeus Stevens became chairman of the House Ways and Means Committee. Meanwhile, the Republican Party platform expanded to include a strong anti-slavery position for Union states, and the party's representatives from Pennsylvania provided the support needed for Lincoln's Emancipation Proclamation, issued in November 1862.

A Secretary of War Resigns An aspirant to the presidency in 1860, Simon Cameron ultimately threw his support behind his party's nominee, Abraham Lincoln, and accepted his rival's offer to join the presidential cabinet as secretary of war. In January 1862, after evidence surfaced of favoritism in the assignment of wartime manufacturing contracts, the president asked Cameron to resign.
Library of Congress, cwp2003000272.

BELOW

A New Secretary of War President Lincoln tapped Edwin McMasters Stanton, a prominent lawyer with strong ties to Pennsylvania, to replace outgoing Secretary of War Simon Cameron. Stanton, who assumed the position on January 20, 1862, masterfully led the War Department to a Union victory. This early 1850s daguerreotype shows Stanton with his son, Edwin Lamson Stanton. *Library of Congress, 2008678327.*

ABOVE

The Great War Governor In his inaugural address on January 15, 1861, newly elected Governor Curtin expressed his opposition to Southern secession and affirmed his support for president-elect Lincoln, calling for "conciliation" between Washington, D.C., and the South. In April, when President Lincoln telegrammed Northern governors for 75,000 volunteers to defend the Union, Curtin was the first state executive to respond. Within days, five companies of Pennsylvania volunteers arrived in Washington, confirming the belief that the "Great War Governor," as Curtin came to be known, would lead Pennsylvania in playing a pivotal role to reunify the country. *Ken Turner Collection.*

CHAPTER 1

Pennsylvania Militia

Ninety years after their formation, the majority of Pennsylvania's scattered local militias—on call in the event of a state emergency and available for federal service—were not trained or equipped to answer a national call to arms. Indeed, most militiamen had never seen battle. In the scramble to create regiments for the rebellion, those with military experience or showing natural leadership qualities would fill the positions of officers. The newly formed regiments would train and, though many would never see battle, their muster sent a message to the Confederacy that the Union would be defended.

ABOVE

James Negley, Brigadier General, Pennsylvania Militia James Negley wears the gray uniform of a brigadier general of the Pennsylvania Militia. A veteran of the Mexican-American War, Negley was given command of the 18th Division in 1861. By November 1862, the Allegheny County native had risen to the rank of major general of volunteers.
Kraus/Messick Collection.

LEFT

Drums of the Militia Throughout military history, drumbeats have kept soldiers in step and signaled a call to arms. These decorated militia drums display the bald eagle from the Great Seal of the United States.

Militia drum, Greenville, Mercer County, c. 1840. Ken Turner Collection.

Militia drum, Lawrence County, c. 1850. Kraus/Messick Collection.

Militia in Formation A company of the Scott Legion—recruited in Philadelphia in April 1861 and composed of Mexican War veterans who had served under General Winfield Scott—poses for a portrait on a rain dampened street. The cap of each soldier displays the state crest, custom-embroidered with metallic thread.
Ken Turner Collection.

CHAPTER 1

LEFT

Sarsfield Rifles An unidentified enlisted man from the militia company known as the Sarsfield Rifles poses for his portrait. Originally organized in Philadelphia in 1858, the mostly immigrant German company was designated as the 1st Brigade, 1st Division of the state militia. In April 1861, the "Rifles" were organized into the 21st Pennsylvania, commanded by Colonel John F. Ballier. Upon reenlistment, the company became part of the 98th Pennsylvania Volunteer Infantry. *Ron Field Collection.*

BELOW

Duquesne Grays William Beal, Jr., was a charter member of the Duquesne Grays, formed in 1831 as part of the Pennsylvania Militia. The Grays fought in the War with Mexico in 1848. At the start of the Civil War they were assigned to Company B of the 12th Pennsylvania Infantry. The Grays produced 69 officers during the war. *Ken Turner Collection.*

CHAPTER 1

OPPOSITE
Antiquated Musket In 1797, Pennsylvania produced 20,000 flintlock muskets patterned after the French model 1763 Charleville. The "CP" stamping identifies this one as property of the Commonwealth of Pennsylvania. Despite being out-of-date, these muskets were the primary arm issued to the militia at the start of the Civil War. *Bill Jacobson Collection.*

BELOW
Infantry Tactics Manual Published in 1836, the *Manual for the Militia* was an essential guide to military know-how. Chapters covered such topics as "Troop Maneuvers on the Field" and "Procedures for Delivering Fire." Illustrations accompanied the often complex text. *Kraus/Messick Collection.*

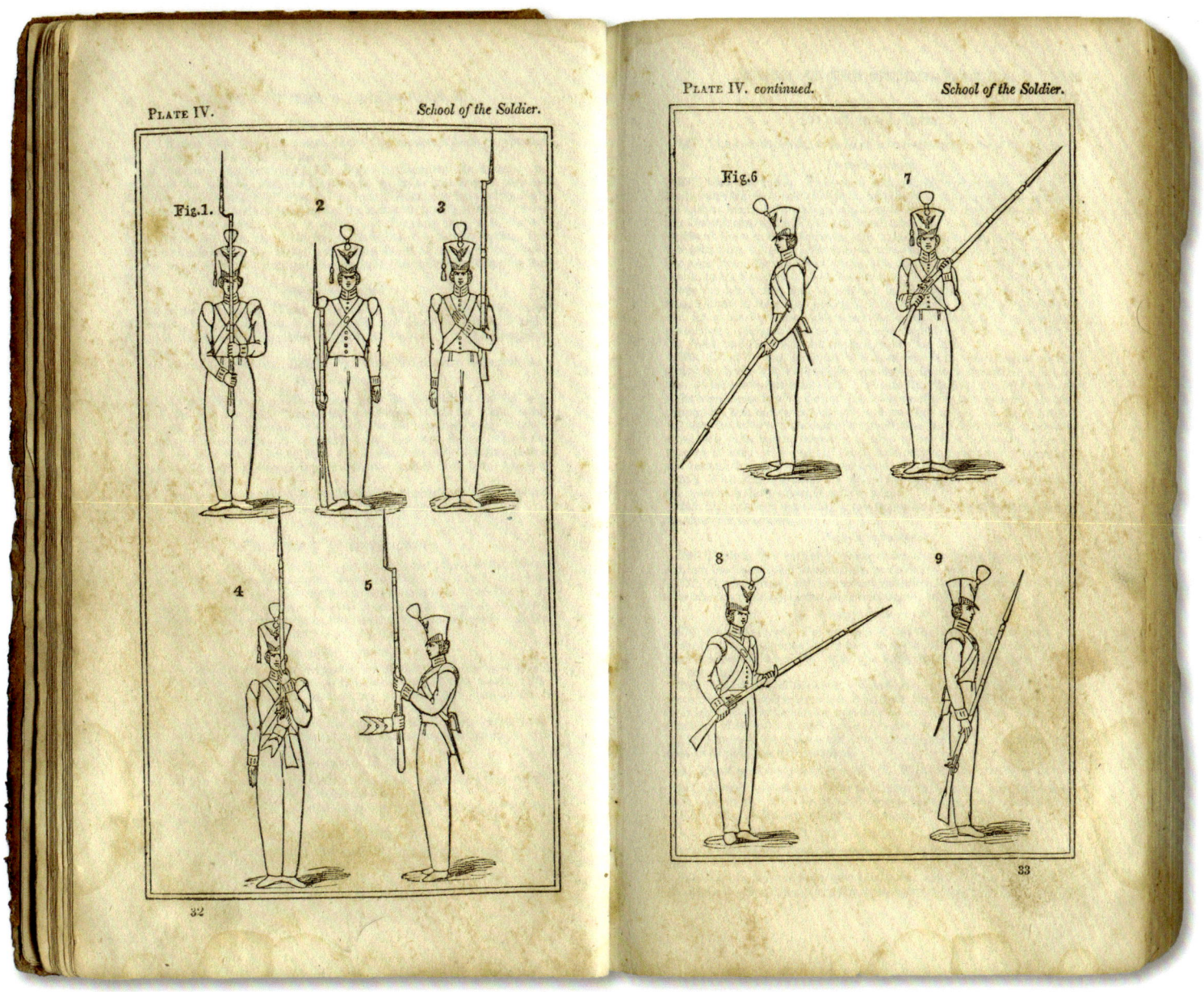

RIGHT

Militia Uniform Uniforms among the Pennsylvania Militia were as individual as the soldier groups wearing them. Militias such as the Pumpkintown White Coats, Mercer Blues, and Gray Reserves often wore uniforms to match their colorful names. This swallow-tail coatee, worn by a Westmoreland County militiaman, dates from before 1858, when infantry trim was white. *Richard Moore Collection.*

BELOW

Marksmanship Medal At least once a year, militia companies gathered for a festive day of training, exhibition drill practice, and marksman competitions. This 1860 silver Best Marksman medal was awarded by the Turtle Creek Guards on such a Militia Muster Day. *Ken Turner Collection.*

Wayne Guard Backpack More decorative than functional, this soldier's knapsack is typical of equipment purchased by individual militia units before the war. Constructed of canvas on a wooden frame and waterproofed with a tar-like paint, the pack was lettered in gold leaf. A leather cylinder on the bottom held a rolled thin blanket. *Ken Turner Collection.*

12th Pennsylvania Volunteers After his three-month term, 21-year-old Private Samuel Baldwin Marks Young (far right) of Company K "City Guard," 12th Pennsylvania Volunteer Infantry would reenlist as a commissioned captain of the 4th Pennsylvania Cavalry. Young rose to the rank of major in 1862, colonel in 1864, and brevet rank of brigadier general of volunteers in 1865. Young also became first president of the Army War College, Carlisle, and first chief of staff of the U.S. Army. *U.S. Army Military History Institute.*

Approximately 500 men left Harrisburg for Washington on April 18, 1861.

CHAPTER 1

CALL FOR VOLUNTEERS

Three days after the Confederates fired on Fort Sumter, President Lincoln issued a proclamation. Lincoln utilized a law first enacted in 1795 to quell the Whiskey Rebellion in Western Pennsylvania, which authorized the president to call state militia into federal service.

The New York Times
APRIL 15, 1861:

Whereas; The laws of the United States have been for some time past, and now are opposed, and the execution thereof obstructed in the States of South Carolina, Georgia, Alabama, Florida, Mississippi, Louisiana, and Texas, by combinations too powerful to be suppressed by the ordinary course of Judicial proceedings, or by the powers vested in the Marshals by law, — now, therefore, I, ABRAHAM LINCOLN, President of the United States, in virtue of the power in me vested by the Constitution and the laws, have thought fit to call forth, and hereby do call forth, the militia of the several States of the Union to the aggregate number of seventy-five thousand, in order to suppress said combinations, and to cause the laws to be duly executed.

Taking Command One day after Lincoln's call for volunteers, Governor Curtin appointed 69-year-old veteran Robert Patterson commander of Pennsylvania volunteers. On July 2, Patterson led his army into Virginia, meeting Confederate forces under Thomas J. Jackson and J.E.B. Stuart.
Library of Congress, cwpb-07077.

FROM FRONTIER COLONY TO THE THRESHOLD OF WAR

RIGHT

First Blood Among the ranks of First Defenders was Nicholas Biddle, a 65-year-old former slave who accompanied the Washington Artillery from Pottsville, Schuylkill County, as a uniformed aide to Captain James Wren. As the Pennsylvanians marched through Baltimore on April 18, 1861, a mob of Confederate sympathizers gathered. A brick thrown from the crowd knocked Biddle to the ground, spilling the first blood of the war. The following day, as President Lincoln welcomed the troops, the chief executive spoke to Biddle about the blood-soaked bandage on his head. In this portrait, Biddle's bandage is stuffed into his coat pocket; drops of blood can be seen on the coat's chest and arm. *Library of Congress, 3c26417.*

TOP FAR RIGHT

Colonel Francis E. Patterson Francis Patterson, son of General Robert Patterson, led the 17th Pennsylvania Infantry in his father's campaign into Virginia. Wearing the distinctive army issue "Quaker Hat," Patterson rose to the rank of brigadier general. An accidental discharge from his own pistol took his life in November 1862. *Ken Turner Collection.*

BOTTOM RIGHT

Colonel John White McLane John White McLane, veteran militia officer, responded to Lincoln's call by recruiting some 800 men from the northwest corner of the state. The Erie Regiment was billeted first at the inadequately appointed Camp Wilkins, and then transferred to Camp Wright, but, like many eager regiments, saw their term end before being called to the front. After returning to Erie in July, McLane recruited the 83rd Pennsylvania Volunteer Infantry and led it into battle as their colonel. He was killed in action on June 27, 1862, at the Battle of Gaines' Mill, Virginia. *Ken Turner Collection.*

CHAPTER 1

Bordered by the pro-Southern states of Virginia and Maryland, Pennsylvania stepped forward to protect the Union and defend its state border. Approximately 500 men left Harrisburg for Washington on April 18: the National Light Infantry and Washington Artillery (both from Pottsville), the Ringgold Light Artillery (Reading), the Logan Guards (Lewistown), and the Allen Rifles (Allentown). These Pennsylvania volunteers adopted the moniker First Defenders.

ABOVE

Flag of the Logan Guards "Presented by the Ladies of Lewistown to the Logan Guards" is emblazoned on this painted silk flag, carried by the Logan Guards as they entered Washington, D.C., on April 18, 1861. A placard, added later, identifies the flag as the first to arrive in the nation's capitol in defense of the Union. *Ken Turner Collection.*

LEFT

Colonel Phaon Jarrett, 11th Pennsylvania Infantry Colonel Phaon Jarrett commanded the 11th Pennsylvania Volunteer Infantry, one of 18 three-month Pennsylvania regiments assigned to the federal army under General Robert Patterson. Jarrett led the 11th at the Battle of Falling Waters, Virginia, on July 2, 1861, a small action that saw the unit pitted against Southern forces led by future Confederate generals Thomas J. "Stonewall" Jackson and J.E.B. Stuart. *Ken Turner Collection.*

Cannons from Pennsylvania The Phoenix Iron Company of Phoenixville, Chester County, was the principal manufacturer of the three inch ordnance rifle, or cannon; approximately 1,000 were produced during the Civil War. Leaning on the left wheel is Lieutenant Robert Clarke of Battery A, 2nd U.S. Artillery, formerly an officer in the 8th Pennsylvania Reserves. The group was photographed near Fair Oaks, Virginia, during the Peninsula Campaign, June 1862. *Library of Congress, cwpb-01024.*

CH. 2

1862: WAR

Between fall 1861 and spring 1862, after the first three-month volunteer regiments returned from their short term of service, tens of thousands of Pennsylvanians volunteered to fight for the Union Army. These men came from all walks of life and the overwhelming majority were untrained in the technique of warfare, nor were they prepared for the grinding routine of army life and the grim reality of war. All believed however that the fight to preserve the Union was their just calling. While battles were the most memorable events of military service, armed engagements were only a part of the soldiering. The majority of time was spent in camps where the men trained and drilled, and battled disease and long periods of unbearable boredom. To combat war weariness, soldiers engaged in a variety of sanctioned and unsanctioned pastimes. By far the most popular activity was letter writing. On the Union side alone, some 135,000 letters were dispatched per day. The monotony of camp life, the endless dust and long marches, the loss of comrades, the horrors of the battlefield, and uncertainties about the future helped forge a brotherly bond among soldiers. Whether a soldier returned home after three months or three years of service, wounded or uninjured, all returned changed.

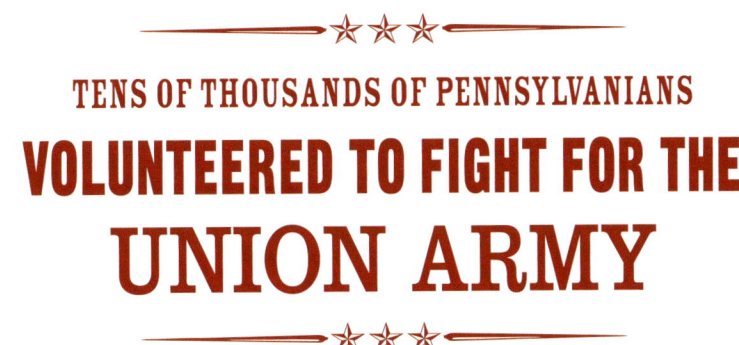

Robert Cornelius, early daguerreotypist
Applying his knowledge of chemistry and metallurgy, Philadelphian Robert Cornelius perfected the art of the daguerreotype. In October 1839, Cornelius took this photo outside his family's store, the first known self-portrait.
Library of Congress, 3g05001.

Photography of the 19th Century

In September 1839, news arrived in New York City detailing an innovation by Frenchman Louis Daguerre: the first commercially successful photography process. The daguerreotype process created an image directly on a silver-plated sheet of copper when exposed to mercury vapor. The process required great care and the result was easily damaged, so daguerreotypes were mounted in glass cases or picture frames.

Americans immediately began experimenting with daguerreotypes. Within weeks, Philadelphia engraver Joseph Saxton likely asked metallurgist Robert Cornelius to create a silver plate so he could make a daguerreotype of the Pennsylvania State Arsenal and Central High School. The image, taken within days from his window at the U.S. Mint just off Penn (then Center) Square in Philadelphia, is the earliest surviving American photograph.

Cornelius began his own experiments and created a grainy self-portrait—the first posed photograph of a person. Within months, he established a photography studio in Philadelphia at the corner of 8th Street and Lodge Alley, one of the first in the United States (today it is noted by a state historical marker). Photographers opened studios across Pennsylvania, with formal portraiture comprising most of their business.

In 1840, Robert Cornelius established a photo studio in Philadelphia.

CHAPTER 2

LEFT
Ambrotype: Sisters Freckle-faced sisters in identical dresses sit for their portrait. The ambrotype photographic process utilized clear or ruby-tinted glass in place of iron or paper, and was a simpler and far less expensive process than the labor-intensive daguerreotype. *Kraus/Messick Collection.*

BELOW
Daguerreotype: African American York Studio This daguerreotype of an unnamed man was taken by African American photographer Glenalvin Goodridge in York. The subject's blank expression and stiff pose were required for the lengthy exposures needed (as long as 40 seconds) even in a well-lit studio. A head brace was used to ensure little to no movement. The red velvet padding in the case is embossed with the name of Goodridge's studio. *Kraus/Messick Collection.*

By the late 1850s, the ambrotype, a less costly yet much-improved product, replaced the daguerreotype in popularity. At the outbreak of the Civil War, hundreds of thousands of citizen soldiers flooded studios to "have their likeness taken." Enterprising photographers followed soldiers to the battlefront, erecting field studios in camps and even setting up equipment on battlefields to record the aftermath.

ABOVE
Stereograph Stereographic images, popular since the early 1850s, appear three-dimensional when viewed through a stereoscope. Stereographic production grew during the Civil War as the demand for war-related images increased. This c. 1861 view of a group at Altoona, Blair County, includes Mary E., Sue Wilson, Henry Wilson, Mary H., and Mary Wilson. *Library of Congress, 1s01499.*

LEFT
Carte-de-Visite Because it utilized a wet plate process that created a negative from which copies could be made, the carte-de-visite became an affordable and popular photographic keepsake, such as this portrait of a child from Bethlehem, Northampton County. *Kraus/Messick Collection.*

CHAPTER 2

Photographer Frederick Gutekunst
Frederick Gutekunst was one of Philadelphia's premier photographers. His Arch Street gallery maintained a large soldier clientele.
Friends Historical Library of Swarthmore College, Truman-Underhill Album Collection.

1862: WAR

134th Pennsylvania Infantry photo album

During the war years, soldiers collected carte-de-visite images of their comrades and family, storing the keepsakes in specially designed albums. This handsome example was presented by the Beaver County men of Company E, 134th Pennsylvania Infantry, to their commanding officer, Captain J. Adams Vera. Bound in leather, with the cover embossed in gold letters, the album contains photos of nearly 100 soldiers.

Ken Turner Collection.

The Complex Effort to Record History

Field photographers such as Mathew Brady used a complicated wet plate process that meant a photograph had to be snapped within 10 minutes, before the plate dried. That was just the beginning of a complex process using dangerous chemicals.

1. In a darkened tent or wagon, wet a glass plate with collodion and silver-nitrate solution.
2. Place wet plate in camera.
3. Outside, attach camera to tripod, aim at subject, and expose to light for up to 30 seconds.
4. Back in complete darkness, develop with acid and set with chemical "fixer" solution.
5. Wash with water, creating a negative.
6. Allow negative plate to dry.
7. Place plate on photographic paper and expose to sunlight for up to 60 minutes.
8. Fix, wash, and dry the paper to produce a photograph.
9. Tone, fix, dry, and mount the photograph.

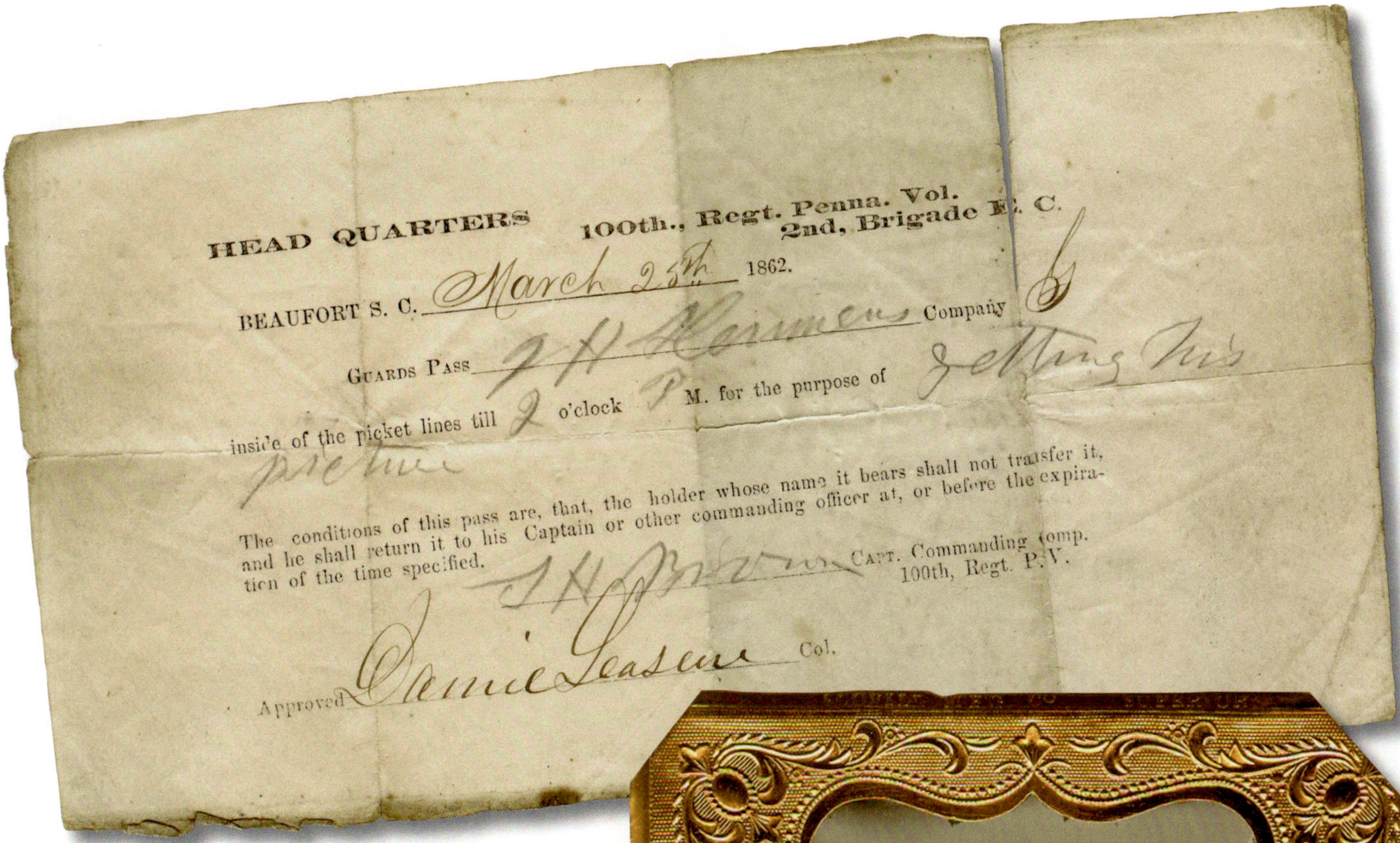

HEAD QUARTERS 100th., Regt. Penna. Vol.
2nd, Brigade E. C.

BEAUFORT S. C. March 25th 1862.

Company G

Guards Pass J H Slemmons

inside of the picket lines till 2 o'clock P M. for the purpose of getting his picture

The conditions of this pass are, that, the holder whose name it bears shall not transfer it, and he shall return it to his Captain or other commanding officer at, or before the expiration of the time specified.

[illegible] Capt. Commanding Comp.
100th, Regt. P. V.

Approved Daniel Leasure Col.

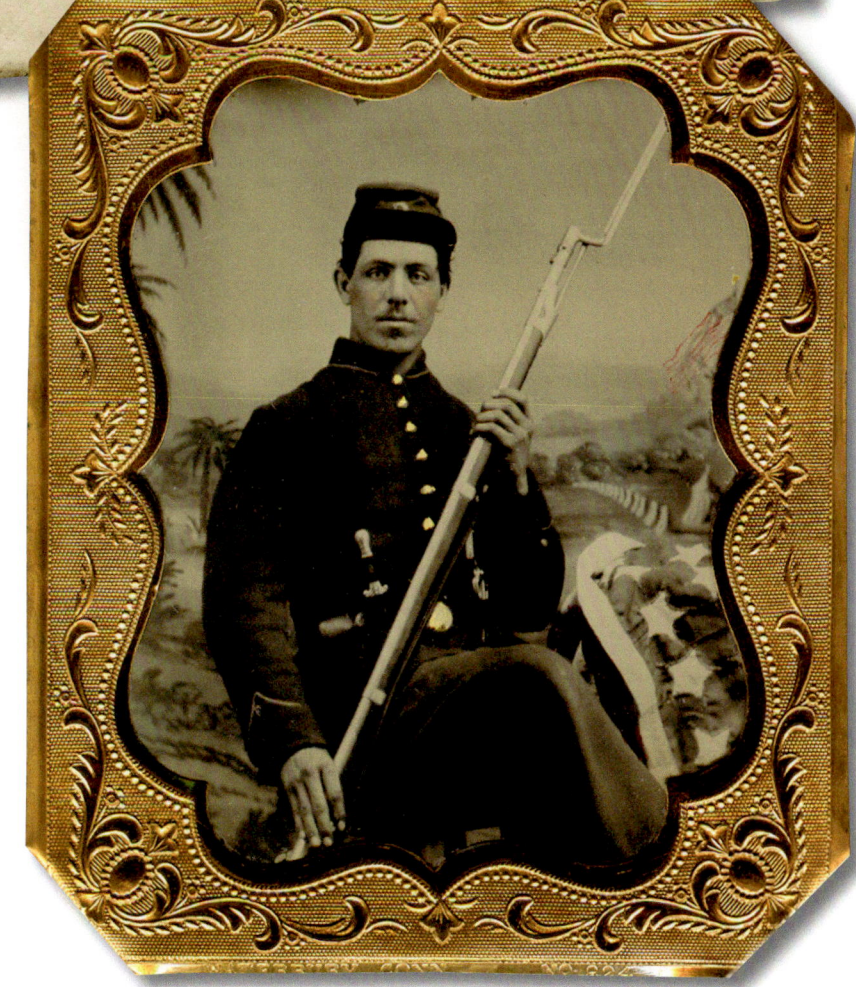

"Got my likeness taken" A visit to a photographer's studio was a significant event for most soldiers. Private Joseph Slemmons' diary entry, dated March 25, 1862, reads, "I got a pass this forenoon [above] and went down in town and got my likeness taken." Slemmons, a Mercer County member of Company G, 100th Pennsylvania Volunteer Infantry, was serving in Beaufort, South Carolina, when the photograph was taken. The image was developed on a thin sheet of colloidal-coated iron. *Kraus/Messick Collection.*

ABOVE

Mock combat Upon enlisting in the army in 1861, Thomas Lemmon, Henry Stewart, and Lemuel Brady (left to right), Company A, 61st Pennsylvania, stage a fight for the camera. All three would perish at the Battle of the Wilderness on May 5, 1864. *Ken Turner Collection.*

ABOVE RIGHT

William Lucas, Company G, 28th Pennsylvania Volunteer Infantry Uniformed in dress frock coat complete with shoulder scales, young Private William Lucas of Allegheny County, Company G, 28th Pennsylvania Infantry, displays a saber bayonet. Lucas's name is scratched into the photo's emulsion above his head. *Ken Turner Collection.*

Volunteers

The Union Army was composed of three different military structures: the federal army, a force of approximately 16,000 that would expand to nearly 23,000 during the war; the militia, an instrument of state law subject to nationalization; and, most important to the Union war effort, the United States Volunteers. The majority of the 2.2 million soldiers in Union armies served as volunteers, originating with regiments raised in their states. At the end of 1861, regiments from the commonwealth numbered 115, totaling nearly 110,000 men in service or preparing for it. By war's end, more than 337,000 Pennsylvania men, including 8,600 African Americans, served. The state mustered 185 infantry regiments and 24 cavalry regiments, five artillery regiments (one light and four heavy), and raised dozens of militia units.

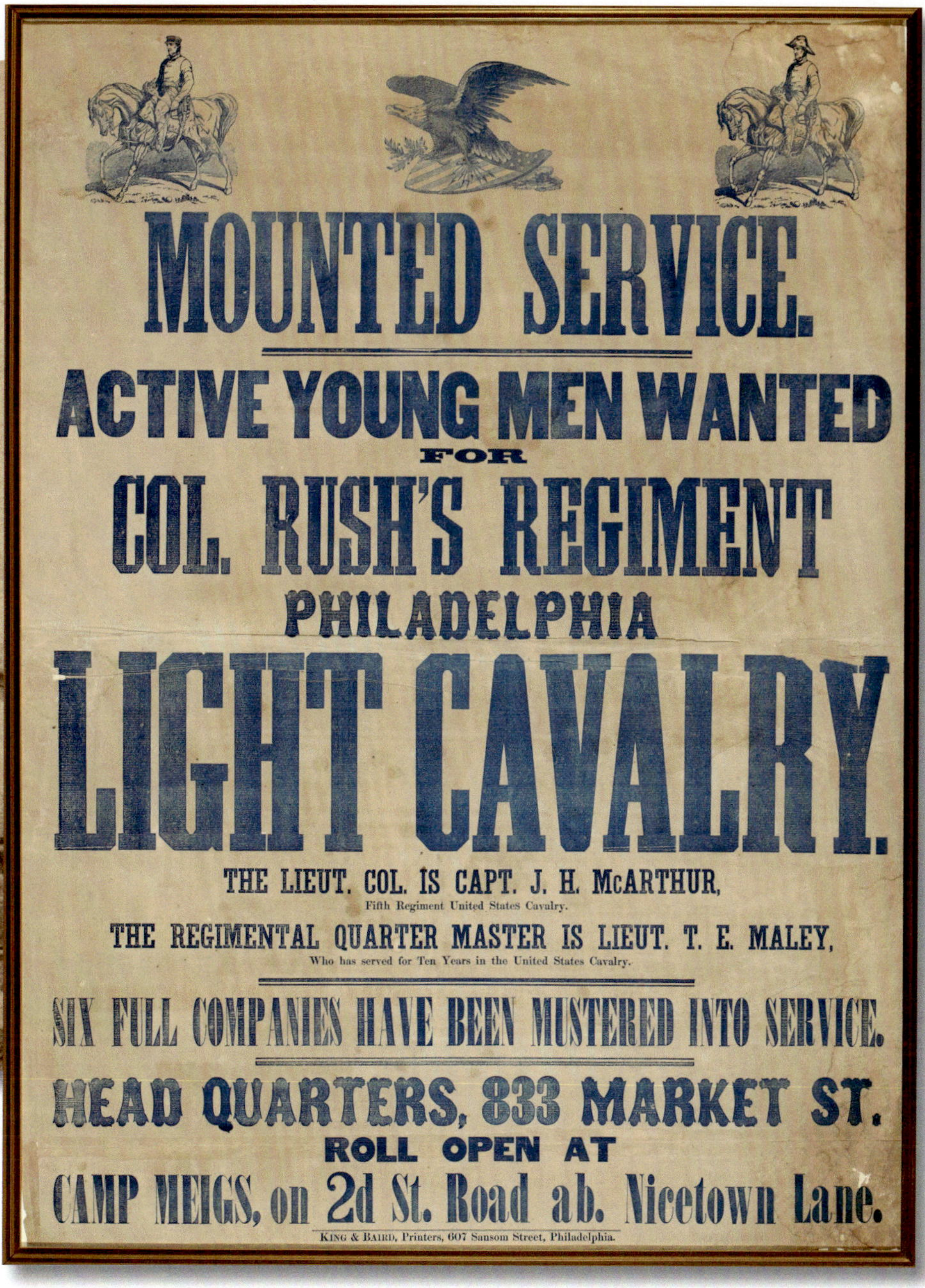

CHAPTER 2

Colonel Richard Rush A prominent Philadelphian and 1846 West Point graduate, Richard Rush capitalized on his social status to raise and outfit the 6th Pennsylvania Cavalry. Rush drew many of his men from the First Troop Philadelphia City Cavalry, a militia company tracing its roots to the Revolutionary War. Rush's Lancers were armed with 10-foot-long cavalry lances, useful only in close combat; by 1863, lances were abandoned in favor of the breech-loading cavalry carbine. *Ken Turner Collection.*

70	McClain W. A.	74			
71	McCune John	95	Steward Benjamin	26	
72	McClintock Alex 35	96	Smith John		
73	Muse James 32	97	Shoaf J. M.	25	
74	Needs Matthias	98	Taylor J.	76	29
75	Newlin W. W. 25	99	~~Thomas~~ Henry Thomas		
76	~~Neill~~ Neill William 20	100	Tomer Adam	30	
77	Patterson George 28	101	Turley Robert	22	
78	Palmer L. 20	102	~~Watson~~		
79	Perkins Thomas 19	103	Weaver H. G.	22	
80	Pinkerton Joseph 21	104	Weddle George	21	
81	Parks Monzi 20	105	Williard Albert	18	
82	Prescott William 24	106	Williard A. G.	18	
83	Queary John 17	107	~~White~~		
84	Reed William 20	108	White Samuel	19	
85	~~Reddick J.~~	109	Weimer H. F.	24	
86	~~Report Retford~~	110	Zimmerman William	37	
87	Saner Harrison 20	111	Warren Benjamin	23	
88	Shannon Wm 18	112	Nish Andrew	19	
89	Shaner John 18	113	Woodward J. H.	24	
90	Shaner J. H. 28	114	Burkhart Samuel	23	
		115	Taylor J. H.	18	
		116	Christy W. K.	21	

State of Pennsylvania
County of Westmoreland

I do certify that the above and foregoing Persons were duly sworn into the Service of the United States by the undersigned one of the Justices of the Peace in and for said County according to the prescribed form Witness my Hand and Seal this third day of September A.D. 1861   A. C. Hamilton J. P. [Seal]

Enlistment Roll of the 11th Pennsylvania Infantry, September 1861. *Kraus/Messick Collection.*

CHAPTER 2

BELOW
Colonel J. Bowman Sweitzer, 62nd Pennsylvania In late summer of 1861, Major J. Bowman Sweitzer and Adjutant Joseph Brown of the 62nd Pennsylvania were photographed by Mathew Brady for a series titled *Illustrations of Camp Life*. Sweitzer mustered out as colonel on July 13, 1864. Brown opted out in fall 1862. *Ken Turner Collection.*

ABOVE
Lancaster Fireman and Engine In large cities, firefighters often answered the call to arms by enlisting together. Such infantry companies, composed of men used to working together under dangerous conditions, proved especially effective during the challenges of military life. Baxter's Fire Zouaves of the 72nd Pennsylvania was comprised entirely of Philadelphia firemen. *Ken Turner Collection.*

Major General George F. McCall Governor Andrew Gregg Curtin demonstrated the foresight of a strategic commander when he proposed a reserve corps be mustered from the overflow of Pennsylvania's first wave of volunteers. The state legislature adopted the plan to organize, equip, and train men to be deployed as needed. In May 1861, 13 regiments of infantry, one of cavalry, and one of artillery, known as the Pennsylvania Reserves, were created. The governor's initiative proved prescient; on July 22, 1861, one day after the defeat of Union forces at Bull Run, the Pennsylvania Volunteer Reserve Corps (PVRC) was sworn into federal service.

Retired regular army Colonel George A. McCall of Philadelphia was given command of the corps. He was commissioned major general only to be wounded and captured at the Battle of Charles City Cross Roads in Virginia on June 30, 1862. He was held in Richmond, Virginia's, notorious Libby Prison until exchanged for Confederate prisoner General Simon Bolivar Buckner. *Ken Turner Collection.*

CHAPTER 2

ABOVE

Silas Baily, 8th PVRC A jeweler from Waynesburg, Greene County, 25-year-old Silas Baily was commissioned captain in the 8th PVRC in 1861. Rising quickly through the ranks, Baily was promoted to major in June 1862, then colonel in March 1863. At Gaines' Mill, Virginia, he was wounded in the face, and surgeons deemed him unfit for duty. Baily recovered, however, and returned to lead the 8th until they mustered out in May 1864. Baily was brevetted to brigadier general for his actions at Wilderness and Spotsylvania, Virginia. *Ken Turner Collection.*

ABOVE

William McClurg, 9th Pennsylvania Reserves Beaver County native William McClurg was attending Yale University when the call for troops drew him home to enlist in the 9th Pennsylvania Reserves. McClurg, an accomplished mathematician capable of translating Greek and Latin, was the mess mate of Chaplain Eli Torrance, who described the college student as a perfect gentleman and brave beyond criticism. While storming the heights at South Mountain, Maryland, on September 14, 1862, McClurg was struck down by Confederate bullets; he was transported to a hospital in Washington, D.C., and died of his wounds 26 days later. *Ken Turner Collection.*

By July 1862, it was clear that a swift resolution to the war was impossible, and with no end in sight, fresh troops were needed. As an incentive for recruits, the state raised 16 new infantry regiments for a relatively short nine-month enlistment, enabling eligible men to serve without abandoning their families and livelihoods for a protracted period of time.

LEFT

Pastor and Colonel John B. Clark, a Presbyterian pastor in Allegheny City, Allegheny County, challenged the young men in his congregation to fight for the Union. Three days later, Clark had gathered three full companies of volunteers. After 10 days, seven more companies were organized—the pastor had raised enough soldiers to form the 123rd Regiment of Pennsylvania Volunteers. *Ken Turner Collection.*

CHAPTER 2

OPPOSITE
Infantry Kit Seneca Yoder of Berks County relaxes as he displays his infantry kit for the camera. Yoder was captured at Chancellorsville, Virginia, when Confederates tricked the 128th Pennsylvania into surrendering. He managed to escape, finish his enlistment, and sign on for a second term in the 51st Pennsylvania.
Ken Turner Collection.

VOLUNTEERS
WERE CRUCIAL
TO THE
UNION WAR
EFFORT

Colonel Edward O'Brien In August 1862, Edward O'Brien was commissioned in the 134th Pennsylvania Volunteers; just four months later he was promoted to colonel. Following orders, O'Brien led his men in the final assault on Marye's Heights at Fredericksburg. The charge cost the regiment 139 men killed, wounded, or missing. O'Brien survived the charge but died years later in an insane asylum. *Ken Turner Collection.*

CHAPTER 2

UNIFORMS

Military supplies, including uniforms, were in short supply at the onset of war. Scrambling to outfit troops, Pennsylvania manufactured and issued gray coats and trousers typical of the state militia. The state soon conformed to the union blue, though variations remained such as the Zouaves, whose colorful red jackets and pants were modeled after those of French Algerian troops.

BELOW
Hennon Cap Joseph W. Hennon's cap, worn in his 1861 portrait. *Kraus/Messick Collection.*

BELOW RIGHT
Joseph W. Hennon Tintype Joseph W. Hennon from Irish Ripple, Lawrence County, wears the gray uniform of the early Pennsylvania troops. The youthful soldier was killed at South Mountain, Maryland, in the Antietam Campaign. *Kraus/Messick Collection.*

1862: WAR

ABOVE
James Probasco, 33rd Independent Pennsylvania Infantry Mathew Brady's camera recorded Private James Probasco of the 33rd Independent Pennsylvania Infantry in this portrait made in late summer 1861. The private, dressed in a state-issued gray uniform, displays a burnished M1842 musket at a camp near Washington, D.C. *Ken Turner Collection.*

LEFT
Alexander Barr, Hampton's Battery Alexander Campbell Barr, Allegheny County, served in Hampton's Battery F, Pennsylvania Independent Artillery. His regulation short jacket, trimmed in red piping, was designed for comfort while riding. Barr's cap is embellished with a stamped brass insignia featuring the crossed cannons of the light artillery. *Ken Turner Collection.*

ABOVE

Benjamin F. Landan, 3rd Pennsylvania Heavy Artillery Benjamin Landan, 3rd Pennsylvania, wears his regulation frock coat adorned with brass shoulder scales. His hat bears the crossed cannon insignia of the artillery. As a heavy artilleryman, Landan was trained both as a large cannon operator and a foot soldier.
Ken Turner Collection.

RIGHT

J. Reese Moore, 15th Cavalry Most Pennsylvania cavalrymen wore army regulation short shell coats trimmed in yellow. The 15th Pennsylvania Cavalry, however, changed the taping color to orange and added extra rows along the front of the jacket. J. Reese Moore, Company E, poses ready for action with saber and pistol.
Ken Turner Collection.

CHAPTER 2

BELOW
Pennsylvania Infantry Sergeant Major
Dressed more for the camera than war, an unknown Pennsylvania sergeant major carries a non-commissioned officer sword, while wearing a backpack with blanket roll and a shiny new haversack. *Ken Turner Collection.*

ABOVE
2nd Pennsylvania Cavalry Seated astride an extraordinary cavalry horse, Nathan Cheney, 2nd Pennsylvania Cavalry, wears the short jacket preferred by mounted troops. Cheney hailed from Linesville, Crawford County. The horse is muscular, well-groomed, and larger than a typical cavalry horse. *Ken Turner Collection.*

RIGHT
Pennsylvania state seal uniform buttons
Most often worn by field and staff officers of the Reserve Brigade, these state seal buttons identify the wearer as hailing from the Keystone State. *Kraus/Messick Collection.*

ABOVE
Gosline's Zouaves A short blue jacket, double row of buttons, and red trim identify the uniform of the 95th Pennsylvania. Colonel John Gosline contracted with the Schuylkill Arsenal in Philadelphia to outfit his regiment. The unidentified soldier in this photo wears a tasseled fez, characteristic of the Zouave uniform. *Ronn Palm Collection.*

RIGHT
Birney's Zouaves James Walworth, William Everhard, and Matthew Spence of Birney's Zouaves, Company C, 23rd Pennsylvania, wear the distinctive uniform adopted in 1861. Walworth and Everhard would be wounded at Cold Harbor in 1864; Spence survived the war uninjured. *Ronn Palm Collection.*

CHAPTER 2

Chasseur de Vincennes Sergeant Major Charles Saeger of the 62nd Pennsylvania poses for his portrait in the baggy trousers, dress coat, and fatigue cap of the French *Chasseur au Pied* uniform. Two Pennsylvania regiments, Saeger's and the 83rd, were awarded the distinctive military garb for proficiency in drills. The Pennsylvania soldiers, however, found the uniforms unflattering. Before the Army of the Potomac marched from Washington toward Richmond in spring 1862, the uniforms were packed away, never to be worn. *Ken Turner Collection.*

LIFE IN CAMP

Soldiers only spent approximately one-fourth of their time in battle. The rest of the time they drilled, dug trenches, built fortifications, marched, and waited. In the winter and early spring, before the weather improved and military action became possible, the tedium of camp life was an appealing counterpoint to the terror of battle. Army camps were like cities, complete with streets, sutler stores, surgeon's tents, and makeshift chapels. Camps were home for hundreds of thousands of soldiers. When not engaged in military affairs, soldiers found other activities to occupy their time, especially if bivouacked near cities. Dancing and theatrical entertainment were their favorites. Soldiers formed literary societies and debating clubs, and played any game they could devise, including baseball, cards, and boxing. Some soldiers were prone to a number of other pursuits officially frowned upon, such as gambling, drinking, and visiting prostitutes.

Dog Jack The Niagara Volunteer Fire Engine House acquired its mascot when a stray dog wandered into its station and was treated roughly by an annoyed fireman. The dog's pitiful yelps attracted the attention of other firemen who set the stray's broken leg. In 1861, when most of the firemen enlisted in the 102nd Pennsylvania, they took their mascot along. For nearly three and a half years, Jack took part in all battles fought by the regiment. The resilient pet was wounded three times and captured twice – he escaped once and was exchanged for a Confederate prisoner. In December 1864, while in Frederick City, Maryland, Jack disappeared, never to be seen again. *Ken Turner Collection.*

THE HARDSHIPS THEY ENDURED TOGETHER BONDED THE SOLDIERS

CHAPTER 2

ABOVE

Captain Joseph Gerard Bearing a crimson silk sash across his chest, indicating his position as Officer of the Day, Captain Joseph Gerard of Company K, 61st Pennsylvania, poses in camp with his canine companion. His regiment was hit hard at the battle of Fair Oaks on May 31, 1862—262 officers and men were killed, wounded, or missing. Captain Gerard was among the dead. *Ken Turner Collection.*

LEFT

23rd Pennsylvania Camp Scene In the fall of 1862, members of the 23rd Pennsylvania camped near Washington, D.C. Here, they relax on furniture constructed from salvaged wood, surrounded by typical camp possessions— an axe, coffee pot, weapons, and musical instruments. *Ken Turner Collection.*

1862: WAR

CHAPTER 2

Camp took on a different meaning to armies on the move. Frequently, a blanket on the ground was the only overnight accommodation for a soldier on the march. In the field, soldiers often subsisted on rations of hardtack (a flour and water biscuit), coffee, salt pork, rice, and whatever they could forage. Disease was rampant.

The hardships they endured together bonded the soldiers. Years after the conflict, veterans would recall their experiences using the model of an encampment as the venue for reunions. There they swapped stories in familiar surroundings.

OPPOSITE
Camping Camps on the move were substantially different from the extensive encampments in which soldiers drilled and trained. Spacious canvas tents had to be left behind, replaced by shebangs—improvised shelters. In this field photograph, several Western Pennsylvania soldiers relax under a lean-to shelter. *Tom Molocea Collection.*

ABOVE
Dog Sallie In April 1861, Sallie was gifted to the captain of Company I, 11th Pennsylvania, by a man from Chester County. Sallie proved her loyalty after the first three-month enlistment, remaining with the 11th Pennsylvania when her regiment reenlisted. She served another three and a half years until killed in action at Hatcher's Run, Virginia, on February 6, 1865. *Pennsylvania State Archives, MG-218 GPC, Military, Civil War.*

A Unique Memorial A statue of Sallie graces the front of the Eleventh Pennsylvania Infantry Regiment monument, located northwest of Gettysburg on Doubleday Avenue. The dedication in September 1890 is pictured in a booklet, *Monument Number, Historic Souvenir* by the Westmoreland County Soldiers' and Sailors' Veteran Association, 1925. *Sue Boardman.*

1862: WAR

BELOW
Volunteer Refreshment Saloon Pin This unique pin belonged to Dr. Eliab Ward, a prominent Philadelphian physician who cofounded the Volunteer Refreshment Committee. *Ken Turner Collection.*

ABOVE
Union Volunteer Refreshment Saloon, Philadelphia Nearly one million meals were served from 1861 to 1865 at the Union Refreshment Saloon, where washing, sleeping, and writing facilities were available. The Cooper Refreshment Shop, a friendly rival, also provided services to hundreds of thousands of soldiers traveling through the nearby Philadelphia train station. Both establishments were charitable organizations kept running by donations. *Ken Turner Collection.*

RIGHT
Mess Chest This mess chest provided compact and transportable storage of cookware for the officers of the 48th Pennsylvania. *Michael Murphy Collection.*

LEFT AND ABOVE

Sutler Card and Token Camp life most always included a sutler—an army-authorized vendor who set up a small store where soldiers purchased supplies. This Sutler Token, manufactured for use by the 2nd Pennsylvania Heavy Artillery, was worth 25 cents. *Kraus/Messick Collection.*

BELOW

Casey's Infantry Tactics Most volunteers had no previous military service and required training in drills and combat. Members of the new officer corps often needed direction in the delivery of commands. Small manuals of instruction, such as these three volumes of Silas Casey's *System of Infantry Tactics*, could be privately purchased and often accompanied combatants into war. *Kraus/Messick Collection.*

THE CAMP KETTLE.

We know only our Country.

VOL. 1.   SEPTEMBER 21, 1861.   NO. 1.

The Camp Kettle Is published every opportunity by the FIELD AND STAFF of the Roundhead Regiment, Col. Leasure, Commanding.

OUR BOW.

We have little room to spare, and none to waste in the "Camp Kettle," and shall briefly state that it is our intention to publish it as a daily, or weekly, or occasional paper, just as the exigencies of the service will permit. It is our intention to cook in it a "mess" of short paragraphs replete with useful information on a great many subjects, about which new recruits are supposed to be ignorant. We shall endeavor to make it a welcome visitor beside the camp fire and in the quarters, a sort of familiar little friend that whispers kind words and friendly advice to inexperienced men concerning the new position they have assumed, and the new duties that follow. Everything relating to a soldier's duty, and camp life, from mounting guard, to cleaning a musket, will be fit ingredient for the "Kettle." Rules for preserving health and cooking rations will be in place, and all sorts of questions relating to a soldier's duty, and his wants, when respectfully asked in writing, over a responsible name, will find an answer in the next mess that is poured out of the "Kettle."

Some individual expense has been incurred by the Commandant of the Regiment, in purchasing material, press, &c., but he only expects a return sufficient to cover current expenses of paper, ink, and the other necessary expenses of the "Kettle."

To this end, twenty-five numbers will cost twenty-five cents to subscribers in the Regiment, to all other fifty cents, and single numbers will sell for two cents. The number subscribed for in each company, will be delivered to the company postmaster for distribution to subscribers.

GUARDS.

There is no part of a soldier's duty that is so hard to learn, or involves so much responsibility as guard duty.— The "lonely sentinel," or "advanced picket" must be "all eyes and ears," for not only his own, but the safety of an entire army may depend upon him. A few general short rules, are put into the "Kettle," in the hope that they may prove useful to young guards.

A soldier detailed on guard must never leave the guard's quarters, until relieved by his proper officer. He must not go to his company quarters for his meals, but must have them carried to him by his messmates, or must take them with him in his haversack. He must not lay off any of his uniform or equipments, to the end that he may be ready on the instant, to start at the least alarm, or "turn out" on the approach of an officer entitled to be received with ceremony. He must keep himself constantly in a state of preparedness to assist the relief on duty in case of trouble, or make arrests of parties disturbing the peace and good order of the encampment. When on duty as a sentinel he must keep wide awake all the time and note every, even the smallest thing, that seems out of the ordinary way. He must keep on his feet, and carry his arms in such a manner as will enable him to use them effectually at any instant. When he sees an officer approach he must, if a Captain or Lieutenant, carry arms as light infantry and bring his left hand up to his gun at the height of the right

SEE FOURTH PAGE.

RIGHT

Camp Kettle Early in the war, a few Pennsylvania regiments carried portable printing presses into camps. In 1861 and '62, field staff of the Roundhead Regiment published *The Camp Kettle*, a newsletter sold among their ranks. Articles included pieces for novice soldiers such as "Guard Duty" and "How to Clean a Rifle." Later, the escalation of war necessitated leaving such cumbersome equipment behind.
Kraus/Messick Collection.

CHAPTER 2

ABOVE

Stationery Pack This prepackaged stationery kit contained writing paper, envelopes, and quill nibs; it was popular among soldiers for its compactness. *Ken Turner Collection.*

LEFT

Carved Bone A soldier's pocket knife was useful for transforming beef bones strewn around camp into decorative items. Activities such as carving and whittling alleviated boredom and kept nervous hands busy. *Ken Turner Collection.*

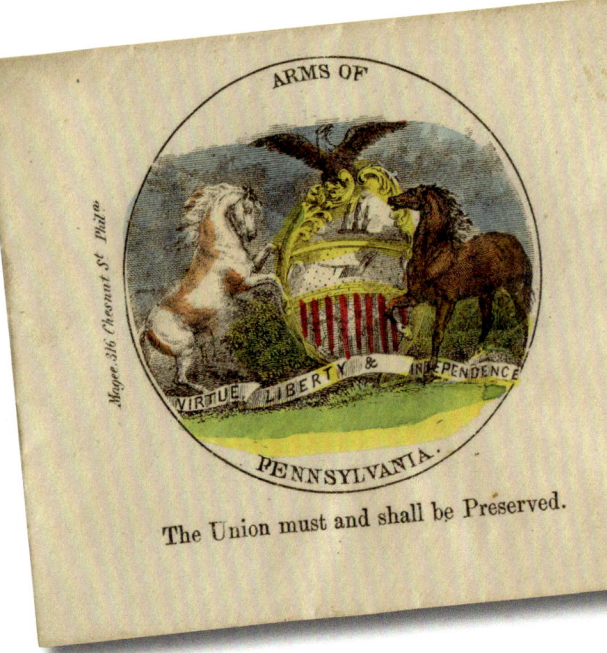

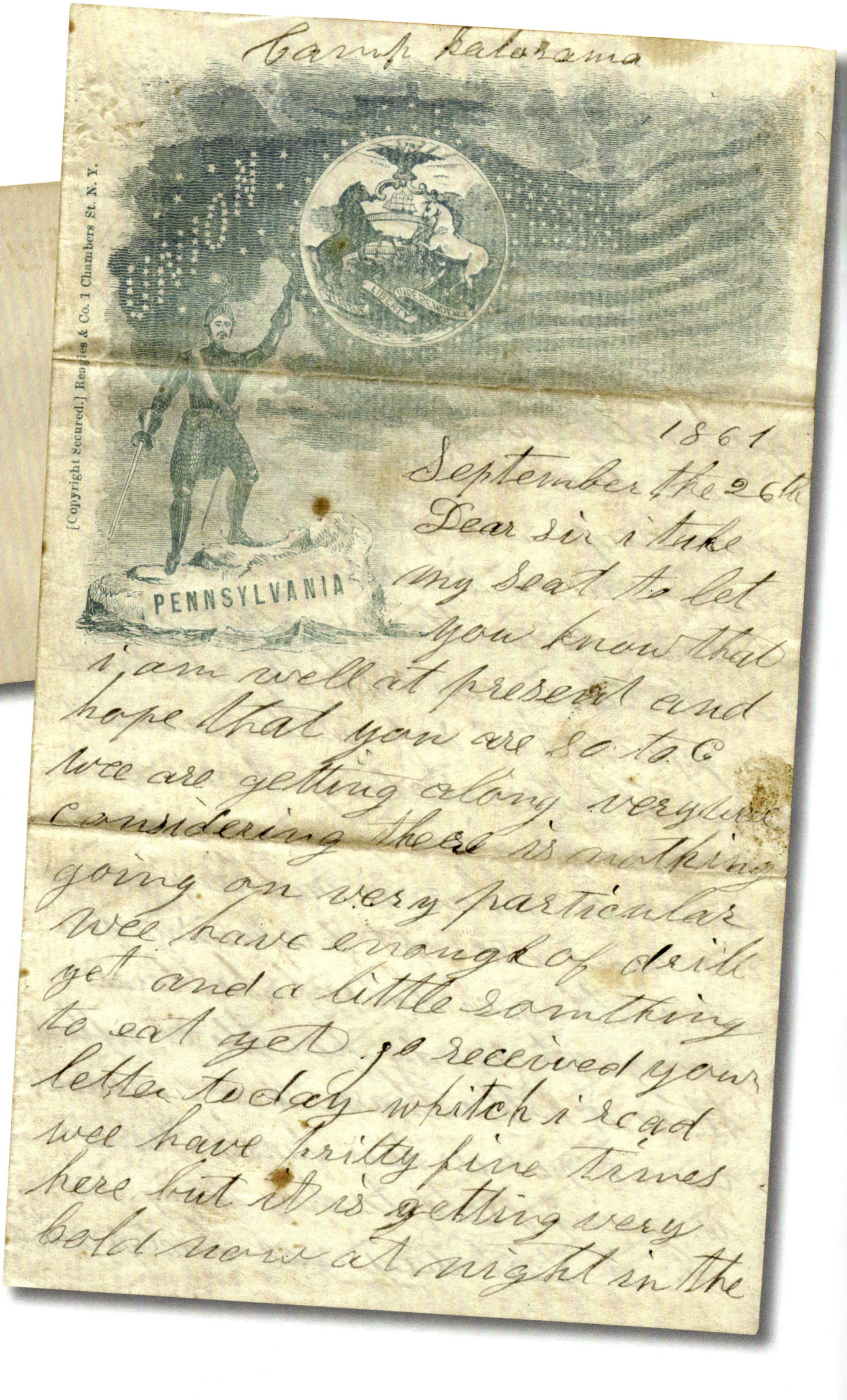

Camp Kalorama

1861
September the 26th
Dear sir i take
my seat to let
you know that
i am well at present and
hope that you are so to
wee are getting along very well
considering there is nothing
going on very particular
Wee have enough of drill
yet and a little somthing
to eat yet. i received your
letter today whitch i read
wee have pritty fine times
here but it is getting very
cold now at night in the

Soldier Letter with Envelope Anyone who could write sent and received letters during the war. Many used illustrated stationery that incorporated patriotic themes.
Kraus/Messick Collection.

CHAPTER 2

UNION BATTLE CRY.

Air: Battle cry of freedom.

By JAMES D. GAY, Army Song Dealer and Publisher, No. 300 North 20th St., Philadelphia, Pa. All of Gay's Army songs sent by Mail.

The Rebels cheered for Mac, when our Army drove them back,
   Shouting the battle cry of freedom.
True soldiers cast your votes, keep Abraham at his post,
   Shouting the battle cry of freedom.
CHORUS: The Union forever hurrah, boys, hurrah,
   Down with the traitors and on with the war,
Yes we'll rally around old Abe, boys, and give him four years more,
   Shouting the battle cry of freedom.

Be honest, brave and true and give honest Abe his due,
   Shouting the battle cry of freedom,
Rebellion must go down and true men in every town,
   Will sent up a holy shout of freedom.   CHORUS.

Come ye loyal men of North, do your work for March the fourth,
   By helping the holy cause of freedom,
Old Abe he must go back, while Grant is on the track,
   Shouting the battle cry of freedom.   CHORUS.

He will prosecute the War and our holy laws restore,
   Shouting the battle cry of freedom,
The Rebels they have swore if we give him four years more,
   They will haul down their seven stars of treason.   CHORUS.

We will capture Gen. Lee and all pirates on the sea,
   Shouting the battle cry of freedom,
When our Union is restored we will sheath the bloody sword,
   Shouting the battle cry of freedom.   CHORUS.

Come ye freemen one and all, cast your votes for Abe this fall,
   Shouting the battle cry of freedom,
Then our Union will be saved and our Banner proudly waved,
   While we shout for the battle cry of freedom.   CHORUS.

Entered according to Act of Congress, in the year 1864, by JAMES D. GAY, in the Clerk's Office of the Eastern District of Pennsylvania.

Song sheet This song sheet doubled as stationery.
Kraus/Messick Collection.

Carved Pipe A soldier in the 78th Pennsylvania whittled this smoking pipe bowl from laurel root and embellished it with the state seal.
Ken Turner Collection.

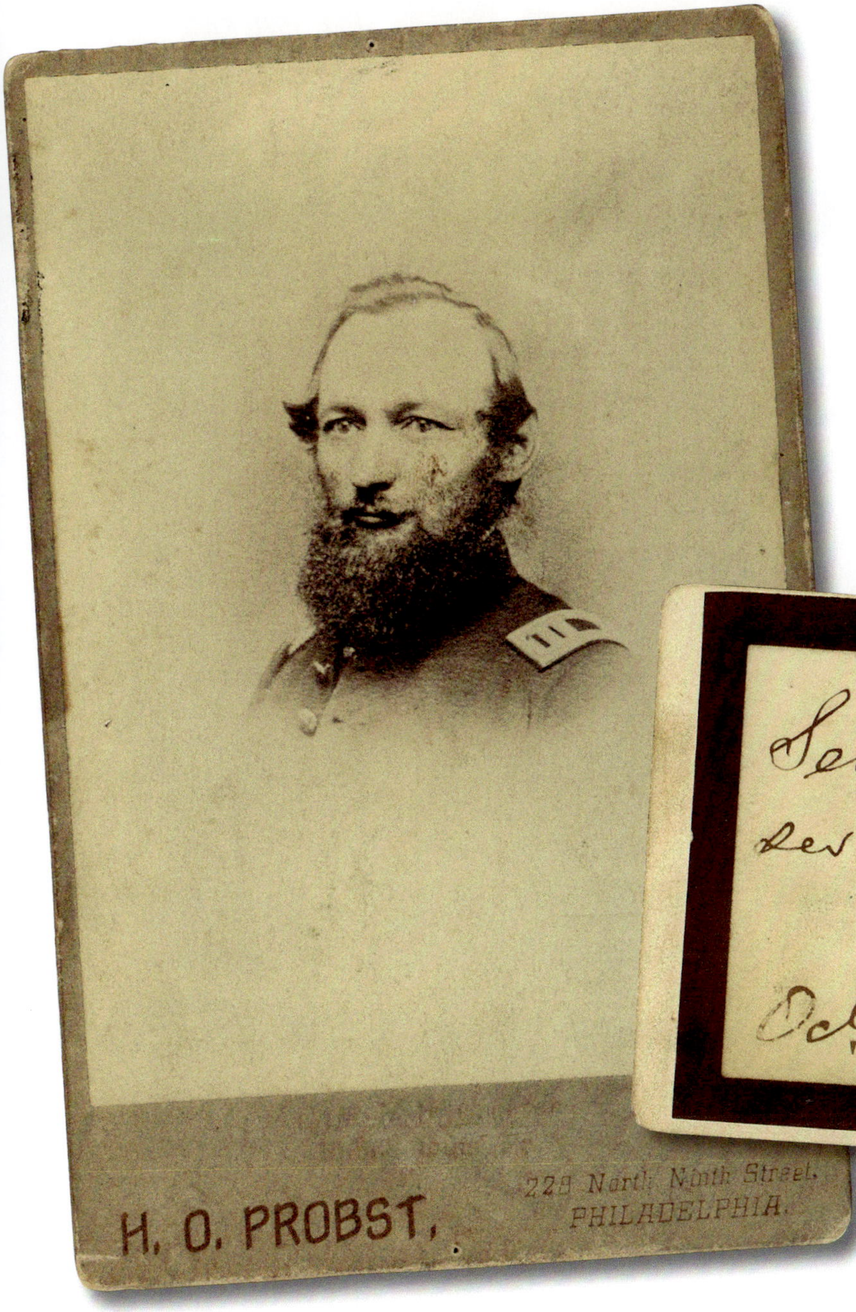

A Friend of Lincoln Captain Henry W. Crotzer's campaign life was interrupted by special assignment. In fall 1862, Crotzer (from Meadville), Captain David V. Derickson, and their two companies of Pennsylvania Bucktails (Companies D and K of the 150th Pennsylvania) were assigned to the post of presidential guard in the nation's capital. Although Crotzer developed a strong personal relationship with the president, he longed for life at the front. (The note below permitted him to see Secretary of War Stanton about his request.) In February 1863, Crotzer and Company D returned to the field; Company K, however, remained in the service of the president until war's end. Below is his presentation sword (made by Tiffany) and scabbard, which include gold detailing *All Ken Turner Collection.*

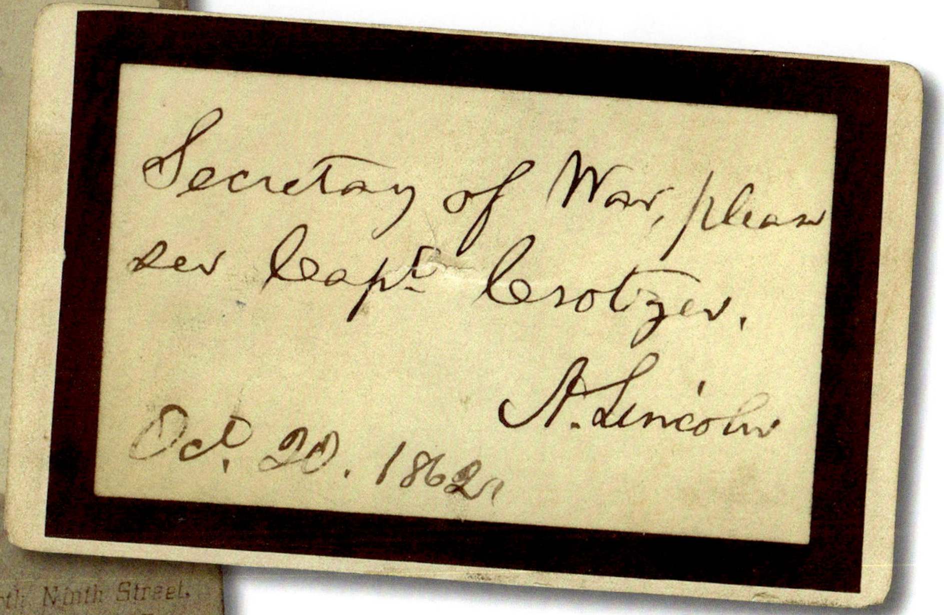
Secretary of War, please see Capt. Crotzer.
A. Lincoln
Oct. 20. 1862.

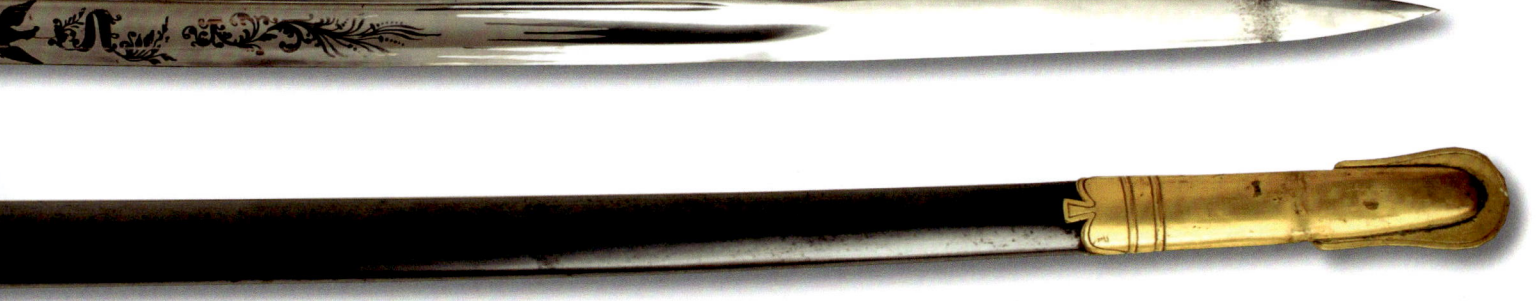

CHAPTER 2

IMMIGRANTS FIGHTING FOR THEIR ADOPTED COUNTRY

The commonwealth's diverse population was represented in the ranks of its military men. From soldiers who could trace their ancestors to colonial days to recent immigrants, regiments were comprised of a rich ethnic mix. For soldiers born on foreign soil, fighting for their adopted country was perceived as a pathway to citizenship. While the occasional regiment formed around a single nationality, such as Pennsylvania's Irish 69th or the German-speaking 74th, the patriotic identity of the Northern army was uniformly American.

OPPOSITE PAGE
Irish Brigade Recruiting Broadside
Philadelphia contributed several regiments of Irish soldiers to the war, among them the 69th and 116th Pennsylvania regiments. This 1861 recruitment broadside makes a direct appeal to the Hibernian community to join Colonel Robert Emmett Patterson's Irish Brigade. *Ken Turner Collection.*

LEFT
Adolpho Fernandaz Cavada In the early days of the conflict, Cuban-born brothers Adolpho and Frederico Cavada enlisted as officers in the 23rd Pennsylvania. Adolpho, a talented writer, kept a diary that later provided insight into his experience of war. At Gettysburg, he noted, "The air full … of flying shot, shell, and canister … and a groan here and there attest [to] their effect."

After the war, the Philadelphia-raised Cavada brothers were appointed consuls to Cuba but later resigned their posts, returning to Cuba to join in the fight to end Spanish rule. Both brothers died in the struggle—Frederico in 1871 by a Spanish firing squad, and Adolpho in battle in 1872. *Ken Turner Collection.*

BELOW
Thomas A. Smyth Born in Fermoy, County Cork, Ireland, Thomas A. Smyth was among thousands of Irish immigrants in Pennsylvania who enlisted. Smyth's first command was as captain in the three-month 24th Pennsylvania Infantry. He rose through the ranks to command a division of the Second Army Corps. *Ken Turner Collection.*

ABOVE
Colonel Gabriel DeKorponay, Soldier, Polka King Gabriel DeKorponay, a Hungarian immigrant with extensive military service, entered the army on June 28, 1861, as lieutenant colonel of the 28th Pennsylvania Volunteer Infantry. DeKorponay was promoted to colonel in April 1862, but ill health forced his discharge from the army less than a year later. DeKorponay was a nationally known dance instructor and had introduced the polka to the United States in the 1840s. *Ken Turner Collection.*

CHAPTER 2

Brigadier General Henry Bohlen
German-born Henry Bohlen, a wealthy Philadelphia businessman, was commissioned colonel of the 75th Pennsylvania Voluntary Infantry at age 50. An experienced military man, Bohlen had served as a staff officer in the Mexican War and had fought for the French in the Crimean War. In April 1862, Bohlen was promoted to brigadier general, only to be killed in action four months later. A Philadelphia newspaper reported, "Thus fell one of Philadelphia's best, bravest, and brightest children." *Ken Turner Collection.*

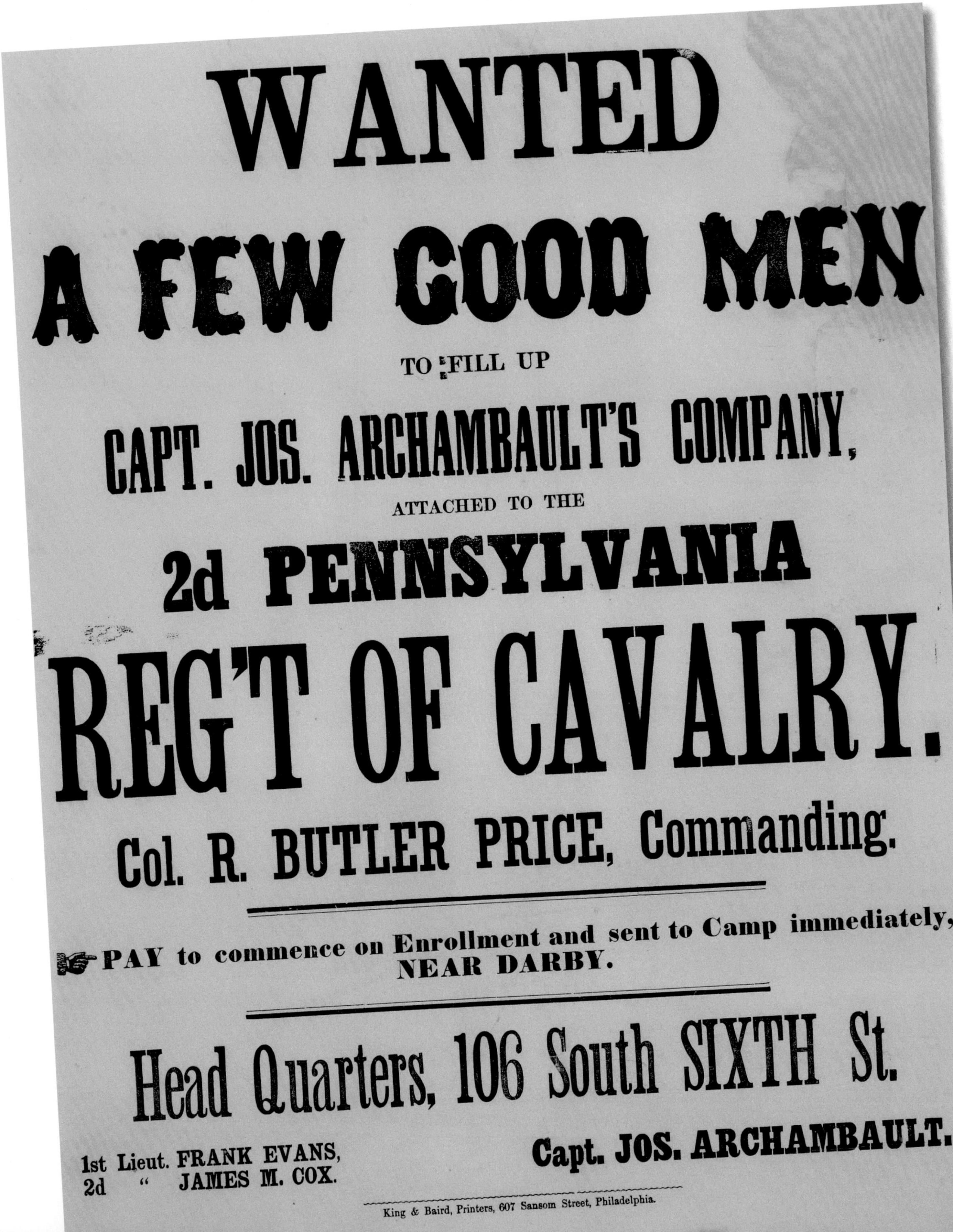

1862: WAR

WANTED
A FEW GOOD MEN
TO FILL UP

CAPT. JOS. ARCHAMBAULT'S COMPANY,

ATTACHED TO THE

2d PENNSYLVANIA
REG'T OF CAVALRY.

Col. R. BUTLER PRICE, Commanding.

☛ PAY to commence on Enrollment and sent to Camp immediately, NEAR DARBY.

Head Quarters, 106 South SIXTH St.

1st Lieut. FRANK EVANS,
2d " JAMES M. COX.

Capt. JOS. ARCHAMBAULT.

King & Baird, Printers, 607 Sansom Street, Philadelphia.

OPPOSITE AND ABOVE

Captain Joseph Archambault with sword and Recruiting Poster Born in France in 1796 and orphaned as an infant, Joseph Archambault attended military school as a ward of the French government, and later served as a valet to Napoleon. Wounded at Waterloo, Archambault was selected to accompany the deposed emperor to exile at St. Helena. Around 1817, the young man came to the U.S., settling in Newtown, Bucks County. After years as a hotel operator, the 65-year-old soldier was commissioned in the 2nd Pennsylvania Cavalry, serving nearly two years for his adopted country. *Ken Turner Collection.*

ABOVE

Colonel John Koltes, 73rd Pennsylvania Infantry In 1861, German-born John Koltes was commissioned colonel of the 73rd Pennsylvania Infantry, a Philadelphia unit comprised primarily of soldiers of German ancestry. On August 30, 1862, while riding at the head of his command, 1st Brigade, 2nd Division, 1st Corps Army of Virginia, Koltes and his horse were fatally hit by a shell fragment in the Battle of Second Bull Run (Second Manassas). *Ken Turner Collection.*

RIGHT
Conrad Seidentopf, 2nd Pennsylvania Cavalry By the time Conrad Seidentopf enlisted in the 2nd Pennsylvania Volunteer Cavalry, he was already a veteran, having served in the Prussian cavalry during the Crimean War. Pictured here in the uniform of quartermaster sergeant, Seidentopf served the 2nd Pennsylvania until discharged in 1865.
Ken Turner Collection.

OPPOSITE PAGE
Herbert Edwards Welsh-born Herbert Edwards was a musician in the 56th Pennsylvania regimental band.
Kraus/Messick Collection.

CHAPTER 2

Chaplains

Army chaplains entered the military from various denominations, as did the men they served. Chaplains provided a source of faith, bringing soldiers much needed comfort. In addition to their spiritual duties, chaplains wrote letters home for illiterate soldiers and were entrusted with mailing army pay to families. They ministered to the wounded on the battlefield and in field hospitals and prayed over the dying. Although considered non-combatant members of the armed forces, these men of the cloth faced death every day; one of them, Chaplain Horatio S. Howell, was killed on the steps of the Christ Lutheran Church during the Battle of Gettysburg.

ABOVE
Chaplain Robert Audley Browne During the battle at Chantilly, Virginia, September 1, 1862, Chaplain Robert Audley Browne rode up and down the regimental front under fierce rainstorms, shouting above claps of thunder and cannon fire, "Boys, remember Cromwell, trust in God, and keep your powder dry!" In this 1861 photo, the fighting Presbyterian chaplain proudly wears the uniform of an infantry officer. *Kraus/Messick Collection.*

RIGHT
Chaplain Charles W. Sanders Chaplain Charles W. Sanders poses with the 5th Corps badge on his watch fob. His regiment, the 131st Pennsylvania, was devastated at Fredericksburg, losing 177 men in a single hour. Sanders reenlisted in September 1864 as chaplain to the 208th Pennsylvania Infantry. His hat displays the 9th Corps badge from that regiment. *Ken Turner Collection.*

CHAPTER 2

Chaplains provided a source of faith, bringing soldiers much needed comfort.

Chaplain Alexander Stewart Chaplain Alexander Stewart of the 102nd Pennsylvania strikes a stalwart pose upon his mare Jessie. Stewart chronicled his war experience in a book, *Camp, March and Battlefield*, in which he defined a chaplain's duty: "to make those under your command better men, and hence better soldiers; to comfort the sick and wounded, and console the dying." *Ken Turner Collection.*

LEFT
Bucktail Drummer This drummer boy wears a deer tail on his cap, the trademark of a Pennsylvania Bucktail regiment. *Tom Molocea Collection.*

BELOW
Jonathan Ocker, Drummer Jonathan Ocker, drummer of Company A, 46th Pennsylvania Volunteers, with his drum that has been embellished per army regulations by an eagle with spread wings. *Ken Turner Collection.*

CHAPTER 2

MUSIC

In the 19th century, the lively sound of music accompanied soldiers marching into war. The stirring call of bugles, fifes, and drums—known as field music—signaled reveille, duty calls, and marching cadences with an established musical or percussive phrase. To lighten military life, popular music by songwriters such as George F. Root and Pennsylvania's own Stephen Foster was often sung by soldiers and played by regimental bands.

ABOVE

Daniel Seeman Far too young to be a soldier, Daniel Seeman of Honesdale, Wayne County, stands beside a drum, military cap in hand. The inscription on the back of the photo reads, "Daniel Seeman, drummer boy."
Kraus/Messick Collection.

LEFT

James Crumleigh, Bugler The job of a bugler, such as James Crumleigh of the 9th Pennsylvania Cavalry, was to deliver notes that could be heard throughout the ranks when a commanding officer's voice could not.
Ken Turner Collection.

Regimental Band, 106th Pennsylvania Before August 1862, regimental bands were formed at the discretion of a colonel, who could appoint as many as 16 non-combatant musicians. These band members from the 106th Pennsylvania display typical over-the-shoulder (OTS) brass instruments and drums. As with other camp comforts, regimental bands were phased out as the war intensified. *Ken Turner Collection.*

CHAPTER 2

LEFT

Musician, Regimental Band of the 114th Pennsylvania A bandsman from the 114th Pennsylvania leans on the bell of an over-the-shoulder bass saxhorn. Regimental bands were positioned in the front of a moving regiment so that the sound of large brass instruments, with their bells positioned backward, projected to the rear. *Ken Turner Collection.*

BELOW

Octarara Coronet Band The Octarara Coronet Band from Lancaster County was an early war militia organization whose members later enlisted in the Pennsylvania Reserve Corps. *Ken Turner Collection.*

Sheet Music Ballad The demand for new songs during the war was met by innovative songwriters who wrote military-themed lyrics to established popular tunes. Cheaply printed song sheets, doubling as stationery, were sold to the ranks by a soldier acting as an agent for the music publishers.
Kraus/Messick Collection.

CHAPTER 2

LEFT
Fifer, 101st Pennsylvania An unknown fifer of the 101st Pennsylvania wears an infantry musician's frock coat. *Ken Turner Collection.*

BELOW
Presentation Fife Unlike military-issued fifes made of rosewood, this comparatively expensive instrument was made of nickel silver and engraved with its owner's name: [Private]W.A. Randolph, Co. B, 6th Pa Heavy Art[tillery]. *Ken Turner Collection.*

Old Iron City Fiddle This fiddle was obviously well-loved by the many men of the 193rd Pennsylvania who signed it.
Ken Turner Collection.

1862: WAR

Cavalry Bugle This cavalry bugle's inscription indicates it was presented to Hiram Keasey by members of Company D, 21st Pennsylvania Cavalry, on October 25, 1864. *Ken Turner Collection.*

Pennsylvania's Battle Flags

For a Civil War regiment, its colors, or battle flags, represented the military heart of the unit. Pennsylvania Infantry regiments were authorized to carry two flags: their regimental colors, embellished with the seal of the United States, and the state colors, a six-by-six-and-a-half-foot version of the national flag with the state crest painted against the blue field and its regimental number on the fourth red stripe. Two Philadelphia firms produced all the state colors of Pennsylvania.

ABOVE
Flag of the 51st Pennsylvania The state colors of the 51st Pennsylvania show battle honors from Fredricksburg, Vicksburg, and Jackson. Remnants of "Antietam" can be seen on the top stripe. On the afternoon of September 17, 1862, this flag, along with two others carried by the 51st, were the first to successfully cross Burnside's Bridge at Antietam under galling enemy fire.
Kraus/Messick Collection.

RIGHT
Flag of the 83rd Pennsylvania Sergeant Alexander Rogers displays the state colors of the 83rd Pennsylvania. Rogers hoisted the colors when one bearer after another was killed during the skirmish at Malvern Hill on July 1, 1862, the last day of the Seven Days Battles near Richmond, Virginia. Rogers continued to carry the colors until he was killed at the Battle of the Wilderness in May 1864.
Ken Turner Collection.

In campaign and battle, the state flag was borne by a regimental color bearer and protected from enemy capture by men of the Color Guard, whose sole purpose was to defend the banner. Once a flag was too battered to carry, it was returned to the state. Its replacement would be issued with well-earned battle honors added to the stripes.

ABOVE
Flag of the 111th Pennsylvania Frank Guy and Alonzo Faust display the battle-worn state and regimental colors of the 111th Pennsylvania. *Ken Turner Collection.*

ABOVE RIGHT
Lithograph of State Flags *Kraus/Messick Collection.*

RIGHT
Flag of the 79th Pennsylvania Corporal John Morton of the 79th Pennsylvania poses with a camp flag. Banners such as these were typically brought from home and carried special meaning to their owners. *Ken Turner Collection.*

1862: WAR

ABOVE
Color Bearer Insignia, 56th Pennsylvania
Handsomely embroidered in silk and metallic thread, these crossed flags were displayed by color sergeants in the notch within their chevrons. This example was worn by Wallace Early of the 56th Pennsylvania.
Kraus/Messick Collection.

RIGHT
Flag of 9th Pennsylvania Reserves Sergeant Henry Blanchard displays the state colors of the 9th Pennsylvania Reserves. Wounded slightly at New Market Cross Roads, Virginia, part of the Seven Days Battles, on June 30, 1862, Blanchard carried the banner until his second more serious wound at Antietam several months later. *Ken Turner Collection.*

OPPOSITE
Secretary of War John B. Floyd On December 24, 1860, Secretary of War John B. Floyd of Virginia ordered thousands of government weapons sent to arsenals in the South. As 124 large cannon were moved from the Allegheny Arsenal in Pittsburh to the wharf, angry protests erupted. Telegrams flooded President Buchanan's office about Floyd's unilateral action. The protests delayed loading of the cannons onto ships until word from Washington superseded Floyd's orders—and prompted his resignation. *Ken Turner Collection.*

CHAPTER 2

Arsenals and Technology

Much of the long-term success of the Union war machine was due to the uninterrupted flow of military supplies. Pennsylvania was home to three federal arsenals, major manufacturers of ammunition and supplies. The Schuylkill Arsenal near Philadelphia turned out uniforms, blankets, and tents; the nearby Frankford Arsenal produced cartridges, cannon fuses, and percussion caps. The Allegheny Arsenal near Pittsburgh churned out rifle and artillery ammunition, leather accoutrements, artillery harnesses for horses, and field carriages for cannon. At its peak, the Schuylkill Arsenal kept 10,000 workers on its payroll, most of them women. "Sewing women" were paid by the piece for each completed uniform they stitched from pre-cut patterns. Their handwork kept soldiers supplied and families fed.

BELOW
Philadelphia Depot Canteens Hundreds of thousands of canteens, many manufactured by the Schuylkill Arsenal, were delivered to the Philadelphia Depot for distribution among Union troops. *Kraus/Messick Collection.*

1862: WAR

> "Without the services of this eminent soldier, the national cause must have been lost or deeply imperiled."
>
> ~Secretary of State William Seward regarding Quartermaster General Montgomery C. Meigs

Quartermaster General Montgomery C. Meigs
Born in Georgia but raised and educated in Philadelphia, Montgomery C. Meigs was a career military man and loyal Unionist. Meigs graduated from the United States Military Academy at West Point in 1836, and, while in the U.S. Army Corps of Engineers, helped construct several forts and supervise the engineering of the Washington Aqueduct, Union Arch Bridge, and the wings and dome of the United States Capitol. In May 1861, Meigs' extraordinary leadership and talent were put to use as U.S. quartermaster general; he supervised a department that expeditiously supplied the northern army of 2.2 million troops. At Meigs' recommendation, Arlington National Cemetery was established in 1864. Both he and his son, Lieutenant John R. Meigs, whose death in combat preceded his father, are interred there. *Library of Congress, cwpbh-03111.*

CHAPTER 2

Rodman Gun While serving at the Allegheny Arsenal, ordnance officer Major Thomas Jackson Rodman devised a process to ensure the even cooling of molten iron during the casting of cannon barrels. His innovation enabled the Fort Pitt Foundry to produce the largest cannons yet cast; each Rodman barrel weighed an astounding 117,000 pounds. This photograph of a Rodman Gun, taken in 1864, emphasized the cannon's 20-inch bore. *Ken Turner Collection.*

ABOVE

Allegheny Arsenal Two city blocks long by one block wide, the Allegheny Arsenal was built east of Pittsburgh in 1814. By the outbreak of the Civil War, it was one of three important federal arsenals in Pennsylvania. Looking downhill across Butler Street from the upper arsenal, this photograph reveals 17 heavy artillery cannon laid on the ground near the arsenal stables. Across the street is the guardhouse and armory.

John L. Carnprobst, Karen S. Urbanek, and Louis E. Wagner.

OPPOSITE ABOVE

Explosion at Allegheny Arsenal In 1862, Allegheny Arsenal employed 1,000 workers, mostly women, who rolled rifle cartridges and armed artillery shells with highly explosive materials. Women were hired as cartridge rollers based on the belief they were more adept at fine handwork. This simple block wood device, belonging to Allegheny Arsenal worker Sarah Finn Millbach, was used to bundle 10 rifle cartridges into a neat package for use in the field. By the end of 1861, arsenal workers were producing 124,000 cartridges per day. Soldiers were issued four packages (40 rounds), which fit into a leather cartridge box worn on the chest or belt.

As demand for ammunition grew, safety standards relaxed, which resulted in grains of gunpowder accumulating on the floors and between cobblestones in the streets. With production at its peak, an errant spark ignited powder, which spread to the laboratory porch and several powder kegs stored there. The first explosion was quickly followed by a second, then a third. Those who weren't killed in the bloody blasts were consumed in the fire that engulfed the wooden structure, killing 78, the single greatest loss of civilian life during the war. However, the disaster was overshadowed by news of the devastation at the Battle of Antietam the same day. In costs to both soldier and civilian lives, September 17, 1862, was indeed the bloodiest day of the war.

Heinz History Center, Gift of Alfred L. Millbach.

CHAPTER 2

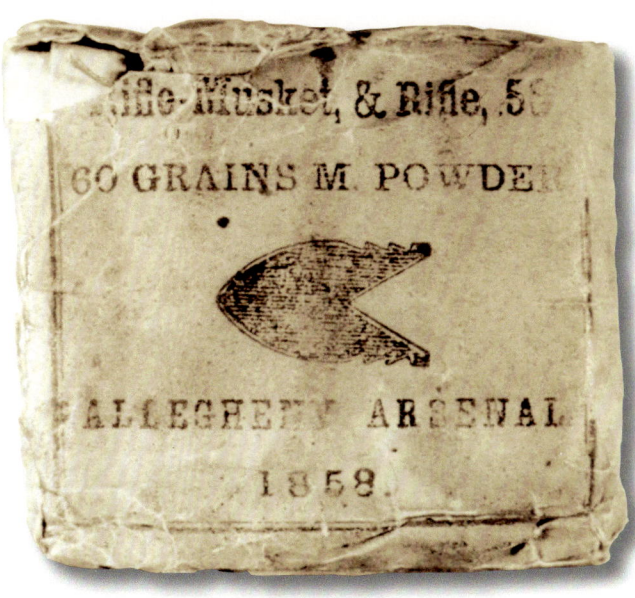

ABOVE
A Rare Artifact
A packet of 10 cartridges, formed in a holder like the one seen here from the Allegheny Arsenal.
Dean Thomas.

LEFT
Arsenal Girls An illustration in *Harper's Weekly*, July 20, 1861, shows young women seated around a table filling cartridges at a federal arsenal.
Heinz History Center, Library & Archives.

1862: WAR

Photograph. By Richards.

Girard House Hotel
Northeast corner of Chestnut & 9th st.
As viewed from the Southwest across the foundation walls of the new Hotel on the S.E. corner of Chestnut and Ninth Street.

Girard House Shortly after the outbreak of war, a former Philadelphia hotel, the Girard House, was converted to a makeshift uniform manufacturing facility. Nearly a thousand local women quickly rallied to work as seamstresses. *Bryn Mawr.*

CHAPTER 2

LEFT

Frankford Arsenal Fuses A package of cannon fuses produced at the Frankford Arsenal near Philadephia. The fuse was inserted into a charged projectile, such as a cannonball, as it was loaded. Upon firing the cannon, the fuse ignited, exploding downrange over its intended target. *Ken Turner Collection.*

RIGHT

Uniform made by the Schuylkill Arsenal Built in 1800, the Schuylkill Arsenal in Philadelphia was one of the largest producers of uniforms and textiles in the nation. Nearly 12,000 employees worked at the arsenal during the Civil War. *Ken Turner Collection.*

115

Herman Haupt and the USMRR

In February 1862, Congress created the United States Military Railroad (USMRR); Pennsylvanian Herman Haupt (West Point, class of 1835) was appointed chief of construction and transportation. Haupt, who specialized in railroad, bridge, and tunnel construction, took the position as a colonel in April, and by September was commissioned brigadier general of volunteers. Under his direction, the USMRR was a key component in the victory to save the Union. Here, Haupt demonstrates a pair of pontoons small enough to be easily carried and concealed, but when assembled, ideal for scouting operations.

Library of Congress, ppmsca-10341.

ABOVE
USMRR Train and Work Crew A train and work party in Virginia.
Library of Congress, ppmsca-07293.

OPPOSITE
Haupt's Torpedo The inventive mind of General Herman Haupt conceived of an explosive demolition device known as a torpedo "for quickly wrecking wooden bridges," as written on the back of this photo. The device (seen here being assembled by a soldier) was inserted into a hole drilled in the truss of a bridge and detonated by wire. *Library of Congress, ppmsca-10403.*

CHAPTER 2

1862: WAR

ABOVE
Colonel Jacob Zeilin, USMC As captain, Jacob Zeilin held second in command of the Marine battalion at the first Battle of Bull Run (Manassas). He survived wounding and in June 1864 was promoted to colonel and named commandant of the U.S. Marine Corps. In 1867, Zeilin was promoted to brigadier general and is credited with authorizing the corps' "eagle, globe, and anchor" insignia, still worn by Marines today. *Ken Turner Collection.*

RIGHT
Colonel John Harris, USMC Chester County native Colonel John Harris, commandant of the Marine Corps when the Civil War broke out, remained the corps' senior officer until his death in 1864. He served 50 years of distinguished service. *Ken Turner Collection.*

THE UNITED STATES MARINE CORPS

The United States Marine Corps (USMC) achieved wartime strength of 4,000 men and officers. For the most part, Marines performed their traditional duties as detachments on board the ships of the U.S. Navy in coastal and blockade operations. Marines who served on land did so in small numbers, and on occasion fought alongside Army troops, most notably at the July 1861 Battle of First Bull Run (Manassas) where, among a battalion of 350 Marines, nearly all were new recruits from Pittsburgh and Philadelphia. Pennsylvania Marines served until the end of the war.

CHAPTER 2

THE UNITED STATES NAVY

During the Civil War, only New York and Massachusetts sent more men into the United States Navy (USN) and Marine Corps than Pennsylvania. More than 14,000 Pennsylvanians enlisted in these services, fighting up and down the Mississippi, on the Great Lakes, along the Atlantic and Pacific coasts, in the Gulf of Mexico, and off the coast of France. The vital private shipbuilding yards of Philadelphia and Pittsburgh were critical to the Navy's mission, as were the strategic ports of Erie in the west and Philadelphia in the east. Notably, the Navy permitted the enlistment of African Americans long before the Army created the United States Colored Troops.

ABOVE

Joseph F. Baker, USMC Lieutenant Joseph F. Baker was among U.S. Marines stationed at the Philadelphia shipyard who were called to defend Washington. On July 21, 1861, he was struck in the mouth by a bayonet at the Battle of First Bull Run (Manassas), knocking him unconscious. *Ken Turner Collection.*

LEFT

Marcus Lewis, USS *Silver Lake*, USN
Two sailors of the Mississippi Squadron enjoy a cigar while posing for the camera. Marcus (or Mark) Lewis stands beside a seated John E. Nicholson. Both men enlisted from Erie on board the USS *Michigan* in summer 1864 and were quickly sent westward. Assigned to the gunboat USS *Silver Lake* as seamen, the two spent their days patrolling the Tennessee River for wayward rebels. Lewis died of typhoid fever at Smithland, Kentucky, on January 15, 1865; his body was returned home to Erie for burial. Nicholson served until his one-year enlistment expired in August 1865. He returned home to Erie County, where he lived the rest of his life. *Pat Knierman Collection.*

U. S. STEAMER MICHIGAN.

ABOVE
USS *Michigan* The *Michigan* was not only the first iron-hulled warship in the U.S. Navy, but was the only warship on the Great Lakes during the Civil War. The steamer was built in components by Stackhouse and Tomlinson Iron Works of Pittsburgh, then transported by ox cart and canal to Erie, where it was assembled and christened late in 1843 in honor of the recently proclaimed 26th state.

The *Michigan* protected locks, lake commerce, and lakeside cities, with as many as 4,000 recruits coming aboard for transport to various stations during its service. At least two serious Confederate attempts to capture the *Michigan* failed during the war. After a long career, including 61 years of an active naval commission and a name change to *Wolverine*, the steamer was scrapped in 1949. *Ted Karle Collection.*

OPPOSITE
Commodore Andrew A. Harwood, USN
A great-grandson of Benjamin Franklin, Commodore Andrew A. Harwood was chief of the Bureau of Ordnance and Hydrography from 1858 to 1862. Afterward, Harwood commanded the Washington Navy Yard and the Potomac Flotilla until December 1863. In 1869, he was promoted to rear admiral on the retired list. *Library of Congress, 3c10147.*

1862: WAR

RIGHT

Rear Admiral John A. Dahlgren A large number of heavy ordnance aboard navy warships, such as large smoothbore and rifled cannons, were manufactured at the Fort Pitt Foundry in Pittsburgh. Ranging in size from 12-pound howitzers to mammoth 20-inch guns, hundreds of these cannons were designed by Rear Admiral John A. Dahlgren, perhaps the world's greatest inventor of naval ordnance. Born in Philadelphia, Dahlgren's naval career stretched from 1826 until his death in 1870. For 15 years, he developed naval cannons at the Washington Naval Yard. At the outbreak of war, Dahlgren's expertise became critical to the Northern cause; in July 1862, he was named chief of the Bureau of Ordnance and Hydrography, with the rank of captain. Dahlgren finished the war with the rank of rear admiral, commanding the South Atlantic Blockading Squadron.
Library of Congress, cwpb-0580.

OPPOSITE

Dahlgren Rifle Rear Admiral John A. Dahlgren stands next to one of his many inventions—a 50-pound Dahlgren rifle. The photo was taken April 21, 1865, aboard the steamer USS *Pawnee*, anchored in Charleston Harbor, South Carolina; the battered remains of Fort Sumter are barely discernable in the distance. The Fort Pitt Foundry cast many of the 5.1-inch "fifty pounder" iron rifles.
Library of Congress, cwpb-02990.

1862: WAR

BELOW
Commander Napoleon Collins, USN
Commander Napoleon Collins entered the navy in 1834. The Fayette County native was lieutenant aboard the USS *Vandalia* when the Civil War broke out and was promoted to the rank of commander in 1862. Aboard the *Vandalia*, Collins captured the Confederate commerce raider, *Florida*, in the Bay of San Salvador, Brazil, in October 1864.
Ted Karle Collection.

ABOVE
David Dixon Porter, Admiral, USN David Dixon Porter enlisted as a lieutenant and mustered out a rear admiral, one of the two most important officers in the Union Navy. Born in Chester, Delaware County, the son of famed naval officer Commodore David Porter, the younger's achievements included the command of a flotilla at Vicksburg and of the North Atlantic Blockade Squadron, as well as the capture of Forts Jackson and Saint Phillip in Louisiana. On three occasions, Congress voted thanks to Porter for distinguished service.
Ken Turner Collection.

CHAPTER 2

CAMPAIGNS OF 1862

As summer approached, the Northern advance into Confederate territory commenced in earnest. Pennsylvania boys and men took up fighting in Virginia, Maryland, South Carolina, and Tennessee, while their families anxiously awaited news of their fate. Battles throughout the year at Gaines' Mills, Fair Oaks, Antietam, and Stones River left the blood of the Keystone State's soldiers on distant soil, and left the horrors in the collective memory of survivors and those at home.

The Sunken Road at Antietam Filled with human carnage, this sunken farm lane was the site of some of the fiercest fighting at Antietam. *Library of Congress, cwpb-00239.*

RIGHT

Colonel Oliver Hazzard Rippey, 61st Pennsylvania In 1861, Oliver Hazzard Rippey, a veteran of the Mexican War, obtained permission from Governor Curtin to raise the 61st Pennsylvania. Rippey recruited men from Pittsburgh and later from Philadelphia, Indiana, Mercer, and Luzerne counties. Colonel Rippey was commanding the regiment during the fight at Fair Oaks, Virginia, on May 31, 1862, when the regiment was outflanked. Every line officer and half the men were killed or wounded in the battle, including Rippey, whose body was left on the field. After nightfall, the colonel's remains were recovered and returned to his home in Pittsburgh, along with the regimental colors. *Ken Turner Collection.*

OPPOSITE

Colonel James Cameron, First Colonel Killed Brother of Secretary of War Simon Cameron and a native of Lancaster County, Colonel James Cameron commanded the men of the 79th New York, aptly named the Highlanders for their Scots-Irish roots. At Bull Run, Cameron's regiment, advancing under fierce enemy fire, charged three times over the dead and wounded of the 2nd Wisconsin. When they mistook a rebel flag for their own, the Highlanders ceased firing and received an assault that caused them to fall back from the hill. Upon retreat, they found the body of their colonel in the Henry house yard, felled by enemy fire. *Library of Congress, cwpb-05392.*

CHAPTER 2

ABOVE
Captain John Moore, 10th Pennsylvania Reserves On June 27, 1862, at the Battle of Gaines' Mills (or the First Battle of Cold Harbor, the third of the Seven Days Battles near Richmond, Virginia), Captain John Moore of Company K, 10th Pennsylvania Reserves, was severely wounded in the leg. After he was removed to Fortress Monroe, it was necessary for surgeons to amputate the mangled limb above the knee. *Ken Turner Collection.*

ABOVE RIGHT
Sergeant Hiram W. Purcell, 104th Pennsylvania Infantry A native of Upper Black Eddy, Bucks County, Sergeant Hiram Purcell, 24, carried the national colors of the 104th Pennsylvania Infantry into the battle of Fair Oaks, Virginia, on May 31, 1862. While holding the flag high, Purcell saw the color bearer of the state banner fall. As the Confederate battle line advanced, he snatched up the colors, marking himself an even more requisite target. While carrying both flags to the rear, Purcell was shot three times; he collapsed exhausted, but survived his wounds. Purcell died May 13, 1918, and was buried at Laurel Cemetery in White Haven, Luzerne County.
Ken Turner Collection.

OPPOSITE
Gifted but Flawed Major General George Brinton McClellan, a gifted though tragically flawed military leader, was more responsible for the Union's lack of progress than probably any other officer. A native of Philadelphia and an 1846 West Point graduate, McClellan was an able administrator who was beloved by many of his men but proved to be an extremely cautious field commander. After early victories in western Virginia, McClellan was appointed commander of the Army of the Potomac in August 1861. Three months later, he was promoted to General-in-Chief of the Armies of the United States. Despite the rise in rank, McClellan failed to capture Richmond in the spring of 1862—a critical failure. At Antietam, he battled Lee's army to a stalemate, forcing the Confederates to retreat into Virginia. His failure to press Lee's retreating forces after the battle led Lincoln to relieve him of command, effectively ending his military service. He resigned from the army on the day of the 1864 presidential election, in which he lost his bid for the presidency to the incumbent Lincoln.
Library of Congress, ppmsca-08368.

MAJOR GEN'L. GEO. B. McCLELLAN.

Entered according to Act of Congress in the year 1861, by M. B. Brady, in the Clerk's office of the District Court of the District of Columbia.

Sergeant James Fullerton, Battery B 1st Pennsylvania Light Artillery "It is with tears that I pen to you the fate of our noble boys," wrote Sergeant James Fullerton in a letter home after Battery B was overrun at the Battle of Charles City Cross Roads (the sixth of the Seven Days Battles). Fullerton recounted the deaths of Lieutenant Henry W. Danforth and Sergeant James Miller, the latter killed while trying to rescue a third mortally wounded soldier. *Kraus/Messick Collection.*

CHAPTER 2

LEFT
Colonel Hugh Watson McNeil, 13th Pennsylvania Reserves (1st Rifles/Bucktails) Warren County lawyer Hugh W. McNeil was the esteemed commander of the 13th Pennsylvania Reserves, also known as the 1st Rifles and the Pennsylvania Bucktails. On September 16, 1862, in a skirmish at Sharpsburg, Maryland, Colonel McNeil was shot in the lung and killed. *Ken Turner Collection.*

FAR LEFT
Colonel (Brevet-Brigadier General) William Watts Hart Davis, 104th Pennsylvania Volunteer Infantry An 1842 graduate of Vermont's Norwich University, and a pre-Civil War faculty member at the Virginia Military, Scientific, and Literary Academy, Davis first commanded a company in the 25th Pennsylvania Infantry. After the company's three-month term of service expired, Davis raised the 104th Pennsylvania Infantry from Bucks County, leading the regiment for the duration of the war. Davis lost his right-hand fingers during the siege of Charleston; following recovery, he went to Philadelphia to sit on the general courts martial board for the rest of the war. After his service ended in 1865, Davis was brevetted to brigadier general of volunteers. *Ken Turner Collection.*

"It is with tears that I pen to you the fate of our noble boys."

Eagleson Cap and Photo First Lieutenant Andrew Eagleson of Company K, 8th Pennsylvania Reserves, wore this forage cap at the Battle of Antietam. The stick marks the path of an enemy bullet that narrowly missed killing the officer. *Both Ken Turner Collection.*

CHAPTER 2

BELOW
25th Regiment Pennsylvania Militia of 1862 These soldiers of the 25th Regiment were part of the Pennsylvania Militia of 1862, called up by Governor Curtin to guard against Confederate capture of DuPont's Mills, the producer of nearly half the federal army's supply of gunpowder. Lee's invasion of the North however, did not target the mill; therefore, these men, impressively armed with Sharp's rifles (renowned for accuracy and range), served only 16 days before mustering out. *Kraus/Messick Collection.*

ABOVE
Colonel James Childs, 4th Pennsylvania Cavalry A civil engineer before the war, James Childs proved to be a competent military leader. Serving first in the militia, then volunteering for the 12th Pennsylvania Infantry in the first three-month enlistment of the war, Childs went on to raise and command the 4th Pennsylvania Cavalry. On September 17, 1862, at the Battle of Antietam, while Childs conferred with staff officers of a cavalry brigade near Middle Bridge, he was struck in the left hip by a cannonball and thrown off his horse. Severely mangled and losing blood, Childs managed to give his last orders and dictate a message to his wife and children before dying. *Ken Turner Collection.*

FAR RIGHT

Major Frank Zentmyer, 5th PVRC Captain Frank Zentmyer of the 5th Pennsylvania Reserves poses in Alexandria, Virginia, in spring 1862. By August, Zentmyer was promoted to major and took part in the intense Battle of Fredericksburg. The reserves fought hard and gained the right of the Confederate line, but with heavy cost to the regiment. Nearly all the 5th's commanding officers were lost, among them Zentmyer and his brother, Adjutant David Zentmyer. *Ken Turner Collection.*

RIGHT AND BELOW

Lieutenant Colonel Vincent Wilcox, 132nd Pennsylvania and Sword of Colonel Wilcox Raised in August 1862, the 132nd Pennsylvania quickly found itself in Maryland. On September 17, while posted in front of the Sunken Road at Antietam, the regiment's baptism by fire came during some of the most severe fighting yet seen. With their ammunition exhausted, the 132nd and the famed Irish Brigade drove the enemy out of their shielded location at bayonet point, taking 300 prisoners in the melee. Starting the day some 750 strong, only 364 men remained. Among the dead was Colonel Richard Oakford. Command fell to Lieutenant Colonel Vincent Wilcox, pictured cradling the sword seen below. *Both Ken Turner Collection.*

CHAPTER 2

Jacob Barndollar, 133rd Pennsylvania Volunteers For the 133rd Pennsylvania Volunteers, the long painful day at Fredericksburg ended with Humphrey's Division assault on Marye's Heights. In a move known as the "forlorn hope," the division fixed bayonets and charged across the open field and uphill under withering fire from Confederates behind a stone wall above them. In the assault, Jacob Barndollar of the 133rd Pennsylvania Volunteers was struck in the arm. After his recovery, Barndollar went home to Everett, Bedford County, where he later served on the town council.
Ken Turner Collection.

1862: WAR

BELOW

John Geety, 47th Pennsylvania Among other Pennsylvania regiments, the 47th arrived by steamer in South Carolina with hopes of pushing north toward the Confederate capital in Richmond. On October 22, 1862, at the Battle of Pocotaligo, South Carolina, Lieutenant John Geety was struck in the eye by an enemy bullet.
Ken Turner Collection.

ABOVE

Colonel Henry Zinn, 130th Pennsylvania Volunteers After the entire color company (including the color guard) of the 130th Pennsylvania was obliterated by a single volley at the Battle of Fredericksburg, Colonel Henry Zinn took the regimental flag and ordered his broken regiment to rally with him. The intensity of fire too great to bear, Zinn, flag in hand, began to retreat when he was hit below the eye by a bullet. Both Zinn and the riddled regimental flag were carried to the rear; the colonel died within a half hour.
Ken Turner Collection.

CHAPTER 2

Colonel William Sirwell, 78th Pennsylvania Volunteer Infantry
Born at the Allegheny Arsenal in 1820, William Sirwell had ample opportunity as a child to observe military life. His own long and distinguished career began at 19 with enlistment in the state militia, where he was promoted to command four different organizations. In 1855, Sirwell raised the first African American militia company in the state, the Hannibal Guards. The colonel also formed and commanded the 78th Pennsylvania Volunteers. In December 1862, at Stones River, Tennessee, the 78th captured a Confederate artillery battery and the flag of the 26th Tennessee (now in the collections of the State Museum of Pennsylvania).

The State Museum of Pennsylvania.

1862: WAR

Emancipation Proclamation President Lincoln's Emancipation Proclamation, freeing slaves in any state of the Confederacy that remained in rebellion on January 1, 1863, signaled the end of human bondage for millions of black Americans living in the South. Total abolition of slavery was finalized by the 13th Amendment, which took effect in December 1865. Photographs of decorated versions of the document were sold by photographers as commemorative mementos.
Ken Turner Collection.

TOTAL ABOLITION OF SLAVERY
TOOK EFFECT DECEMBER
1865

OPPOSITE

Peter Housum, 77th Pennsylvania On September 28, 1861, Peter B. Housum, who hailed from Chambersburg, enlisted in the 77th Pennsylvania Infantry as a lieutenant colonel. On December 31, 1862, while leading his men through the worst of the Battle at Stones River, Tennessee, Housum was struck down and died of his wounds the following day. *Ken Turner Collection.*

Hays Victorious Following Pickett's Charge at Gettysburg, General Alexander Hays of Pittsburgh famously dragged Confederate battle flags in front of his troops. Aide-de-camp Lieutenant David Shields, left, commissioned this painting around 1910. After Shields' death in 1944, his sister gave away the painting, and it has not been seen since, though one report placed it in a private club in Franklin, Venango County. This print is from Betty Shields, the daughter-in-law of David's brother, Thomas. Their other brother, William, was killed in the Battle of the Wilderness. *Betty G.Y. Shields.*

CH. 3

1863: DEFENDING THE STATE

As 1863 dawned, the Union triumphed at Stone's River, Tennessee, but faltered near Fredericksburg, Virginia. Spring brought the Union siege of Vicksburg, Mississippi, and a defeat at Chancellorsville, Virginia. By summer, Confederates were marching into Pennsylvania.

With husbands and sons away at war, Pennsylvanians struggled to make ends meet, while industries in Philadelphia, Harrisburg, and Pittsburgh thrived by landing lucrative manufacturing contracts. Pennsylvania's transformation to the industrial age was powered by the engine of war.

The New Year's Day enactment of Lincoln's Emancipation Proclamation freed slaves in the South and allowed for the enlistment of African American soldiers in the North. Even with the addition of black regiments, the toll of conflict prompted the United States to initiate its first national military draft.

ALL BELIEVED
THAT THE FIGHT TO PRESERVE THE UNION
WAS THEIR CALLING

Chancellorsville Map

On January 26, 1863, after the loss of 13,000 Union soldiers at the Battle of Fredericksburg, President Lincoln replaced the Commander of the Army of the Potomac, Ambrose Burnside, with General Joseph Hooker. Blue and Gray met four months later near Chancellorsville, Virginia, midway between Washington, D.C., and Richmond, Virginia. The battle from April 30 to May 6 ended in a decisive Southern victory, though at a high cost: the accidental wounding and eventual death of Confederate Lieutenant General Thomas "Stonewall" Jackson.

Kraus/Messick Collection.

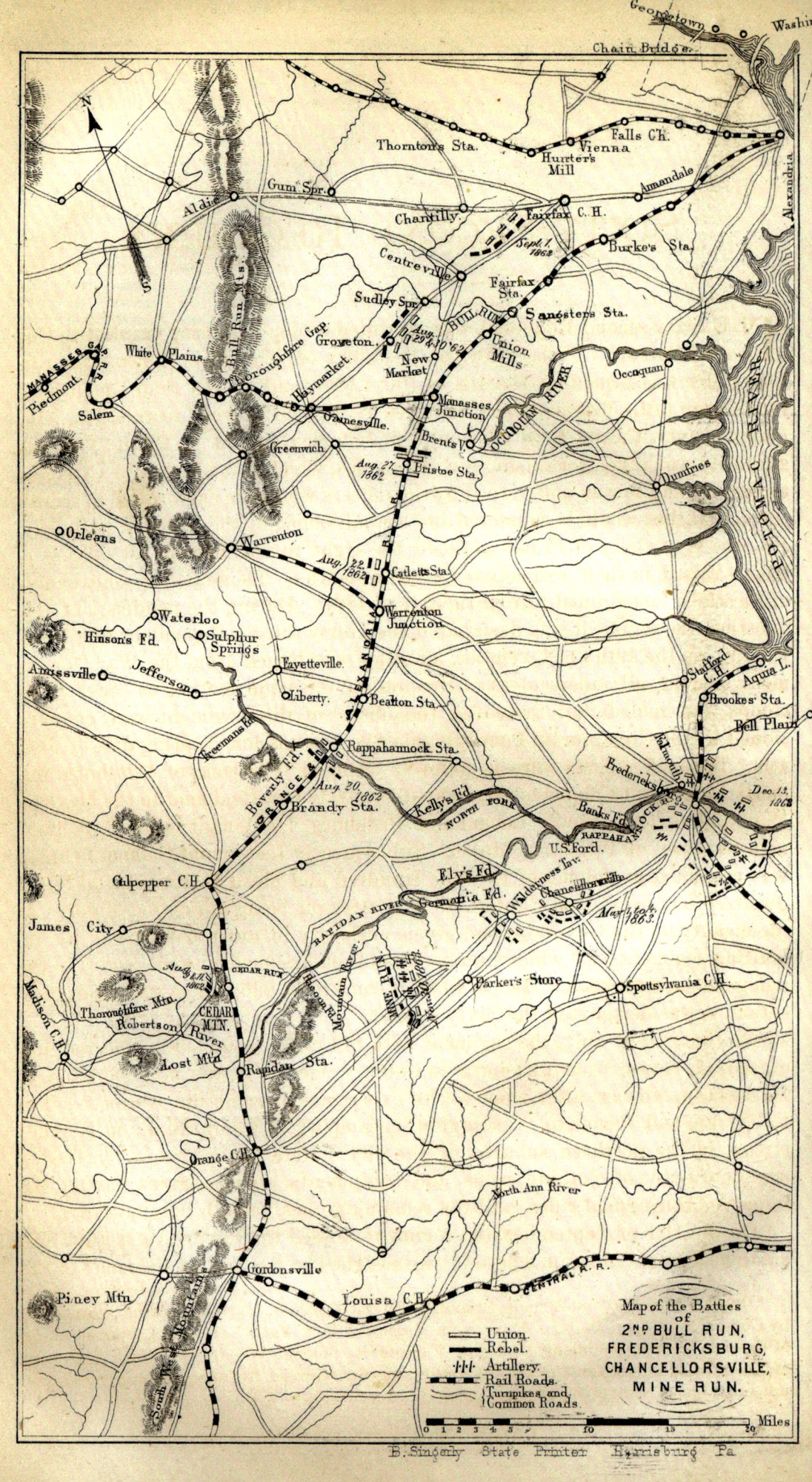

CHAPTER 3

BELOW

Pittsburgh Entrepreneur, Politician, and Captain At age 47, Captain Robert Hampton of Battery F, Pennsylvania Independent Light Artillery, was considered a father figure to his men. Hampton bravely commanded the battery until he was killed on May 3, 1863, at the battle of Chancellorsville. *Ken Turner Collection.*

ABOVE

Zouaves Lose Second Commander Six-foot-three Colonel Gustavus Town assumed command of Gosline's Zouaves from founder Colonel John Gosline, who had died from wounds at the 1862 battle of Gaines' Mill. While leading the 95th Pennsylvania at the second battle of Fredericksburg (Salem Church), Town was killed instantly by a shot through the heart. *Ken Turner Collection.*

At Ease The 8th Pennsylvania Cavalry's Robert Oldham (cap hanging from foot) of Company I and William Corrie, Company F, lounge in a playfully irreverent pose. The 8th Pennsylvania earned distinction at Chancellorsville when it charged Stonewall Jackson's impenetrable column. General Pleasanton reported that the assault "has excited the highest admiration." *Ken Turner Collection.*

CHAPTER 3

Prelude to Gettysburg

In June 1863, Confederate General Robert E. Lee aimed to move fighting out of the South and cap a two-year string of successes with a decisive victory. He hoped an invasion of the North would also resupply his army, weaken Northern morale before the fall elections, and perhaps end the siege around Vicksburg.

The Confederate invasion began on June 15 as Southern General Albert Jenkins' troops rode into Chambersburg. Pennsylvania's inexperienced Emergency Militia was no match for the zealous invaders, and Union cavalry sent to intervene lost ground to the larger Confederate units. A week later, Confederate General Ewell triumphed in a skirmish outside Greencastle, Franklin County, producing the first casualties in the Keystone State – one of whom was Corporal William Rihl, a Pennsylvanian serving in the 1st New York Cavalry. The towns of Shippensburg and Carlisle fell to the rebels on June 25 followed by Mechanicsburg (all Cumberland County) three days later. By June 29, Lee's army was spread out in an arc from Chambersburg to Carlisle to near Harrisburg and Wrightsville, York County, on the Susquehanna River.

Meanwhile Union commander Joseph Hooker marched north over a more easterly route to keep between Washington, D.C., and the Confederates. Hooker's failure at Chancellorsville, however, convinced Lincoln to replace the unfit commander with General George Gordon Meade, who moved his 95,000 troops toward rebel encampments. On June 30, the Union's cavalry encountered J.E.B. Stuart's Confederate cavalry, touching off a fierce fight at Hanover, York County. By the next morning, both armies were converging on Gettysburg where for three days the war would play out on Pennsylvania soil.

West Point "First in Class" York County native William B. Franklin, a skilled engineer and architect, was appointed brigadier general, and, later, major general, of the 6th Corps. The fast-ascending officer gained command of Burnside's Left Grand Division (two corps, under Major Generals John F. Reynolds and William F. Smith) just before their devastating defeat at Fredericksburg. Despite his distinguished record, Franklin was relieved of his command and became the subject of a government inquest. At home in York during the Gettysburg campaign, Franklin was relegated to counseling city leaders on defense strategy of the town.
Ken Turner Collection.

1863: DEFENDING THE STATE

This photo shows the bridge as it looked before the war. Destroyed June 28, 1863.

Columbia–Wrightsville Bridge Knowing the Columbia–Wrightsville Bridge across the Susquehanna would give Confederates access to Harrisburg, Lancaster, Reading, and Philadelphia, Union commander Colonel Jacob Frick ordered his 27th Pennsylvania Emergency Militia to set explosive charges under the structure. As General John B. Gordon moved his Confederate troops onto the 5,620-foot-long span, Frick ordered the charges ignited. Although the explosion was not adequate to bring down the longest covered bridge in the world, Frick's precaution of saturating the span with oil enabled him to burn the bridge. The resulting blaze spread to the town of Wrightsville, forcing the rebel troops back to York. *Ken Turner Collection.*

Preemptive Destruction Having already established himself a war hero at Fredericksburg, veteran officer Jacob G. Frick of the 129th Pennsylvania went on to earn a Medal of Honor at Chancellorsville for regaining his regimental colors after their capture by Confederates. After his term of service expired, Frick was recalled to command the 27th Pennsylvania Emergency Militia. It was Frick and Major Granville Haller who made the strategic decision to burn the Columbia–Wrightsville Bridge before Southern troops could capture and cross it. *Kraus/Messick Collection.*

1863: DEFENDING THE STATE

Defending Philadelphia In June 1863, the people of Pennsylvania braced for an invasion of their capital, Harrisburg, and attacks of strategic targets in Philadelphia and Pittsburgh. Mayor Alexander Henry of Philadelphia ordered the Home Guard to defend the city. *Ken Turner Collection.*

DEFENCE
OF THE
CITY OF PHILADELPHIA

Office of the Mayor of the City of Philadelphia.

BY VIRTUE OF THE AUTHORITY vested in me, by the Act of the General Assembly of the Commonwealth of Pennsylvania, entitled, "An Act relating to the Home Guard of the City of Philadelphia, Approved the Sixteenth day of May Anno Domini one thousand eight hundred and sixty one.

I do hereby require Brigadier General A. J. PLEASONTON, Commander of the **HOME GUARD**, to order out (and into the service of the City of Philadelphia,) THE WHOLE OF THE SAID GUARD, for the preservation of the public peace **AND THE DEFENCE OF THE CITY.** And I hereby call upon all persons within the limits of the said City, to yield a PROMPT AND READY OBEDIENCE to the Orders of the said Commander of the HOME GUARD, and of those acting under his authority in the execution of his and their said duties.

In witness whereof, I have hereunto set my hand and caused the Corporate Seal of the City of Philadelphia, to be affixed, this sixteenth day of June, A. D., one thousand eight hundred and sixty-three.

ALEXANDER HENRY,
Mayor of Philadelphia.

HEAD-QUARTERS, HOME GUARD, CITY OF PHILADELPHIA,
June 16th, 1863.

Under the authority of an Act of the General Assembly of the Commonwealth of Pennsylvania, entitled "An Act relating to the Home Guard of the City of Philadelphia," approved the sixteenth day of May, Anno Domini, one thousand eight hundred and sixty-one, and of the requirement of the HON. ALEXANDER HENRY, Mayor of the City made pursuant thereto, and hereto prefixed, the undersigned assumes the duties "FOR THE PRESERVATION OF THE PUBLIC PEACE AND THE DEFENCE OF THE CITY."

He invites the support and co-operation of his fellow-citizens, and of all the Authorities, National, State and Municipal, in the performance of his responsible duties.

A. J. PLEASONTON,
Brigadier General Commanding in Philadelphia.

Wm. BRADFORD,
Assistant Adjutant General.

King & Baird, Printers, 607 Sansom Street, Philadelphia.

CHAPTER 3

"We would rather give the rascals twice over what we did than have them back!"

~ Cassandra Small

BELOW

Outspoken Lady of York Cassandra "Cassie" Small was indignant the day Confederate Jubal Early secured the surrender of York, the largest Northern town to fall into Rebel hands. Small was especially appalled by Early's threat to burn the town if a ransom of shoes, clothing, rations, and money was not handed over. Two days later, the general rode away with $28,000 of the citizens' cash. "Oh, I could fill sheet after sheet with all their audacious villanies [sic].... It is a matter never to be forgotten."
York County Heritage Trust.

ABOVE

Tenderfoot Defenders With most of Pennsylvania's troops on Southern battlefields, the early burden to defend the state's borders rested with the Emergency Troops, created in 1863 by Governor Curtin. The novice soldiers of the 26th Pennsylvania, commanded by 22-year-old Harrisburg industrialist Colonel William W.W. Jennings, received less than a week of training. Jennings and his men made their way to Gettysburg where, on June 26, they encountered Ewell's seasoned corps. Outnumbered, Jennings' regiment was pushed back and took up position north of town near Bailey's Hill. Remarkably, none of Jennings' men were killed in the skirmish, though he lost 120 to injury or capture. *Ken Turner Collection.*

CHAPTER 3

THE REBELS SHELLING THE NEW YORK MILITIA IN THE MAIN STREET OF CARLISLE, PENNSYLVANIA.—Sketched by Mr. Thomas Nast.—[See Page 478.]

ABOVE
Shelling of Carlisle, July 1, 1863 Fears of a Confederate attack on Carlisle—some 15 miles west of Harrisburg and 25 miles north of Gettysburg—were realized when General J.E.B. Stuart's horse artillery bombarded the town and set fire to the Carlisle Barracks. The Battle of Carlisle was short but significant in that it delayed Stuart, whose late arrival in Gettysburg deprived General Robert E. Lee of valuable reconnaissance. This Thomas Nast illustration depicts the shelling of the New York militia defending Carlisle. *House Divided Project, Dickinson College, Carlisle.*

OPPOSITE
Bridge Restored Virginia Lieutenant Colonel Elijah V. White's 35th Battalion set fire to the Hanover Bridge, cutting off railroad traffic between Harrisburg and Baltimore. Within days, crews from the U.S. Military Railroad repaired it and other structures destroyed by rebel forces. *Library of Congress, cwpb-01537.*

1863: DEFENDING THE STATE

Fearing an attack, Pittsburgh and Philadelphia built earthen defenses.

Earthworks in Philadelphia These earthworks in Philadelphia were hastily constructed as a defense against an anticipated Confederate invasion. Pittsburgh, fearing an attack on its industries, built similar earthen defenses. *Ken Turner Collection.*

CHAPTER 3

Major General George Gordon Meade George Gordon Meade, son of a U.S. Navy agent, was born in Spain and raised in Philadelphia. An 1835 West Point graduate, Meade served for several years as a topographical engineer, but with the outbreak of war, took a command in the army. By Chancellorsville, he had led two different corps through several battles and had risen to command of the 5th Army Corps, proving his skill in handling troops and providing sound strategic decisions. His short temper, however, earned him the nickname "Old Snapping Turtle."

On June 28, 1863, Meade was selected to replace General Joseph Hooker, the third commander of the Army of the Potomac to be replaced by the president. Three days later, Major General Meade defended his home state against the seemingly invincible Confederate Army of Robert E. Lee.
Ken Turner Collection.

1863: DEFENDING THE STATE

ABOVE
Major General John Reynolds After relieving Hooker of his command, the president offered the position to Major General John Reynolds. Knowing the Commander-in-Chief often took a role in army affairs, Reynolds answered that he would take the post if there would be no executive interference. When Lincoln could give no such guarantee, Reynolds turned down the commission, which went to George Gordon Meade. Tactical placement of the 1st Corps was left to Reynolds. As his men encountered advancing Confederates, Reynolds was shot in the back of the head. He was dead before his men could ease him down from the saddle. Reynolds was buried in Lancaster on July 4, 1863. *Ken Turner Collection.*

Battle of Gettysburg: July 1, 1863

Early on the morning of July 1, 1863, Union cavalry videttes (sentries on horseback) clashed with advance elements of the Confederate Army of Northern Virginia along the Chambersburg Pike, west of Gettysburg. The Union's 1st Army Corps soon arrived, followed by the 11th Army Corps several hours later. The 56th Pennsylvania Infantry fired the first infantry volley of the battle.

That first day, 5,857 Pennsylvanians from 19 units participated in the fighting. Significant casualties occurred; in some units, more than 50 percent. The loss in officers was particularly severe, but none more devastating than that of Lancaster native Major General John F. Reynolds.

By 4 p.m., Union troops were overwhelmed by the Confederates' greater numbers. Falling back into the town of Gettysburg, the weary soldiers took up positions just south of town on Cemetery Hill and Cemetery Ridge. The remainder of the Army of the Potomac would arrive under cover of darkness and discover they nonetheless held a superior position.

CHAPTER 3

ABOVE
Devastating Injury Langhorne Wister was 27 when promoted to colonel of the 150th. His regiment was posted near the Chambersburg Pike when, in some of the most intense fighting of the war, his Pennsylvania Bucktails were forced to retreat. Wister was struck in the face by a minie ball, shattering his jaw. Recovering from his Gettysburg wound, Wister returned to duty in August 1863, but resigned his commission by the next February. He passed away in 1891. *Ken Turner Collection.*

LEFT
Captain Alfred Sofield, 149th Pennsylvania Captain Alfred Sofield and his men of the 149th Pennsylvania found themselves in the crossfire of rebel infantry and artillery. As they took cover in a ditch by the Chambersburg Road, an artillery shell landed under the captain, and, by one account, "literally cut him in two, leaving his heels in contact with his head." *Ken Turner Collection.*

OPPOSITE
Seminary The Lutheran Theological Seminary on the western edge of Gettysburg, 1863, scene of fighting on the first day of battle. *Library of Congress, detail of cwpb-01649.*

ABOVE

Harvest of Death Fallen soldiers at Gettysburg, photographed by Timothy O'Sullivan and published in *Gardner's Photographic Sketch Book of the War* (1865) as "A Harvest of Death." *Library of Congress, ppmsc 00168.*

RIGHT

Colonel Robert Cummins, 142nd Pennsylvania Engulfed by A.P. Hill's attack, fragments of the retreating 142nd Pennsylvania collected around their colonel, Robert Cummins. When Cummins was felled by a well-aimed shot, his men strained to remove him from the field while under constant fire. Cummins was carried to a field hospital at the Lutheran Theological Seminary but died within a few hours. *Ken Turner Collection.*

FAR RIGHT

Ready for Action Corporal John Holtzman (Hausman), Company A of the 150th Pennsylvania Bucktails, poses with his Enfield rifle. Holtzman was captured in the fighting west of Gettysburg. *Ken Turner Collection.*

CHAPTER 3

BELOW
A Debt Unpaid Lieutenant Jeremiah Hoffman of the 142nd Pennsylvania was transported to the make-shift hospital at the Lutheran Theological Seminary on the back of a horse given up by his adjutant, Andrew G. Tucker, also wounded. Four days later, Hoffman would watch from his bunk, tears streaming down his face, as Tucker's body was lowered into the ground. *Ken Turner Collection.*

ABOVE
Impassioned Color Sergeant Color Sergeant Benjamin Crippen of the 143rd Pennsylvania stopped several times to shake his fist in defiance, even as his outflanked regiment gave up ground to the oncoming enemy. An easy target, the six-foot-one flag bearer was felled by his pursuers. Although the state colors were recovered, Crippen's body was not. Crippen's likeness in stone, clenched fist raised, now stands on the battlefield as the regimental marker of the 143rd. *Ken Turner Collection.*

ABOVE
Prussian Army Veteran Despite extensive military experience, Brigadier General Alexander Schimmelfennig did not live up to his potential. At Chancellorsville, his brigade of the 11th Corps was overwhelmed. At Gettysburg, the 1st and 11th Corps were overpowered by Confederate infantry and artillery. Retreat turned to rout as Union soldiers fled back into town, closely pursued by Rebel soldiers. Schimmelfennig hid in a shed owned by Anna Garlach for two days before deeming it safe to come out. *Karl E. Sundstrom Collection.*

RIGHT
Colonel Francis Mahler, 75th Pennsylvania Under the command of Colonel Francis Mahler, the predominately German-American 75th Pennsylvania fought off Confederates north of town. After a halting advance through fenced farm fields, the regiment reached a wheat field and charged toward enemy troops. Mahler's horse was killed, leaving the colonel on foot to direct fire toward the approaching Confederates. As the rebels enveloped his men, Mahler was shot, dying from his wounds four days later. *Ken Turner Collection.*

CHAPTER 3

ABOVE
Burns's Musket A close-up of John Burns's flintlock musket (different than the prop in his portrait).
The State Museum of Pennsylvania, Pennsylvania Historical and Museum Commission, 6.2.

LEFT
Eccentric Citizen Soldier John Burns—remembered both as a "true patriot" and "complete humbug"—donned his swallow-tail coat and beaver felt top hat, grabbed his flintlock musket, and joined the 150th Pennsylvania fighting west of Gettysburg. Though wounded three times, the 70-year-old man pushed on and killed three rebels by his own count, then cleverly evaded capture and passed through Confederate lines. While Burns recovered from his wounds, Mathew Brady traveled to Gettysburg and photographed the celebrated local. Brady's images, reproduced as woodcut engravings in *Harpers Weekly*, turned Burns into a folk hero. The old man lived up to his fame, escorting President Lincoln to the Gettysburg National Cemetery dedication, and becoming a sought-after battlefield guide despite, or because of, his colorful rants against fellow citizens who, he complained, failed to take up arms. Burns was awarded a pension by Congress until he died at 78.
Ken Turner Collection.

ABOVE
Dead Horses On the second day of fighting, the Trostle farm was commandeered by Union forces as headquarters for Major General Daniel Sickles, ousting the Trostle family with dinner still on the table. The 9th Massachusetts (Bigelow's) Battery fought here until Confederate infantry was within six feet of its guns, and killing more than 100 of the its horses. *Library of Congress, ppmsca-32844.*

BATTLE OF GETTYSBURG
JULY 2, 1863

Meade prepared for Lee's next attack by dispersing troops along a fishhook-shaped line that began at Culp's Hill on the far right and extended southward down Cemetery Ridge and, by the end of the day, to Little Round Top. Confederates had the most success on the Union left led by James Longstreet's Corps, inflicting high casualty rates in the Devil's Den and nearby peach orchard. They threatened to outflank the northern line on Little Round Top, but hard fighting by defending troops, punctuated by a bayonet charge of the 20th Maine—one of the most fabled episodes in the Civil War—prevented them from succeeding. Approximately 15,000 Pennsylvanians, serving in all seven of the army's infantry corps, defended their state this day. As on July 1, the men persevered despite heavy losses, and the cries of the wounded on the field could be heard throughout the restless night.

LEFT
Zouave D'Afrique Cartridge Sling Insignia The 114th Pennsylvania entered the service as the Zouaves D'Afrique, a tribute to French North African soldiers whose uniforms they replicated. This insignia was recovered near the Sherfy House, one of only two authentic examples of this plate known to survive. *Ken Turner Collection.*

CHAPTER 3

"Steady, men. Fire low. Remember you are Pennsylvanians."

~Colonel Richard Roberts

ABOVE
Richard P. Roberts, Colonel, 140th Pennsylvania Colonel Richard Roberts, widowed father from Beaver County, confided to a fellow officer his premonition of not surviving his next battle. He asked his friend to see that his daughter would be cared for. On the second day of fighting, moments after Roberts' instruction to the 140th— "Steady, men. Fire low. Remember you are Pennsylvanians."—the colonel was struck by multiple bullets and killed. *Ken Turner Collection.*

ABOVE
A General Falls Samuel Kosciuszko Zook recovered from a wound sustained at the Battle of Fredericksburg and returned to his brigade's command to fight at Gettysburg. At the Wheatfield, when Zook rushed his men to shore up an exposed flank of the 3rd Corps, he was felled by a bullet to the abdomen. He died painfully in a rudimentary field hospital. *Ken Turner Collection.*

Negative by T. H. O'SULLIVAN.   Entered according to act of Congress, in the year 1866, by A. Gardner, in the Clerk's Office of the District Court of the District of Co

GATEWAY OF CEMETERY, GETTYSBURG.

ABOVE

First Lieutenant R. Bruce Ricketts and Captain Ezra Mathews Pictured here are Captain Ezra Matthews, (left) and Lieutenant Bruce Ricketts, (right), commanders of Battery F, 1st Pennsylvania Light Artillery. When Matthews received a promotion to major, Ricketts moved up to command the battery. Defending Cemetery Hill, Ricketts fired his cannons at the charging Confederates at nearly point blank range. The rebels kept coming until the two sides were locked in close combat. Despite successfully keeping the hill, Ricketts reported 23 casualties and 20 battery horses lost. *Ken Turner Collection.*

LEFT

Cemetery Gatehouse This impressive structure was erected in 1855 as gatehouse to Evergreen Cemetery, but also served as home to cemetery caretaker Peter Thorn and wife Elizabeth. Upon her safe return home, Elizabeth discovered mangled fencing, broken windows, damaged furniture, and blood-stained bedding. Although pregnant, the caretaker's wife made repairs to the gatehouse and helped bury 105 soldiers while her soldier husband helped pursue the Southern army.

Library of Congress, ppmsca-12560 from Gardner's Photographic Sketch Book of the Civil War, image 86, July 1863.

RIGHT

Surgeon and Brigadier General Franklin County native and University of Pennsylvania graduate Samuel Crawford began his military career in 1851 as a surgeon. When war broke out, Crawford transferred to the infantry, gaining brigade command, and, for a brief time at Antietam, division command. After recovering from severe battle wounds, Crawford led the Pennsylvania Reserves at Gettysburg, where he grabbed the colors of the 1st Reserves and led his men across Plum Run, through the Valley of Death.
Ken Turner Collection.

OPPOSITE

Allegheny Stone Cutter Private James Tudhope of Company A, 62nd Pennsylvania, is pictured wearing the Chasseur de Vincennes uniform that the regiment was awarded in 1862. Tudhope was among 175 men in his regiment who were killed, wounded, or captured in the Wheatfield; 29 were killed by rifle and bayonet in brutal, hand-to-hand fighting. *Ken Turner Collection.*

CHAPTER 3

1863: DEFENDING THE STATE

Fortunate Survivor The 140th Pennsylvania advanced through the Wheatfield to Stoney Hill before its lines on the left and right were broken and the regiment was forced to retreat. Comprised of men from Beaver, Greene, Mercer, and Washington counties, the 140th lost 241 soldiers that day. Private John A. Dickey, back row, left, was wounded in the shoulder in the brutal fight. *Ken Turner Collection.*

"DON'T GIVE AN INCH!"
~ Colonel Strong Vincent

LEFT
Colonel Strong Vincent, Hero from Erie
Colonel Strong Vincent took initiative and directed his brigade up the slope of Little Round Top to defend the hill against the onslaught of Law's Brigade. The colonel climbed onto a boulder and cried out, "Don't give an inch!" but a bullet struck Vincent, breaking his right thigh bone. As the colonel was carried from the field, reinforcements arrived and Little Round Top was saved; however, Vincent fell in and out of consciousness over the next five days, and then succumbed to his wound. His pregnant widow, Elizabeth Carter Vincent, gave birth to their baby girl two months later, but she would lose daughter Blanche Strong Vincent nine days before the child's first birthday. *Ken Turner Collection.*

BELOW
Vincent's Sword The sword and scabbard of Strong Vincent.

Smithsonian Institution, National Museum of American History.

RIGHT

Oliver Wilcox Norton, 83rd Pennsylvania
Following Colonel Strong Vincent's orders, brigade bugler and standard bearer Oliver Wilcox Norton kept himself and the brigade headquarters flag hidden behind a large boulder as the fight for of Little Round Top raged. Norton was devastated to learn that Vincent, his commander and mentor, was struck by a bullet; Norton later located the dying colonel to reassure him that their brigade had held the hill. After the war, Norton penned the definitive work on the battle, *Attack and Defense of Little Round Top*, in which he profiled his hero. As a further tribute, Oliver Norton named his son Strong Vincent Norton.
Ken Turner Collection.

OPPOSITE

Surgeon James Penrose Burchfield, 83rd Pennsylvania James Penrose Burchfield and his bride, Eva Marie Nourse, pose for their portrait as newlyweds. Burchfield, a surgeon of the 83rd Pennsylvania, managed a field hospital at a Gettysburg farmhouse; he attended the mortally wounded Strong Vincent but was unable to prevent the colonel's painful five-day decline that ended in death. Personal tragedy struck Burchfield himself in 1864 when his wife, Eva, died after giving birth to their son James. *Kraus/Messick Collection.*

CHAPTER 3

Breastworks at Little Round Top This view of the breastworks on Little Round Top was photographed less than two weeks after the fighting. Looking southward toward Big Round Top, a group of civilians perch on a boulder just yards ahead of where Colonel Strong Vincent fell rallying his men.

Library of Congress, cwpb-04001.

PENNSYLVANIA TROOPS PLAYED A PIVOTAL ROLE IN THE VICTORY

RIGHT

Commander of Stature Before the War Between the States, John White Geary was a civil engineer and railroad man. He was elected first mayor of San Francisco and, later, governor of Kansas Territory. Geary capitalized on his celebrity to recruit the 28th Pennsylvania, which drew enough volunteers to also form an artillery battery. Knaps' Battery, named for Captain Joseph Knap, accompanied Colonel Geary and the 28th Pennsylvania into service.

At six-foot-five, Geary was an easy target for enemy sharpshooters. Struck twice at Cedar Mountain, the brigadier general was again injured at Chancellorsville. As division commander in the 12th Corps at Gettysburg, Geary and his men endured arduous fighting on Culp's Hill's rocky slopes, successfully resisting several Confederate advances.

Geary was elected governor of Pennsylvania in 1867 and became known as champion of the people. He secured a coal mine safety bill, vetoed special interest bills, and reduced political corruption. Geary died at 53, two weeks after his second term as governor ended. *Ken Turner Collection.*

OPPOSITE

Gettysburg, Day 3 An oil painting by Edwin Forbes depicts Pickett's Charge looking westward from the Union lines to the Angle, the Copse of Trees, and thousands of onrushing Confederates. *Library of Congress, ppmsca-22571.*

CHAPTER 3

Gettysburg: July 3, 1863

At daybreak on July 3, the Union battle line stretched from Culp's Hill (where heavy fighting greeted the morning) across Cemetery Hill and down the spine of Cemetery Ridge to Little and Big Round Top. Lee planned another assault on the Federal lines but delays, miscommunication, and a dispute with Longstreet about the wisdom of the attack slowed the Confederates. At 1 p.m., Confederate artillery opened fire on the center of the Union line on Cemetery Ridge, marked by a small grove of trees. Ninety minutes later, more than three divisions of Confederate infantry surged forward. Commonly known as Pickett's Charge, few Confederate soldiers would breach the Union line, turned back by the concentrated fire power of thousands of muskets and scores of cannon. At the center of the storm fought the Philadelphia Brigade (the 69th, 71st, 72nd, and 106th Pennsylvania regiments) under the command of Brigadier General Alexander Webb. The battle ended with the Army of Northern Virginia stymied in its effort to defeat the Union on Northern soil. Pennsylvania troops played a pivotal role in the victory: 23,412 men fought but 5,886 were left dead, wounded, captured, or missing.

ABOVE

Albert's Image After he was killed in the repulse of Pickett's Charge, Albert B. Neill, Company K, 72nd Pennsylvania, also known as Baxter's Fire Zouaves, would be remembered by his family with this photograph.
Ken Turner Collection.

Colonel Dennis O'Kane (right) and Lieutenant Colonel Martin Tschudy (below), 69th Pennsylvania *Both Ken Turner Collection.*

From the Regimental Monument of the 69th Pennsylvania positioned at the stone wall by the Copse of Trees, where the regiment lost 137 of its 258 men:

In memoriam of our deceased comrades, who gave up their lives in defense of a perpetual Union. On this spot fell our commander Col. Dennis O'Kane, his true glory was victory or death, at the moment of achieving the former, he fell victim of the latter. While rallying the right to repulse Armistead, the Lieut. Col. Martin Tschudy was killed. He was also wounded on the previous day, but nobly refused to leave the field.

CHAPTER 3

Major General Winfield Scott Hancock
Arriving on the battlefield at Gettysburg on July 1, Pennsylvania native Major General Winfield Scott Hancock oversaw the occupation by Union troops of Cemetery Hill. The strategic landform south of town would be a vital component of the Union lines in the coming days and the scene of significant combat. On July 2, Hancock resumed command of his 2nd Army Corps, positioning it on Cemetery Ridge, from which on July 3, his men helped repulse Pickett's Charge. Commanding from the front line, he was wounded when a rebel bullet struck his saddle, driving a nail and other debris deep into his thigh. With a painful wound that never completely healed, the veteran officer began using a converted horse-drawn ambulance in the field so he could continue his command through the end of the war. *Ken Turner Collection.*

1863: DEFENDING THE STATE

CHAPTER 3

LEFT

Last Request While serving on the staff of fellow Pennsylvanian Major General Winfield Scott Hancock, Henry Bingham, 140th Pennsylvania, participated in one of the more memorable events of Pickett's Charge of July 3. Shortly after the attack was repulsed, Bingham came upon several men carrying Confederate General Lewis Armistead to the rear. Speaking to the mortally wounded general, Bingham offered to take care of his personal possessions. Armistead identified himself as an old friend of Hancock's and purportedly asked Bingham to relay a message to the general, relating his deep regret for fighting for the Confederacy. Captain Bingham served through the war, being captured once and wounded three times. He received the Medal of Honor for his actions at the Wilderness. Bingham then served 17 terms in the U.S. House of Representatives from 1879 to 1912. *Ken Turner Collection.*

OPPOSITE

Virginia "Jennie" Wade Gettysburg's only civilian casualty, 27-year-old Mary Virginia "Jennie" Wade, was reportedly baking bread for famished Union soldiers holding positions near the home. While kneading dough early on July 3, a bullet ripped through two wooden doors and into the woman's back, killing her instantly. Despite the story's lack of corroborative evidence, Wade became a symbol of peace, struck down while baking the staff of life. This photo with Jennie on the right is the only photograph of her known to exist; a cropped version showing just her face has been reproduced millions of times, ensuring Jennie Wade the stature of a permanent icon of Gettysburg lore.
Library of Congress, 17020743, The true story of "Jennie" Wade, a Gettysburg maid, *by J. W. Johnston, 1917.*

Jennie Wade, Gettysburg's only civilian casualty, became a symbol of peace.

ABOVE

General Alexander Hays' Presentation Sword Elaborately decorated swords, such as this gift to Brigadier General Alexander Hays from his admirers in Pittsburgh, were typical of the awards bestowed on venerated commanders. Tiffany & Company of New York crafted and hand-engraved the sword, which reads, in part, "Presented to General Alexander Hays By The Citizens of Pittsburgh, 1863." *HHC 92.14.*

RIGHT

Brigadier General Alexander Hays Western Pennsylvanian Alexander Hays commanded the 3rd Division of the 2nd Corps on Cemetery Ridge, holding the right of the corps' line against an assault led by Confederate brigades of generals James Pettigrew and Isaac Trimble. Hays' confident leadership broke the momentum of the attack, and the defeated Confederates withdrew. The brigadier general's division reported 21 captured enemy flags, more taken than in any other single day of fighting. To the cheers of his men, Hays and two aides rode along the division's lines dragging captured battle flags behind their horses. *Ken Turner Collection.*

CHAPTER 3

Confederate Prisoners on Seminary Ridge, July 15, 1863 One of the most studied Mathew Brady photographs is this image of three Confederate prisoners completely outfitted except for weapons. Researchers have identified the location as Chambersburg Pike, across from Lee's Headquarters, July 15, 1863. This unique untrimmed print shows more of the scene than later cropped versions. *Ken Turner Collection.*

Happy Family of Cell No. 1 Five Kentucky cavalrymen pose outside Western Penitentiary in Allegheny City, Pennsylvania. The tableau and pencil inscription identifying the group as "Happy Family of Cell No. 1" make a sardonic comment on the treatment received by prisoners. From left: William E. Curry, Captain, 8th Kentucky Cavalry (who would later escape by jumping from a prison train in October 1864); unidentified; First Lieutenant Leland Hathaway, 1st Battalion, Kentucky Mounted Rifles; First Lieutenant Henry D. Brown, 7th Kentucky Cavalry; and First Lieutenant Will Hays, 2nd Kentucky Cavalry.
Ken Turner Collection.

Kentucky Cavalrymen Incite Panic

While Lee was invading Pennsylvania from the south, elements of Brigadier General John Hunt Morgan's Confederate cavalry swept through Kentucky, southern Indiana, and southern Ohio, inciting panic. Nonetheless, on July 26, less than a month after the raids began, approximately 300 of Morgan's cavalrymen surrendered near New Lisbon, Ohio. High ranking officers were sent to Ohio State Prison; 118 landed at Western Penitentiary in Allegheny City.

CHAPTER 3

BELOW
Kentucky Doctor Lieutenant Will Hays, 2nd Kentucky Cavalry—one of the "Happy Family"—was 27 when he enlisted. The former physician had his image taken by well-known Pittsburgh photographer R.M. Cargo. *Ken Turner Collection.*

ABOVE
Photographed in Pittsburgh While incarcerated, Lieutenant Carneal Warfield and many of his fellow Kentuckians received new uniforms and funds from home. Warfield is seen here wearing new boots, which he, no doubt, wore when walking into town on an "honor" pass from prison. Treating the prisoners like notorious celebrities, many locals gathered and gawked at the Confederate officers until the cavalrymen returned to the penitentiary. *Ken Turner Collection.*

1863: DEFENDING THE STATE

CHAPTER 3

LEFT
Citizens Volunteer Hospital, Philadelphia One of the first military hospitals in Philadelphia, The Citizens General Hospital was also one of the smallest, with fewer than 400 beds. The Ladies Aid Society visited recovering soldiers to supply shirts, slippers, and other goods to make their hospital stay more comfortable. *Ken Turner Collection.*

Military Hospitals

Pennsylvania was not initially equipped to care for the massive number of injured soldiers returning from war. Philadelphia became home to approximately 24 new military hospitals and nearly that many small civilian facilities. The largest built to accommodate the war wounded was Satterlee Hospital, with 4,500 beds. Other major military hospitals sprang up in Chester, York, White Hall, and Pittsburgh.

The relatively unknown practices of embalming and undertaking took hold in the United States during the Civil War. Among the earliest recorded embalmer-undertakers was a Pennsylvanian, Dr. Richard Burr, who served briefly in the 72nd Pennsylvania Volunteer Infantry. In western Pennsylvania, the only embalmer for 50 years was William DeVore who contracted his services to the U.S. Army. DeVore embalmed not only battle deaths, but also fallen Pennsylvania Railroad workers and those killed in the 1862 Allegheny Arsenal explosion.

OPPOSITE
Fifteen Dollars for Damages Like other free blacks fearful of capture and enslavement, Abraham Bryan fled the modest clapboard home in Gettysburg that he had purchased six years earlier. Bryan's 12-acre farm turned to battlefield as Pettigrew's Brigade surged on Union lines. The farmer returned to restore his battered house, fences, and crops. Years later, the federal government awarded Bryan only $15 of his $1,028 claim for damages. The unpaid balance represented Confederate liability, which was never compensated. *Library of Congress, cwpb-01860.*

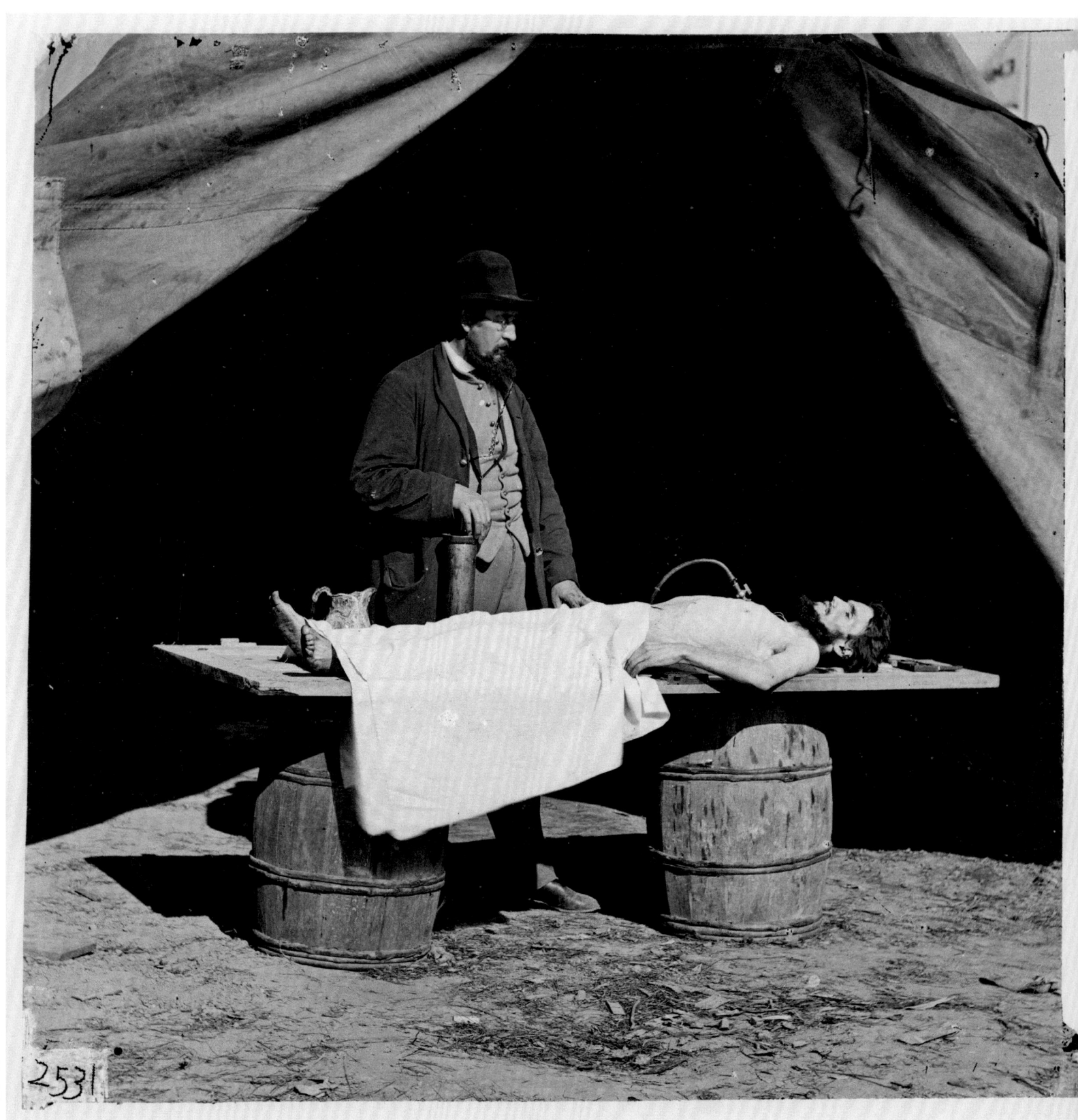

CHAPTER 3

OPPOSITE

Dealing with the Dead Embalming and undertaking began in earnest during the Civil War. Following the battle at Antietam in late 1862, Dr. Richard Burr, a physician shown here demonstrating on a fallen soldier, created and distributed handbills offering "Embalming for the Dead," and inviting the public to watch. *Library of Congress, cwpb-01887.*

RIGHT

Founder of The Episcopal Hospital The Reverend Alonzo Potter was the third bishop of the Pennsylvania Episcopal Church. Potter worked tirelessly throughout the 1850s to raise funds for a new hospital in Philadelphia. In 1860, the Hospital of the Protestant Episcopal Church was opened and, during the Civil War, the institution took in thousands of wounded soldiers and officers. It continues today as Temple University Hospital-Episcopal Campus. *Ken Turner Collection.*

BELOW

Free from Odor and Infection As embalmers followed armies into war, temporary embalming stations such as this one were set up to preserve and ship home deceased soldiers whose families could afford the fee. Of those who were hastily buried on the battlefield, some were reinterred in proper graves; most, however, without any form of identification, remained buried in shallow graves where they fell. *Ken Turner Collection.*

1863: DEFENDING THE STATE

CHAPTER 3

OPPOSITE
Fifer Shenkel In battle, Jacob Shenkel's military role would change from fife playing to attending the wounded. As the Union Army pursued Lee out of Gettysburg, Shenkel and fellow martial musicians from the 62nd Pennsylvania stayed behind to assist at Camp Letterman Military Hospital. Shenkel's November 1863 diary entries reveal he and friends also found time to drink, meet girls, and pose as dead soldiers. *Ken Turner Collection.*

ABOVE
Playing Dead The second "dead" man from the left is Jacob Shenkel on detached duty from the 62nd Pennsylvania, who, along with comrades, posed for photographer Peter Weaver. This view was taken on boulders across from Devil's Den, November 11, 1863. *Ken Turner Collection.*

Fresh Air Wards At the Hospital of the Protestant Episcopal Church, its grid of whitewashed buildings with open windows and roof vents was typical of modern hospital design when stagnant air was thought to contribute to the spread of germs and bacteria. A patient in the window of the building in the forefront appears to be taking in "good air." *Ken Turner Collection.*

CHAPTER 3

BELOW
Episcopal Hospital, Saving Bodies and Souls
Nearly 100 portraits of Union soldiers, all casualties of the three-day Battle of Gettysburg, fill the photographic album of the Hospital of the Protestant Episcopal Church in Philadelphia. An occasional note can be found penned next to a soldier's identification that reads "Baptized" or "Converted." *Ken Turner Collection.*

ABOVE
Sister of Mercy This portrait of an unidentified nun appears on the first page of the photograph album of the Hospital of the Protestant Episcopal Church in Philadelphia. *Ken Turner Collection.*

1863: DEFENDING THE STATE

CHAPTER 3

OPPOSITE

Lincoln poses before traveling to Pennsylvania President Abraham Lincoln posed for Mathew Brady just days before traveling to Gettysburg to deliver his address.
Library of Congress, ppmsca-19191.

ABOVE

Lincoln's Dedicatory Address, November 19, 1863 At the dedication of the Soldiers National Cemetery in Gettysburg on November 19, 1863, President Lincoln's remarks honored the sacrifice made on Pennsylvania soil, concluding that the dead did not die in vain. His words charged the living to remember the cause for which they fought. Lincoln can be seen just left of center, bareheaded and looking down. Other speakers included Edward Everett, who preceded the president's short speech with a two-hour oration.
Library of Congress, cwpb-07639.

1863: DEFENDING THE STATE

WESTERN THEATER OF OPERATIONS

In 1863, a handful of Pennsylvania regiments from Burnside's 9th Corps were sent west to take part in campaigns in Kentucky, Mississippi, and Tennessee. These veterans from the 100th Pennsylvania Volunteers saw action at Vicksburg and Jackson, Mississippi, and Knoxville and Fort Sanders, Tennessee, where some fought against Longstreet's men, whom they had faced many times back east.

A Day Before Battle Phineas Bird and Adison White, members of the 100th Pennsylvania, were photographed on October 9 in Knoxville, Tennessee, one day before fighting at nearby Blue Springs. *Kraus/Messick Collection.*

CHAPTER 3

Escape from Libby Prison After capture at the Battle of Chickamauga, Georgia, Colonel Thomas Rose of the 77th Pennsylvania was detained at the notorious Libby Prison, a converted warehouse in Richmond, Virginia, known for its harsh conditions. A former school principal from Pittsburgh, Rose masterminded a plan to escape. After a month of digging with improvised tools, he and 109 other prisoners fled through a narrow shaft; 48 were recaptured, including Colonel Rose. *Ken Turner Collection.*

BELOW

Negley's Turn of Fate A graduate of Western University of Pennsylvania (now University of Pittsburgh), James Negley had both an interest in and talent for military service. Negley's pre-war rank of brigadier general in the Pennsylvania Militia qualified him for command in the Union Army. After success at Stones River, Tennessee, Negley was promoted to major general and went on to drive Confederate General Braxton Bragg's army from Tennessee. His demise came not from enemy fire but from fatal error. In the Battle of Chickamauga, September 19–20, 1863, Negley commanded the 2nd Division, 14th Army Corps. On September 20, his division, like much the Union Army, was subject to a massive Confederate attack and forced to fall back. Withdrawing to Snodgrass Hill, Negley directed his battered division from the field without orders, resulting in censure and a military court of inquiry. Though cleared of wrong-doing, Negley never again held field command. *Kraus/Messick Collection.*

William Wardle Barker, smuggler of supplies Captain William Wardle Barker, a jeweler from Pittsburgh, played a key role in saving the Union Army in late 1863. From a base in Stevenson, Alabama, Barker had the daunting task of bribing Confederate locals so food and supplies could be smuggled to Union soldiers in the besieged city of Chattanooga, Tennessee. Barker's sleight of hand, added to General Grant's famous "Cracker Line" initiative, helped feed 40,000 starving Union troops and their animals. Barker, who served with the U.S. Commissary and Subsistence Department, is seated front right with General James Negley (standing beside his headquarters flag) and Negley's staff. *Ken Turner Collection.*

CHAPTER 3

Chattanooga Campaign October 1863

Lookout Mountain Having distinguished itself at the Battle of Stones River, the 78th Pennsylvania served in Tennessee as part of the 14th Corps. Here members of the regiment sit atop Lookout Mountain, overlooking Chattanooga. *Ken Turner Collection.*

CHAPTER 3

OPPOSITE TOP

Benevolent Despot In late 1863, Brigadier General John Geary posed with his 12th Corps staff near Murfreesboro, Tennessee. The general regarded his handpicked team as a surrogate family. However, Geary was a strict leader; he had his staff prepare lengthy battle reports portraying their division commander in a consistently positive light. Ordnance officer Henry H. Wilson (rear left) stands next to his uniformed son, Ashton; they lived together in camp. *Ken Turner Collection.*

OPPOSITE

Boy Soldier Young Ashton Wilson stands by his horse near 12th Corps field headquarters. *Ken Turner Collection.*

RIGHT

Father's Tears Lieutenant Edward Geary of Knap's Battery accompanied his father west for the siege of Chattanooga. Geary's division was positioned in a small valley, known as Wauhatchie, protecting the approach to Chattanooga. At midnight on October 29, 1863, when Confederates from Longstreet's Corps launched a surprise attack, the Union artillery withstood the assault. General Geary's troops turned back the Confederates but when dawn arrived, the general was found weeping over his son's lifeless body. *Ken Turner Collection.*

1863: DEFENDING THE STATE

BADGES OF CIRCLES, CLOVERS, DIAMONDS, AND MORE

Corps Badges In March 1863, the Army of the Potomac adopted the use of prescribed insignia, called corps badges, to differentiate the seven corps under its command. The first army badges made of cloth were coded by color: red, 1st Division; white, 2nd Division; and blue, 3rd Division. Entrepreneurs saw a market for personally engraved metal corps badges, and many Pennsylvanians eagerly purchased and wore the pins with pride. *Kraus/Messick Collection.*

— 200 —

CHAPTER 3

LEFT, TOP TO BOTTOM

Sergeant Frank H. Wentz Sergeant Frank H. Wentz, 107th Pennsylvania, a cabinet maker from Philadelphia, was among those wounded at Gettysburg on Oak Ridge on July 1. *Ken Turner Collection.*

Adjutant Frederick Gerker Adjutant Frederick Gerker, 90th Pennsylvania (National Guards). *Ken Turner Collection.*

Chalkey Fox Chalkey Fox, 88th Pennsylvania, hailed from Conshohocken, Montgomery County. *Ken Turner Collection.*

First Corps (above) The circular 1st Corps insignia was adopted in March 1863. At Gettysburg, the corps was under the command of Lancaster native John Reynolds until his death in the opening hours of the battle.

Second Corps (right) Formally called a trefoil, this clover-shaped insignia was one of the most recognizable of the war. Three Pennsylvanians commanded the 2nd Corps throughout its history, among them Winfield Scott Hancock at Gettysburg.

ABOVE
James Thompson, 106th Pennsylvania James Thompson's richly engraved corps badge indicates he was a private in Company H. Along with other regiments of the Philadelphia Brigade, the 106th fought in the Angle on July 3, taking the brunt of Pickett's Charge. *Ken Turner Collection.*

ABOVE
Elaborate Memento This intricate gold and silver jeweler-made pin belonged to Captain John D. Rogers of the 71st Pennsylvania. The names of past brigade commanders are engraved within each lobe of the trefoil. The 71st, part of the Philadelphia Brigade, fought at the Angle at Gettysburg on July 3, helping to repulse the Conferdate attack.
Ken Turner Collection.

RIGHT
Wounded at the Angle The large 2-shaped silver identification pin represents the 2nd Army Corps, which defended the Angle at Gettysburg. The words Vigilant 1819 refer to a Philadelphia fire station which was home to many of the enlistees like John Fullerton of the 72nd Pennsylvania (Baxter's Fire Zouaves).
Ken Turner Collection.

CHAPTER 3

Fifth Corps (below) A Maltese Cross was adopted as the badge of the 5th Corps in March 1863. Pennsylvanian George Gordon Meade was in command of the corps when assigned to lead the Army of the Potomac.

LEFT

Presented to Lieutenant Joseph Aldred
A gift from the men of Company L of the 62nd Pennsylvania to their lieutenant, this 5th Corps badge is a beautiful example of a jeweler's painstaking craftsmanship. Gold, with applied red enamel, the pin's shield-shaped drop is skillfully engraved on both sides with the names of battles from April 1862 to June 1864.
Ken Turner Collection.

BELOW

George W. Henry, 26th Pennsylvania
George W. Henry of Philadelphia served with the 26th Pennsylvania in Carr's Brigade. On July 2, while posted along the Emmitsburg Road on the rightmost end of the 3rd Corps line, the 26th was outflanked and charged by Perry's Florida Brigade. Henry survived but the regiment sustained more than 60 percent casualties. Henry's silver 3rd Corps badge reflects the regiment's one-time association with "Hooker's Old Division." *Ken Turner Collection.*

Third Corps (right) A lozenge, or diamond, was chosen in March 1863 as the insignia of the 3rd Corps. Pennsylvania regiments in the 3rd Corps sustained some of the highest casualties of the war.

203

1863: DEFENDING THE STATE

ABOVE
Six-Point Star This pin belonged to Lieutenant Jacob Shafer of the nine-month 134th Pennsylvania. Shafer, at 47 years, received an early disability discharge in March 1862, before corps badges were adopted. His distinctive six-point star pin was a personal addition to his uniform.
Ken Turner Collection.

ABOVE
Rudolf M. Graeff Rudolf M. Graeff's 31st Pennsylvania Regiment of the 2nd Reserves Corps nearly missed the battle at Gettysburg when the depleted regiment was left behind in Maryland. Only after insisting they be included in the march to Pennsylvania did the 232 men get the opportunity to defend their state.
Ken Turner Collection.

ABOVE
Davids' Watch Fob Corps badges were worn various ways; this one served as a pocketwatch fob. Its owner, Captain Richard P. Davids, was with the 118th Pennsylvania during the close fighting at the Trostle Farm on July 2. As Confederate skirmishers made their way toward Davids' men, one knelt and fired, killing the captain. *Ken Turner Collection.*

CHAPTER 3

Sixth Corps (this page) A cross with equal length arms was adopted as the insignia of the 6th Corps. More than a dozen Pennsylvania regiments were a part of the corps.

ABOVE

Corporal James Butler, 82nd Pennsylvania
Corporal James Butler's corps badge has a recessed center, painted red, delineating the 82nd Pennsylvania in the 1st Division of the 6th Corps. *Ken Turner Collection.*

LEFT

Casper Kaufman, 61st Pennsylvania Casper Kaufman's 6th Corps badge has a miniature captain's insignia affixed to its face. It is inscribed "Co. B; 61 Reg.; 3rd Brig."
Ken Turner Collection.

OPPOSITE

The 11th and 12th Corps Combined The 73rd Pennsylvania belonged to the 11th Corps, whose crescent insignia was hung with the star of the 12th Corps when the two units were combined. Curiously, Charles U. Jann, the name inscribed on this badge, is not found on the 73rd Pennsylvania roster.
Ken Turner Collection.

ABOVE

Unidentified Soldier and Companion An unknown soldier of the 87th Pennsylvania, wearing a cloth 6th Corps badge, sits beside his unidentified female companion. *Kraus/Messick Collection.*

RIGHT

Cross Bottony Although an official Corps Badge was not adopted until 1864, some 9th Corps men wore a Cross Bottony—a symmetrical cross whose arms terminate in a clover-like design. Most likely, the insignia was inspired by the example found on the Maryland State Seal, as the 9th Corps was heavily engaged in Maryland campaigns in 1861 and '62. This rare unidentified 9th Corps cross hangs from a yellow ribbon that descends from a banner inscribed with the name Burnside, the commander of the 9th at the time the pin was manufactured. *Ken Turner Collection.*

CHAPTER 3

Eleventh Corps (right) The 11th Corps adopted the Crescent as its insignia in 1863. Many German American regiments were found in this corps, including several from Pennsylvania.

Twelfth Corps (below) A star was chosen as the insignia for the 12th Corps. The Second Division of the 12th—often called the White Star Division—was commanded by Westmoreland County native and future Pennsylvania governor Brigadier General John White Geary.

LEFT AND ABOVE
Gillen's Star William Gillen's badge displays an expertly cut 29 within a five-pointed star. Gillen, a Philadelphian, was wounded in the shoulder at Lookout Mountain. He would die, reportedly of infection, at the military hospital in Chester, Delaware County. *Ken Turner Collection.*

— 207 —

Recruiting Poster A photo of the 25th Regiment USCT at Philadelphia's Camp William Penn in February 1864 was transposed into this hand-tinted lithograph and used as a recruiting broadside for colored regiments. *Historical Society of Pennsylvania, DAMS 242, call# Bb 54 P544.*

CH. 4

HOME FRONT AND BATTLEFRONT

Tens of thousands of Pennsylvania troops fought in nearly all the military operations of 1864, from far-flung battlefields to naval clashes. In May, newly appointed commander of Union forces General Ulysses S. Grant began his offensive in Virginia. The bloody battles of the Wilderness, Spotsylvania, and Cold Harbor followed. Fighting moved to Petersburg where Confederate forces dug in behind elaborate fortifications for an agonizing nine-month siege. Further south, General William T. Sherman blazed a path across Tennessee and Georgia, aiming for Atlanta and intent on crushing the South. Active on all these fronts were the men of the United States Colored Troops, who brought real meaning to Lincoln's Emancipation Proclamation by literally fighting to free the men, women, and children still in Southern bondage. Some 179,000 black men would serve in the U.S. Army (10 percent of the total) and another 19,000 in the Navy. Nearly 40,000 of them would perish before the war ended. Meanwhile, the United States Sanitary Commission was working to bring comfort to bivouacked soldiers. Sanitary Fairs in large cities helped raise funds for the ongoing demand for supplies.

GENERAL WILLIAM T. SHERMAN BLAZED A PATH INTENT ON CRUSHING THE SOUTH

HOME FRONT AND BATTLEFRONT

RISE OF THE UNITED STATES COLORED TROOPS

In addition to proclaiming freedom for slaves in the Confederacy, President Lincoln's Emancipation Proclamation decreed that African American men "of suitable condition, will be received into the armed services of the United States to garrison forts, positions, stations, and other places, and to man vessels in said service." They initially received less pay than white soldiers and were prohibited from holding the rank of officer.

Hundreds of African American men from Pennsylvania volunteered for the 54th and 55th Massachusetts Regiments. With less than two months' training, they gathered in Boston Commons to the cheers of well-wishers lining the streets. Facing enslavement or execution if captured, the "colored troops" nevertheless proudly boarded a transport ship for the slave-trading port of Charleston, South Carolina.

ABOVE

Fighting for Freedom Sergeant Major Thomas Hawkins received the Medal of Honor for retrieving this flag after the color bearer was killed in the battle of New Market Heights. The reverse of this banner of the 6th United States Colored Troops flag features another of black artist David Bowser's hand-painted images.
Ken Turner Collection.

RIGHT

Rather Die Freemen African American artist David Bowser of Philadelphia painted powerful images on the front and back of each of the 11 Pennsylvania Colored Troops' flags. The flag of the 3rd Regiment, the first of the black units to be trained at Camp Penn, features Bowser's depiction of the Goddess of Liberty handing the Union's flag to an African American soldier.
Ken Turner Collection.

CHAPTER 4

LEFT

Camp William Penn Commander Lieutenant Colonel Louis Wagner, a wounded hero of the 88th Pennsylvania, requested and received command of Camp William Penn. He fought also for equal treatment and pay for black soldiers. *Ken Turner Collection.*

BELOW

Chaplain Asher Jeremiah Asher, minister of the Shiloh Baptist Church in Philadelphia, volunteered as chaplain to the newly formed 6th U.S. Colored Troops regiment. He served his soldiers' needs during battle and through the painful horrors of hospitalization. Minister Asher died July 27, 1865, of typhoid fever, likely contracted from sick Union soldiers. Asher's grandfather, Gad, born in Africa, died a slave in the New World. *Ken Turner Collection.*

Lincoln once chided an opponent of emancipation: "You say you will not fight to free Negroes. Some of them seem willing to fight for you." Indeed, many African Americans, free and enslaved, had fought for independence in the Revolutionary War. Eventually, some 8,600 free blacks from the commonwealth entered the Union army—more than from any other state.

HOME FRONT AND BATTLEFRONT

ABOVE

Camp William Penn By June 1863, the imminent Confederate invasion of the North had spurred the opening of Camp William Penn, the first training camp for black soldiers in Pennsylvania. It was founded just north of Philadelphia in Cheltenham on land owned by Edward M. Davis, a leader of the Union League, an exclusive club of pro-Union white men. Davis was also the son-in-law of Lucretia Mott, a well-known abolitionist whose husband had helped found the American Anti-Slavery Society. The camp was in view of the Mott estate, "Roadside," a major stop on the Underground Railroad.

Camp William Penn was home to 11 U.S. Colored Troop regiments who had committed to a three-year enlistment. It was the state's only training camp for blacks and the largest of 18 in the nation. Of the nearly 11,000 African American soldiers trained in Pennsylvania, more than 1,000 of them would be killed in action or die of disease. *Library of Congress, ppmsca-10898.*

LEFT

Leroy Hilton Leroy Hilton of Pittsburgh enlisted in Company H of the 54th Massachusetts. Hilton was wounded in action at the failed attack on Fort Wagner, South Carolina, on July 18, 1863—the battle immortalized in the movie *Glory*. *Ken Turner Collection.*

CHAPTER 4

"You say you will not fight to free Negroes. Some of them seem willing to fight for you."

~ Abraham Lincoln

RIGHT
Lincoln to Stanton A note from Lincoln to Secretary of War Edwin Stanton (who was an attorney in Pittsburgh before the war) encouraging the use of "colored troops."
HHC L&A, G. William Bissell collection, 2004.0003.

BELOW
Camp Entrance Guards and visitors stand near the entrance to Camp William Penn, likely the winter of 1863 or '64.
Historical Society of Pennsylvania, DAMS 1426, file# 1426_v63_ba54p544_1.

HOME FRONT AND BATTLEFRONT

OPPOSITE

William Catlin, 32nd USCT Free blacks from Monongahela, Washington County, tried to enlist together but were forced to split up. William Catlin joined the 32nd USCT, trained at Camp William Penn, and shipped out to South Carolina to fight in the Battle of Honey Hill and later the occupation of Charleston. After the war, Catlin became one of the first three African American officers in the Pennsylvania National Guard, commissioned in 1871 as captain of Company F, 10th Pennsylvania Infantry. Catlin and his fellow officers were the first of their race to serve as officers in any Northern states' National Guard. Captain Catlin and his African American company served until 1878. *Ken Turner Collection.*

BELOW

Unknown Soldier The identity of this young soldier is unknown other than the pencil inscription on the back of the photograph which indicates he served in Pennsylvania Independent Battery E as Captain Joseph M. Knap's orderly. *Ken Turner Collection.*

ABOVE

Joseph Kiddoo Very few officers in the war served in as many capacities as Joseph Barr Kiddoo. Born in Sewickley, Allegheny County, Kiddoo joined the war as a private in a three-month unit. After serving as sergeant of the 63rd Pennsylvania, Kiddoo was commissioned colonel of the 137th Pennsylvania and fought at Antietam, Fredericksburg, and Chancellorsville. Kiddoo led the 6th USCT in late 1863 and the 22nd USCT in 1864. Promoted to brevet brigadier general and, later, brevet major general, Kiddoo retired from military service in 1870 and worked for the Freedmen's Bureau in Texas, where he encouraged education for African Americans. *Ken Turner Collection.*

The New York Times
JUNE 2, 1864:

The Pittsburgh Sanitary Fair Business was suspended this afternoon on the opening of the Sanitary Fair. There was a grand military and civic procession, the largest ever known. The streets on both sides were crowded in the whole line of the procession, from the Monongahela Hotel, in Pittsburgh, to the fair ground in Allegheny City. Gov. Curtin delivered the oration which was enthusiastically received. The Hyatt Cadets, from the West Chester Military Academy, excited considerable interest.

HELP FROM THE HOME FRONT— UNITED STATES SANITARY COMMISSION

In addition to the threat of injury and death, war brought disease to field camps due to poor sanitary conditions. The United States Sanitary Commission, a civilian organization, worked with local clergy and ladies' aid organizations to improve the quality of life for bivouacked soldiers. The Philadelphia branch (one of three in the East) distributed volunteers' handmade clothing to soldiers passing through the city. As the war dragged on, two Chicago women answered the need for continued supplies by organizing a large fair, raising crucial financial support. In 1864, Pittsburgh and Philadelphia joined in the fund-raising by hosting their own Sanitary Fairs.

CHAPTER 4

OPPOSITE

Monitor Building Of particular interest was a miniature lake inside the Monitor Building at Pittsburgh's Sanitary Fair. Fairgoers were delighted by mock battles of steam-powered ironclad models, which began when the small-scale monitor and two mortar schooners sailed by water batteries along the shore. *Carnegie Library of Pittsburgh, Pennsylvania Room.*

ABOVE

Commission Wagon Number 13 A Sanitary Commission wagon prepares to leave Washington, D.C., in April 1865, carrying supplies gathered by hundreds of Pennsylvania volunteers. *Library of Congress, cwpb-04159.*

ABOVE
Refreshment Hall Staff The African American wait-staff of the Great Central Fair's Refreshment Hall in Philadelphia.
Library Company of Philadelphia, 5781.F.165 f.

OPPOSITE
A Few Minutes Rest Workers relax in front of "The Home" Sanitary Commission Lodge for Invalid Soldiers in Washington, D.C., June 1863. In the field, most work was done by men, but in Pennsylvania's wards, boroughs, and townships, it was the Ladies Aid branches of the Commission that worked tirelessly to make shirts, socks, and other articles for soldiers far from home. *Library of Congress, cwpb-04155.*

CHAPTER 4

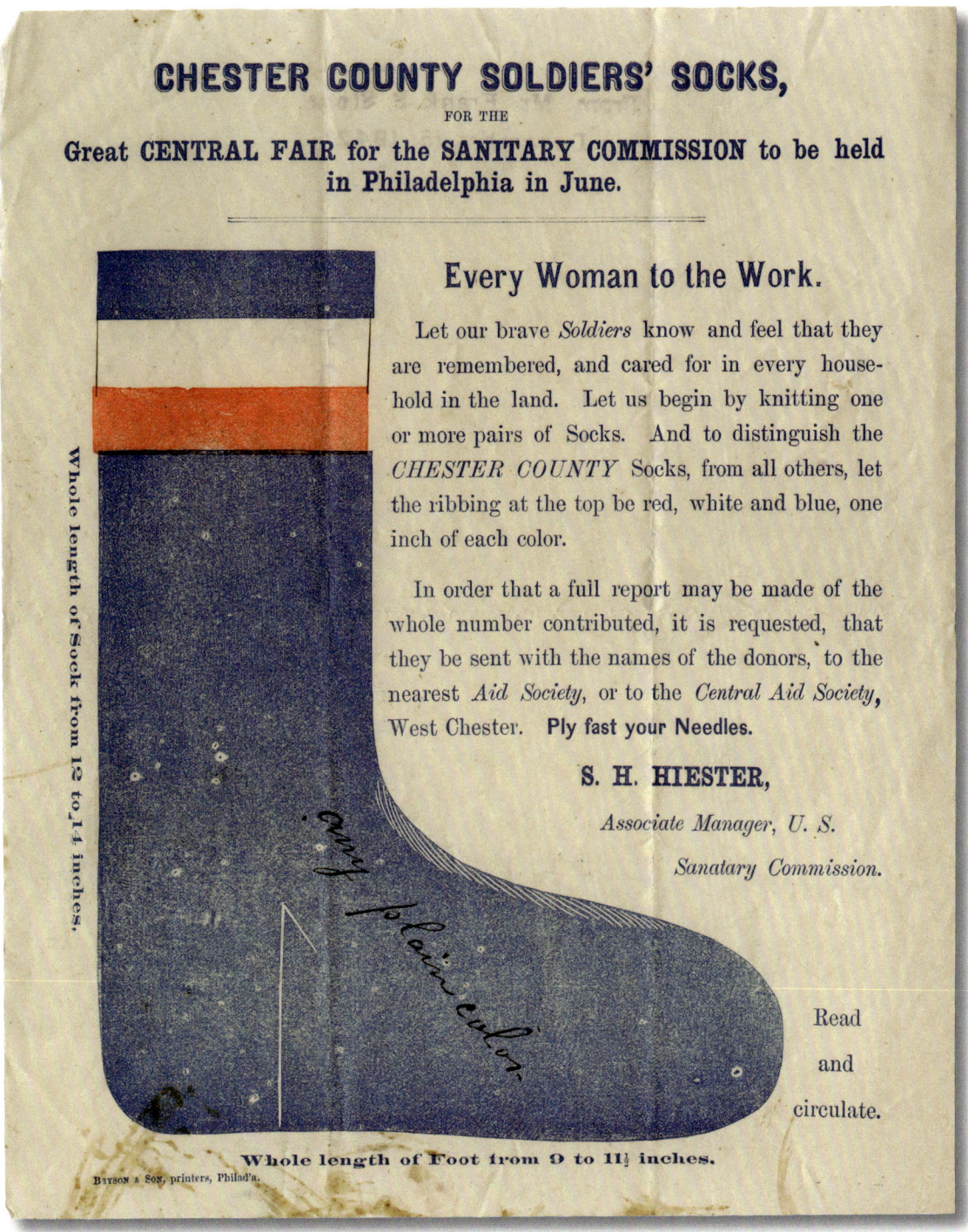

OPPOSITE
Pittsburgh Sanitary Fair Opened on June 1, 1864, the 20-day Pittsburgh Sanitary Fair raised more than $320,000—more money per capita than any other city's fair. Housed within six large temporary buildings, the exhibits and activities related to war, inventions, hand-crafts, and fund-raising attracted some 22,000 visitors daily. African Americans were barred from attending, though many held behind-the-scenes service positions. *Both HHC L&A MSQ008.*

ABOVE
Socks for Soldiers This promotional poster, requesting Chester County women to "Ply fast your Needles," asks for donations of patriotic-themed hand-knit socks. *Historical Society of Pennsylvania, U.S. Sanitary Commission Philadelphia Branch collection (679), box 2, DAMS 50139.*

LEFT

Sanitary Fair Matron Many of the women who organized the Great Central Fair in Philadelphia also volunteered in various stations within the complex. Several ribbons pinned to this woman's jacket indicate she was associated with the Floral Committee, Historical Autographs (display), and "Our Daily Fare" refreshment area.

Historical Society of Pennsylvania, Horace Howard Furness collection on the Great Cent [0224], Box/Folder 5.3 (Dams 5098).

CHAPTER 4

OPPOSITE
Great Sanitary Fair of Philadelphia Logan Square in Philadelphia was the site of the Great Central Fair, which raised more than $1 million. Appearing from the outside like a walled city, the fair featured a huge central building, 540 feet long by 60 feet wide. Inside, merchants and manufacturers displayed and sold products alongside patriotic exhibits and works of art. President and Mrs. Lincoln were among the hundreds of thousands of visitors.
Ken Turner Collection.

ABOVE
A Chance to Showcase a Product Among the scores who rented space at the Great Central Fair to showcase innovative products, this vendor demonstrates a sewing machine attachment that held fabric in place without the need for basting. Later, vendors used stereographs like this to promote their business.
Library Company of Philadelphia, 5781.F.168f.

CHAPTER 4

UNITED STATES CHRISTIAN COMMISSION

Philadelphia was the national headquarters for the United States Christian Commission, an off-shoot of the Y.M.C.A. The organization, founded in 1861, worked with military chaplains to provide for the spiritual welfare of soldiers. In the field, volunteers distributed religious materials and provided care for wounded soldiers. As the war escalated, the commission worked for better treatment of prisoners of war and aided in accumulating burial records. The Y.M.C.A. continued these roles after the war.

ABOVE
Christian Commission Agent Silver pins, such as this well-preserved example, identified agents of the Philadelphia branch of the Christian Commission, giving them access to military camps, battlefields, and hospitals. *Ken Turner Collection.*

OPPOSITE
Busy Day at the Christian Commission Activity around the Christian Commission offices in Washington stops as the photographer captures the diversity of people milling about. Commission headquarters in Philadelphia sent countless boxes to Washington filled with religious tracts and comfort items for distribution to field agents, who in turn handed them to needy soldiers. *Library of Congress, cwpb-04357.*

RIGHT
USCC Field Tent A Christian Commission camp at Germantown, a neighborhood of Philadelphia, September 1863. *Library of Congress, ppmsca-12574.*

OPPOSITE
James Powell's Journal Pocket-sized ledger books carried by agents of the Christian Commission documented their missionary work. Philadelphia college student James Powell kept this diary from May 16 to June 9, 1864, recording the words of wounded and dying soldiers, which he later copied into letters and sent home to their loved ones. The transcribed letter **(bottom right)** was found in the pages of Powell's book.

Fitch, a member of the 10th Vermont Infantry, had been wounded at Cold Harbor, Virginia. He died four days after this letter was written.
Kraus/Messick Collection.

Washington June 5th/64

Mrs Fitch your husband wishes me to write the following. I got wounded very badly on the first of June through my lungs. If I do not recover put your trust in God, hold on to the good cause in which you have begun. I met with a good Christian society who are very kind to me. I am feeling pretty comfortable at present and hope that under good care which I hope to obtain in this place I may get well. Should I never see you on earth I hope to meet you in heaven.

From your affectionate husband

Charles P. Fitch
Mrs. Chas. P. Fitch
Bennington Co. Vt.

Money and Politics

ABOVE

Jay Cooke and Company Financier Jay Cooke, seen here in 1864 with son Jay Cooke, Jr., sold war bonds to patriotic investors from all walks of life. His Philadelphia firm raised hundreds of millions of dollars for the Union.

Historical Society of Pennsylvania, DAMS 4964, file# 0132_0026_004, Jay Cooke papers [0148], Box FF 92.1, 2, 3, 5.

RIGHT

McClellan for President After being relieved of his command of the Army of the Potomac, Philadelphian George B. McClellan ran against his commander-in-chief in the presidential election of 1864. Although his party platform favored a negotiated end to the war that would allow slavery to continue, McClellan promised to keep fighting until the country was reunited. The once-popular general and running mate George Pendleton were soundly defeated, securing only 30 percent of the military vote.

Library of Congress, ppmsca-17561.

CHAPTER 4

ABOVE

Anna Dickinson During the 1864 presidential campaign, 21-year-old Anna Dickinson became the first woman to address Congress, where she received a standing ovation. The social advocate from Philadelphia was already a popular speaker, promoting a radical Republican, pro-Union, anti-slavery message. Dickinson was known to criticize the president for being too moderate and setting inadequate goals for the war. *Ken Turner Collection.*

LEFT

A Soldier's Vote Far from home, Pennsylvania soldiers completed 1864 presidential election ballots for delivery back to local election authorities. After years of brutal war, the fall of Atlanta in September may have led the military's rank and file to overwhelmingly choose Lincoln over the Democratic peace platform. *Kraus/Messick Collection.*

Veteran Volunteers

In early 1864, the Union's three-year regiments approached the end of their contracted service. To stem the loss of one-third of its most experienced soldiers, the government offered each regiment a 30-day furlough if it would return with the majority of its men. Those regiments would also receive the honorary title of "Veteran Volunteers." Wounded soldiers who wished to remain in the military replaced guards of government installations in Washington and other cities. These new members of the Veteran Reserve Corps freed combat-ready soldiers for service at the front.

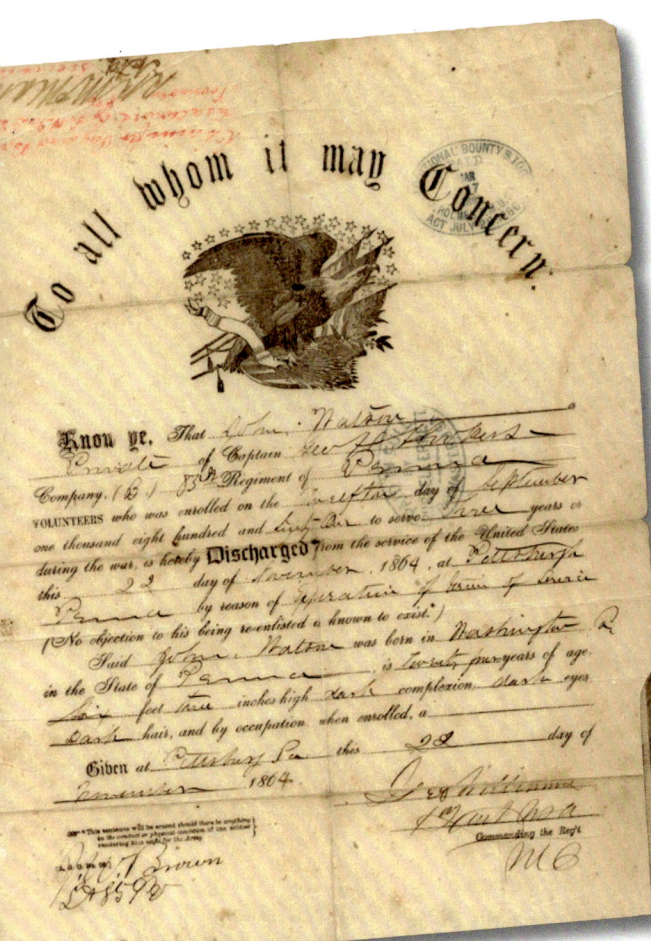

ABOVE
Discharge after Three Years John Watson, Washington, Washington County, who enlisted in 1861, Company B, 85th Pennsylvania Volunteers, mustered out of service in November 1864 after his three-year commitment was fulfilled. A note in the upper left written 23 years later states claims for pay and bounty were disallowed. *Don and Mary Lou Watson.*

RIGHT
William Curvin William Curvin, photographed in his 1864 uniform with veteran stripe, sports a cap with the barely discernable brass letters "PVV" (for Pennsylvania Veteran Volunteers), designating the 56th Pennsylvania as a veteran regiment. *Ken Turner Collection.*

ABOVE RIGHT
Alonzo Bennett Just visible on the left side of Alonzo Bennett's uniform is his empty sleeve. A veteran of the 81st Pennsylvania, Bennett lost his arm at the Battle of Chancellorsville. In 1864, he transferred to the Veteran Reserve Corps, whose light blue uniforms were a mark of distinction. *Ken Turner Collection.*

CHAPTER 4

KEYSTONE MEN FOR DIXIE

Whether by circumstance, for the cause, or in allegiance to marriage vows, some Pennsylvanians relinquished their loyalty to the Union and took up arms for the South.

John C. Pemberton, CSA Born in Philadelphia, Lieutenant General John C. Pemberton was the highest ranking Pennsylvanian in the Confederate Army. After graduating West Point in 1837, Pemberton married a Virginia woman and resigned his commission in the U.S. Army on April 24, 1861. Pemberton's Confederate troops surrendered to General Ulysses S. Grant at Vicksburg, Mississippi, on the same day Lee's defeated army withdrew from Gettysburg—July 4, 1863. The surrender at Vicksburg would result in Pemberton's demotion. He died in 1881 and was buried in Laurel Hill Cemetery in Philadelphia. *Ken Turner Collection.*

" In going over the field after action, I saw a rebel colonel lying on his face. I had him turned over, and was more than surprised when I recognized in him an old townsman and schoolmate. He was **Charlie Collins**, of Pittsburgh."

~ Captain Charles MacConnell, 5th U.S. Artillery

Colonel Charles R. Collins, 15th Virginia Cavalry The destiny of Colonel Charles Read Collins exemplifies the tragic irony of a country at war with itself. Born near Pittsburgh in 1836 and graduated from West Point in 1859 (see photo), Collins married Susan Mason of Virginia in 1860 and ultimately resigned his United States Army commission to join the Confederacy. In 1863, Major Collins was assigned to the 15th Virginia Cavalry. The following year, he was promoted to colonel. On May 7, 1864, Collins was killed at the battle of Todd's Tavern, Virginia. His body was discovered by Union Army Captain Charles C. MacConnell—one of Collins' childhood friends. The rebel Yankee was given a battlefield burial by his fellow Pennsylvanian, then was later re-interred in King's County, Virginia. *Ken Turner Collection.*

BELOW

George W. Scott, 5th Battalion Florida Cavalry CSA George Washington Scott, born in Huntington County, Pennsylvania, was the son of Congressman John Scott, a member of the House of Representatives from 1829 to 1831. The younger Scott settled in Leon County, Florida, and by 1861 had achieved success as a merchant and plantation owner. During the Civil War, Scott served in the 2nd Florida Cavalry and rose to lieutenant colonel of the 5th Battalion Florida Cavalry. His brother, John, was elected to the U.S. Senate from Pennsylvania in 1868.
David Wynn Vaughan Collection.

ABOVE

Josiah Gorgas, CSA Josiah Gorgas, chief of the Confederacy's ordnance department, was born in Dauphin County, Pennsylvania. After marrying a woman from Alabama, the West Point graduate joined the fight for the South. He was instrumental in overcoming considerable obstacles to supply the Confederacy with arms and ammunition. *Library of Congress, B8171-2719x.*

CHAPTER 4

Drayton's Slaves Photographed on Confederate General Thomas Drayton's plantation, these enslaved men, women, and children, surrounded by bolls of cotton, were freed after the U.S. Army occupied Hilton Head, South Carolina. Among the commanders fighting against Drayton and the Confederates was U.S. Navy Lieutenant Percival Drayton—the slave-owner's brother from Philadelphia.
Library of Congress, ppmsca-04324.

LEFT
Thomas Robinson Sharp, CSA
Born in Mount Carbon, Schuylkill County, young Thomas Robinson Sharp moved to Virginia. Like his father, Sharp worked for the railroad and, under General Stonewall Jackson, served the Confederacy as the military railroad superintendent. Captain Sharp directed the "Great Train Raid of 1861," a plan hatched by Jackson and approved by General Robert E. Lee in which federal locomotives, cars, rails, and telegraph wire were stolen, breaking communication along the Baltimore and Ohio Railroad. After the war, Sharp returned to the railroad business, working for the B&O, the same line he targeted during the war.
Courtesy of the Descendents of Gertrude Virginia Sharp Myer and The Eden Historical Museum.

OPPOSITE
William McComb, CSA On February 13, 1865, Colonel William McComb (originally of Mercer County, Pennsylvania) was promoted to brigadier general in the Confederate States Army. McComb—wounded both at Antietam and Chancellorsville—surrendered his brigade of Tennessee troops at Appomattox in April 1865.
Library of Congress, ds-01084.

CHAPTER 4

"Farewell, Percy . . .
Defend the soil of Pennsylvania,
if you will. There, you and I will never meet
as armed foes; cross her southern boundary
with hostile purpose—and we shall face
each other as brothers never should."

RIGHT

Brother Against Brother Thus wrote Confederate Brigadier General Thomas Drayton [top] to his brother, Percival [bottom], a lieutenant in the Union Navy. Drayton's sibling would, in fact, cross Pennsylvania's southern boundary and, on October 7, 1861, brother would fight brother at Port Royal, South Carolina. The Pennsylvania Confederate's land troops returned fire at Percival's Union gunboat. *Both Ken Turner Collection.*

—235—

FIGHTING ON

ABOVE
A Noble Record "His was a noble record" stated an early-20th century biography of Colonel Orpheus S. Woodward of the 83rd Pennsylvania Volunteer Infantry. Woodward advanced from captain in 1861 to colonel in 1864. On May 5, 1864, at the Battle of the Wilderness, Woodward's stellar military career ended when a wound to his right leg necessitated its amputation. *Ken Turner Collection.*

RIGHT
Mourned by His Friend "Poor, Patterson! I shook hands and spoke with him just before the advance was ordered, and a moment afterwards he received a bullet through the brains," wrote Lieutenant Colonel William Moody, after the death of his friend, Colonel John Patterson of the 102nd Pennsylvania Infantry. Patterson [pictured here] fell on May 5, 1864—his 29th birthday—at the Battle of the Wilderness. *Ken Turner Collection.*

Lincoln's Stand-In Anyone drafted into U.S. military service could be lawfully freed of that obligation by paying a $300 commutation fee or by hiring a substitute to serve in his place. From October 1862, when the draft began, through the end of the war, approximately 17,000 Pennsylvania soldiers were classified as draftees or substitutes.

After serving in the 176th Pennsylvania and being discharged with typhoid fever, John Summerfield Staples of Stroudsburg, Monroe County, was asked to reenlist. President Lincoln, who was eager to express unity with Union soldiers, desired a soldier to symbolically represent him in the ranks of the army. From October 1, 1864, through the end of the war, Staples served as Lincoln's stand-in in the 2nd District of Columbia Volunteers.

Monroe County Historical Association.

" We arrived at the famous Libby at 7:30 p.m. and was turned over to the tender mercies of Major T.P. Turner. . . we were searched and everything in my possession was an old comb. I asked them if they did not want my clothes, when they coolly told us we would be hanged in a few days and they would get the clothes then."

- Reuben Bartley

Reuben Bartley Born on a farm near Portersville, Butler County, Reuben Bartley joined the nine-month 123rd Pennsylvania in August 1862. After mustering out, the lieutenant reenlisted in the U.S. Signal Corps, volunteering for the now legendary Kilpatrick-Dahlgren expedition to liberate captives from Richmond prison camps. On March 2, 1864, Bartley was riding with Dahlgren when the unit was ambushed. Despite being captured and held in Libby Prison, Bartley refused to give up any information about the expedition's planned explosions and bridge burnings. One year later, when Bartley was released in a prisoner exchange, the lieutenant weighed only 118 pounds. *Ken Turner Collection.*

RIGHT

Felled at St. Mary's Church The son of a Congressman, George Hay Covode was robust and athletic when he joined the 4th Pennsylvania Cavalry; he would rise to the rank of colonel in 1864. At the Battle of Falls Church, Virginia, Covode brazenly saber-slashed his way out of certain capture. However, at St. Mary's Church, Virginia, June 24, 1864, the nearsighted colonel confused Confederate skirmishers for his own men. Realizing his mistake too late, Covode retreated, but was hit by a fatal volley.

Ken Turner Collection.

LEFT

John N. Gamble's Red Diamond John N. Gamble, McKeesport, Allegheny County, joined the 63rd Pennsylvania Infantry on August 19, 1861. Gamble was wounded in the Battle of the Wilderness in Virginia on May 12, 1864. In this photograph, Gamble displays his forage cap with the red diamond badge of the 3rd Corps.

Ken Turner Collection.

CHAPTER 4

LEFT

Ulric Dahlgren One of the most daring raids of the war was led by Brigadier General Judson Kilpatrick and a young Pennsylvania colonel, Ulric Dahlgren, son of Rear Admiral John. A. Dahlgren (see page 123). Their goal was liberation of Union prisoners of war. On February 28, 1864, Kilpatrick and 21-year-old Dahlgren (who had lost a leg at Hagerstown in the Gettysburg Campaign) launched a raid on Richmond from Stevensburg, Virginia. A few days later, Dahlgren's men were ambushed and the young colonel was killed. The Rebels found papers on his body that reportedly were instructions to assassinate Confederate President Jefferson Davis and his cabinet. The resulting scandal in the newspapers incited a political furor. A villain in the eyes of Southerners, Dahlgren's remains were hastily disposed of. Only when Elizabeth Van Lew, a spy for the North, located Dahlgren's body was it returned north for burial in Philadelphia. *Ken Turner Collection.*

RIGHT

Frederick Pettit "Men were being killed and wounded faster than you could count. No one flinched until we were ordered back," wrote Frederick Pettit of Hazel Dell (now Ellwood City, Beaver and Lawrence counties) to his parents after the 100th Pennsylvania fought its way toward the enemy at Spotsylvania, Virginia. Two months later, Pettit was killed by a sharpshooter while sitting in the trenches at Petersburg. *Kraus/Messick Collection.*

ABOVE

Cooper's Battery This well-known photo of Cooper's Battery (B) 1st Pennsylvania Light Artillery, was taken June 21, 1864, at Petersburg, Virginia. In 1911, Lieutenant James A. Gardner of Cooper's Battery vividly recalled the scene, locating it about one-third of a mile in front and to the right of Confederate Colonel Avery's house, which served as headquarters southeast of the town for General Gouverneur Warren. Standing at center in straw hat is photographer Mathew Brady.

National Archives, T252, Mathew B. Brady Collection of Civil War Photographs, RG 111, B-86.

RIGHT

Private John W. Shelow, Company A, 110th Pennsylvania Infantry This image graphically displays the destruction wrought by small arms fire. On June 18, 1864, John W. Shelow, a private from Blair County, serving in Company A of the 110th Pennsylvania Infantry, was struck in the face by an enemy bullet. Tragically, the one ounce slug of lead destroyed both his eyes.

Ken Turner Collection.

CHAPTER 4

ABOVE
James A. Beaver James A. Beaver's Civil War service paved the way for his election to governor of Pennsylvania, just as with three of his predecessors. Beaver's distinguished war career included three months in the 2nd Infantry, followed by a year as Lieutenant Colonel of the 45th Pennsylvania Infantry. After taking command of the 148th Pennsylvania, Beaver lost his right leg in combat at Reams Station, Virginia, in 1864. Beaver became governor in 1887. His name lives on at Beaver Stadium on the Pennsylvania State University campus in State College. *Ken Turner Collection.*

ABOVE
"A Model Gentleman and Commander"
This hand-tinted photographic portrait memorializes Colonel George A. Cobham, born in England and reared in Warren, Pennsylvania. The beloved commander was killed at Peachtree Creek, Georgia, on July 20, 1864, leading the 2nd Brigade, 2nd Division of the 20th Army Corps. His former regiment, the 111th Pennsylvania Infantry, also mourned his death. *Ken Turner Collection.*

Her Soldier It appears this unidentified Altoona woman is ready to march into war but the photo brooch at her neck suggests she posed to honor a much-loved military man. Whether the officer who owned the saber, pistol, and gloves has died or is recovering from battle wounds is not clear; nor is the stalwart lady's message. Perhaps she wished to have marched by his side or take his place at the front. *Ken Turner Collection.*

CHAPTER 4

ABOVE

The Burning of Chambersburg War crossed the borders of Pennsylvania for the third time on July 30, 1864, when Chambersburg was burned by Confederate cavalry in retaliation for the Union torching of civilian buildings in the Shenandoah Valley. After destroying more than 500 structures, Brigadier General John McCausland's men were pursued by Union cavalry, who defeated the rebels in Moorefield, West Virginia.

Chambersburg was extensively photographed after its destruction. This image is described as a "View of Baptist Church, Iron-bridge, and Surrounding Buildings; at juncture of Water and Queen sts" taken from the "West Market St. Bridge." *Ken Turner Collection.*

LEFT

Elliot Emerges Unscathed Fergus Elliot, color sergeant for the 109th Pennsylvania during the Atlanta Campaign, grabbed the flag at the battle at Peachtree Creek and made a stand against a fierce Confederate advance. The men of the 109th rallied on the banner and held back the onslaught, which had bettered surrounding regiments. Elliott and a few of his men turned two cannons and fired point blank, repulsing the enemy and turning the tide of the battle. *Ken Turner Collection.*

BELOW

Frank M. Eastman Frank Eastman from Beaver County was 18 when, in September 1861, he enlisted as a corporal in the 102nd Pennsylvania. In 1863, Eastman was injured at Salem Church but recovered to fight again. On October 19, 1864, a minie ball tore into his left arm, necessitating its amputation. While recovering, Eastman wrote on the back of this photo, "April 14, 1865 — Today our flag floats proudly over Fort Sumter." Eastman returned to Beaver County, married, and became a lawyer and teacher. *Ken Turner Collection.*

ABOVE

Each Lost a Leg Posed at a hospital between Lieutenant Colonel Robert Avery (102nd NY) and Captain Greene (ADC) is First Sergeant Joseph Goodman, 147th Pennsylvania Infantry, who lost his left leg at the battle of Ringgold, Georgia, on November 27, 1863. Above is Goodman's inscribed corps badge. *Ken Turner Collection.*

CHAPTER 4

BELOW
Unconventional Doctor In June 1861, Dr. Louis Wentag Read, a graduate of the University of Pennsylvania, joined the 1st Pennsylvania Reserves. In December 1863—on leave from his position as director of the McKim U.S. Hospital in Baltimore—Read saved the life of General Winfield Scott Hancock by propping the wounded hero on a kitchen chair and successfully extracting the minie ball that had festered in his groin since the Battle of Gettysburg.
Ken Turner Collection.

ABOVE
Intrepid Colonel Four wounds over three years could not keep Colonel Calvin Craig, 105th Pennsylvania, from the front. In August 1864, at the Battle of Deep Bottom, Virginia, the intrepid colonel received a fatal shot to the head. *Ken Turner Collection.*

ABOVE LEFT
Wounded Zouave This wounded soldier can be identified only as a member of the 155th Pennsylvania; his unit adopted the unique zouave uniform in 1864. *Ken Turner Collection.*

ABOVE RIGHT
Stanton Cousin Dr. David Stanton, surgeon of the 1st Pennsylvania Cavalry, was cousin to Secretary of War Edwin Stanton. *Ken Turner Collection.*

CHAPTER 4

6th Pennsylvania Heavy Artillery Caleb Maratta and William Caldwell, members of the 6th Pennsylvania Heavy Artillery, stand proudly with rifles and a 100-pound spherical cannon shell. *Ken Turner Collection.*

RIGHT

Major Weidner Spera Major Weidner Spera of the 17th Pennsylvania Cavalry commanded a detachment of troopers serving as escort to Major General Philip Sheridan during the Shenandoah Valley Campaign of 1864. On October 19, twenty men from the 17th accompanied Sheridan on the final leg of his famous ride from Winchester to Cedar Creek.
Ken Turner Collection.

BELOW

Killed at the Battle of Cold Harbor Montgomery County lawyer Edwin Schall was killed in battle on June 3, 1864. A fellow officer wrote that he "was universally loved by the whole regiment, and his loss was severely felt."
Ken Turner Collection.

Hell on Earth for Prisoners of War

As the war dragged on and the prisoner exchange system broke down, prison camps became as deadly as battlefields. After separating officers from enlisted men, Union prisoners were moved south to makeshift, overcrowded facilities enforced by cruel guards. One notorious prison, Andersonville in Georgia, holds the remains of 1,849 Pennsylvania prisoners of war who never came home.

CHAPTER 4

ABOVE
Captured and Re-Captured In early 1864, Plympton A. White and 108 others captives successfully broke out of the infamous Libby Prison in Richmond, Virginia. White was recaptured only four days later. Transferred to the prison camp at Florence, South Carolina, White later served as a human shield in the Union bombardment of Charleston. Surviving that ordeal, the second lieutenant of Erie County's 83rd Pennsylvania died in prison on September 13, 1864.
Ken Turner Collection.

ABOVE
Dead Line at Andersonville Fourth Pennsylvania cavalryman William Unversagt, a German immigrant from Allegheny County, wandered too close to the guard towers at Andersonville Prison, accidently stepping over the "Dead Line." He was shot and killed by a guard, and is buried at the Andersonville National Military Park Cemetery.
Ken Turner Collection.

RETURN OF REGIMENTAL FLAG TO STATE OF PENNSYLVANIA,
Independence Hall, Philadelphia, July 4, 1866.

Return of the Flags As the volunteer regiments were mustered out, Philadelphia observed the return of Pennsylvania's battle flags on July 4, 1866, with a grand parade through the city. Pennsylvania generals, including George Meade and Winfield Scott Hancock, stood alongside Governor Curtin at Independence Hall to receive the battle-torn colors in front of thousands of spectators. War widows and orphans were recognized with special seating near the stage.
Kraus/Messick Collection.

Ch. 5

AFTERMATH

As 1865 dawned, thousands of Pennsylvanians were among Union forces battling the last Confederate strongholds. Pennsylvanian Admiral David Porter led an armada to capture Fort Fisher in North Carolina. General William T. Sherman marched northward from Savannah, Georgia, through the Carolinas, overcoming Southern resistance along the way.

In Virginia, the besieged Confederate army at Petersburg launched a last-ditch assault at the Union's Fort Stedman, but they were turned back, in part by a division of Pennsylvania troops from the 9th Army Corps. By April 1, Union soldiers smashed the Confederate line at the Battle of Five Forks. The next day the Northern army broke through the Petersburg defenses with a massive attack that ended the siege, and Richmond surrendered. In the Appomattox Campaign a week later, General Ulysses S. Grant accepted the surrender of Lee's Army of Northern Virginia. Two weeks after that, Sherman's campaign culminated with the surrender of General Joseph Johnston's Confederate army in North Carolina.

GENERAL ULYSSES S. GRANT ACCEPTED THE SURRENDER *of* LEE'S ARMY

CHAPTER 5

Industrial Might

BELOW

George Laughlin Standing behind General Charles Griffin, commander of the 5th Corps, are his aides, including 22-year-old George Laughlin (left). On the General's order, Laughlin delivered the "Cease Fire" command at Appomattox, ending four years of war. The young soldier, son of James Laughlin of Jones and Laughlin Steel, would himself become a powerful industrialist. *Ken Turner Collection.*

ABOVE

The USS Cricket No. 6 The stern-wheeler *Cricket*—built in 1860 in Washington County—was purchased by the U.S. Navy in 1862 and armored with iron plates, also manufactured in Pennsylvania. An April 1864 attack on the Red River in Louisiana left 12 killed, 19 wounded in 5 minutes, but the "tinclad" (in comparison to its sturdier sisters, the ironclads) withstood the bombardment and remained afloat.

HHC L&A, Official Records of the Union and Confederate Navies in the War of the Rebellion, E591.u58 032, Vol. 26.

OPPOSITE

Pennsylvania Locomotive The *Governor Nye* takes on supplies at the wharf in City Point, Virginia, for distribution to Union troops in the South. This locomotive, manufactured in 1862 by Norris and Sons of Philadelphia, was one of countless war contributions furnished by the industrial and manufacturing sectors of Pennsylvania. *Library of Congress, cwpb-01853.*

Four of Six Were Casualties Of six messmates seated for their portrait in 1862, only two of the "Bucktails" (Company D, 149th Pennsylvania) would return home without injury. By 1863, Joshua Momyer (standing left) was discharged for disabilities; Shadrack Phillips (standing center) died of tuberculosis; Frank Dorrington (standing right) and David Philips (seated center) were wounded at Laurel Hill the following year. Only bugler Ustick Rothrock (seated left) and Robert May (seated right) would emerge unscathed. The loss of four of these six men mirrors the percentage of casualties in the Union Army as a whole. *Ken Turner Collection.*

Last to be Counted

The tally of losses to Pennsylvania regiments continued to rise through the last actions of war in 1865. Of the 315,017 Pennsylvanians sent to war, roughly ten percent (33,183) perished.

CHAPTER 5

"Never mind me—keep on and give them hell."

~Colonel John W. Moore

BELOW
Colonel John W. Moore — January 15, 1865 Colonel John W. Moore was in command of the 203rd Pennsylvania Infantry when he was mortally wounded at Fort Fisher on January 15, 1865. As Moore went down he shouted to his men, "Never mind me—keep on and give them hell." The 29-year-old Philadelphian had previously served as major of the 99th Pennsylvania Infantry, which he commanded at Gettysburg. *Ken Turner Collection.*

ABOVE
Asbury Secrist — April 1, 1865 For three years, Asbury Secrist of the 155th Pennsylvania fought without injury. Eight days before Lee's surrender, Secrist was killed at Five Forks, Virginia. *Ken Turner Collection.*

ABOVE
Samuel Robinson — March 13, 1865 After serving unharmed for three-and-a-half years with the 15th Pennsylvania Cavalry, Samuel Robinson was wounded by Confederate guerillas. With the war in its last days, Robinson died in an Army hospital on March 13, 1865.
Ken Turner Collection.

AFTERMATH

RIGHT
Alfred Corman — April 12, 1865 Sergeant Alfred Corman, striking a carefree pose, was captured in Raleigh, North Carolina, while his regiment (9th Pennsylvania Cavalry) was pursuing General Joseph Johnston's army.
Kraus/Messick Collection.

LEFT
Galusha Pennypacker General Adelbert Ames' praise of Galusha Pennypacker recalled the colonel's bravery at the Battle of Fort Fisher, North Carolina, on January 15, 1865. The Chester County officer had raced ahead of his brigade and planted the 97th's flag on the ramparts of the Confederate fort. Pennypacker was wounded and not expected to survive; however, the 20-year-old recovered and for his actions received the Medal of Honor. His promotion to brigadier general of volunteers made Pennypacker the youngest general in the history of the United States Army. *Ken Turner Collection.*

> "Colonel Pennypacker's conduct ... placed him second to none for gallantry that day."
>
> ~ General Adelbert Ames

ABOVE
Norman Ball — April 7, 1865 Two days before Lees's surrender, Second Lieutenant Norman Ball of the 16th Pennsylvania Cavalry was wounded at Farmville, Virginia. *Ken Turner Collection.*

RIGHT
William Montgomery — April 9, 1865 A paid substitute, William Montgomery of the 155th was the last soldier killed from the Army of the Potomac, just after a flag of truce passed through Union lines, the first phase of Lee's surrender. The 15-year-old was loading his rifle near Appomattox, Virginia, when he was struck in the shoulder by a cannonball. His face, pasted on the body of a zouave soldier, appeared in the regiment's published history. *Kraus/Messick Collection.*

WILLIAM MONTGOMERY.

AFTERMATH

RIGHT

Sergeant James McCarty, 97th Pennsylvania Infantry In January 1865, Admiral David Porter of Pennsylvania led a Union armada (in combination with Army, Navy, and Marine ground assaults) in bombarding Fort Fisher in North Carolina. Sergeant James McCarty was carrying the state colors of the 97th Pennsylvania Infantry when he was struck by enemy fire and wounded. The colors were picked up by Galusha Pennypacker, colonel of the 97th—until he too was disabled. *Ken Turner Collection.*

LEFT

Time Worn Sergeant James McCarty's faded military kepi evokes the hard service endured by the 97th Pennsylvania during the last months of the war. McCarty added the heart shaped pin insignia of the 24th Corps to the top. *Ken Turner Collection.*

CHAPTER 5

RIGHT

McCandless and Cat Captain William McCandless of Company I, 6th Pennsylvania Heavy Artillery, spent the last months of the war at Fort Ethan Allen, near Washington. The photographer's cat sleeps peacefully under the skylight that illuminated the studio.
Ken Turner Collection.

LEFT

McCabe of "Sheridan's Scouts" Late in the war, General Philip Sheridan successfully used a number of scouts to penetrate Confederate lines and return with critical information. Sergeant James McCabe, Beaver Falls, Beaver County, of the 17th Pennsylvania Cavalry's Sheridan's Scouts led several daring raids, one resulting in the capture of Brigadier General Rufus Barringer at Namozine Church, Virginia, on April 3, 1865. *Ken Turner Collection.*

AFTERMATH

RIGHT

First in Richmond As a member of one of the first Union regiments to enter the Confederate capital, Josiah Huston wore this "Red Heart Corps Badge" of the 1st Division, 24th Corps of the Army of the James.

On June 25, 1865, Brigade Commander General G.B. Dandy addressed the 206th Pennsylvania in his Farewell Order: Under your gallant commander, Hugh H. Brady, you were the first to enter Richmond, display in that capital of traitors the Stars and Stripes of your country. Bring home with you to your children and your children's children, the Red Heart "Corps Badge." . . . It is the symbol of deeds that will live when this and many succeeding generations have passed away. *Ken Turner Collection.*

LEFT

Hugh H. Conway, 3rd Pennsylvania Heavy Artillery After former Confederate States President Jefferson Davis was captured on May 10, 1865, Hugh H. Conway, 3rd Pennsylvania Heavy Artillery, served as his guard at Fortress Monroe. Conway delivered meals to Davis and attended to his needs. After the war, as a hotel owner in Ellwood City, Conway would write that the Southern leader ate well, was studious, and quiet. *Ken Turner Collection.*

CHAPTER 5

OPPOSITE
Stoddard's Enfield Rifle At the close of war, Robert Stoddard of Company D, 149th Pennsylvania, carved the names of his battles—Chancelersville (sic), Gettysburg, Wilderness, Laurel Hill, N. Anna River—into the stock of his Enfield rifle. *Ken Turner Collection.*

RIGHT
John H. Berlin, 83rd Pennsylvania, Memento of Surrender Appomattox was especially meaningful to John Berlin, an Erie soldier who had been wounded, captured, and released nearly a year before. Berlin cut a sliver of the apple tree under which Grant and Lee discussed terms of the surrender, then fashioned this small shield as a memento of his service. *Ken Turner Collection.*

AFTERMATH

RIGHT

Last to Go Home Private Enoch Pyle spent the entire war with the 77th Infantry, the last Pennsylvania command still in federal service on January 16, 1866. For their final six months, Pyle and his regiment were stationed in Victoria, Texas, defending the border from a possible French incursion via Mexico. *Ken Turner Collection.*

LEFT

"Thank God a Citizen once more" After the war, Phillip Killian, who served 3 years, 11 months, and 16 days in the 52nd Pennsylvania, had his portrait taken in street clothes, and, touchingly, captioned the print with gratitude for his return to civilian life. *Ken Turner Collection.*

CHAPTER 5

MEDAL OF HONOR

On December 21, 1861, an Act of Congress authorized the Secretary of the Navy to bestow Medals of Honor upon those who "distinguished themselves by their gallantry in action and other seamanlike qualities." Providing such honors was thought to "further promote the efficiency of the Navy."

Seven months later, a similar Act of Congress created the same provisions for Army soldiers. William Wilson & Sons of Philadelphia was contracted to cast the medals, the first of which was awarded on March 25, 1863. Medals of Honor were awarded to 1,522 servicemen for acts of valor during the Civil War, many awarded posthumously, some presented decades after the states reunited. Pennsylvania soldiers and sailors were awarded 211 Congressional Medals of Honor. An additional 44 Pennsylvania-born heroes, who fought under the banners of other Northern states, also received the medal.

The following Pennsylvania men are recipients of the Medal of Honor. The quotes below each name are excerpts from that soldier's Medal of Honor citation.

Soldiers who distinguished themselves by their Gallantry in Action.

ABOVE RIGHT
Landsman John Lawson, USS Hartford, United States Navy At Mobile Bay, Alabama, August 5, 1864. *Library of Congress, USZ62-118553.*

"Wounded in the leg . . . Lawson, upon regaining his composure, promptly returned to his station and, although urged to go for treatment, steadfastly continued his duties throughout the remainder of the action."

RIGHT
Army Medal of Honor, Private Higby's Medal
Private Charles Higby of the 1st Pennsylvania Cavalry received this Medal of Honor for the capture of a Confederate flag, and meritorious service, during the Appomattox Campaign of March 29 to April 9, 1865.
Higby Family Descendants.

Trophy of War The regimental staff of the 1st Pennsylvania Cavalry sit for their portrait a final time before mustering out. Standing center, holding a torn Confederate flag, is Chaplain Harvey Beale. The capture of an enemy flag in battle was recognized with the captor receiving a Medal of Honor. Lieutenant Colonel Hampton Thomas, seated below the flag, lost a leg at Amelia, Virginia, while helping to capture an artillery battery and several flags, for which he received a Medal of Honor. *Ken Turner Collection.*

CHAPTER 5

ABOVE
Assistant Surgeon Jacob F. Raub, 210th Pennsylvania Infantry
At Hatcher's Run, Virginia, February 5, 1865. *Ken Turner Collection.*

"Discovering a flanking movement of the enemy, appraised the commanding general at great peril, and though a noncombatant voluntarily participated with the troops in repelling the attack."

ABOVE
Major Charles C. Davis, 7th Pennsylvania Cavalry At Shelbyville, Tennessee, June 27, 1863. *Ken Turner Collection.*

"Led one of the most desperate and successful charges of the war."

CHAPTER 5

ABOVE
Major Robert L. Orr, 61st Pennsylvania Infantry At Petersburg, Virginia, April 2, 1865. *Ken Turner Collection.*

"Carried the colors at the head of the column after two color bearers had been shot down."

OPPOSITE
First Sergeant Alexander Kelly, 6th United States Colored Troops At Chapin's Farm, Virginia, September 29, 1864. *Library of Congress, USZ62-118563.*

"Gallantly seized the colors, which had fallen near the enemy's lines, raised them and rallied the men at a time of confusion and in a place of the greatest danger."

ABOVE
Sergeant Major Thomas R. Hawkins, 6th United States Colored Troops At Chapin's Farm, Virginia, September 29, 1864. *Library of Congress, USZ62-118559.*

"Rescue of Regimental Colors."

AFTERMATH

ABOVE
Colonel James M. Schoonmaker, 14th Pennsylvania Cavalry
At Winchester, Virginia, September 19, 1864. *Ken Turner Collection.*

" At a critical period, gallantly led a cavalry charge against the left of the enemy's line of battle, drove the enemy out of his works, and captured many prisoners."

ABOVE
Charles Shambaugh, 11th PVRC For seizing the Confederate flag on June 30, 1862, during the Battle of Charles City Cross Roads, Prussian-born Corporal Charles Shambaugh would receive the Medal of Honor. In August 1862, Shambaugh lost his left leg at Second Bull Run. *Ken Turner Collection.*

CHAPTER 5

MEDALS FROM WITHIN

Along with the federal government's official medal for valor, several army organizations at the division and corps levels authorized their own unofficial awards for gallantry within the ranks.

ABOVE

Kearny Cross The Kearny Cross, a "cross of valor" created by order of General David Birney in March 1863, was awarded to enlisted soldiers of his 1st Division of the 3rd Corps, Army of the Potomac. Many of the recipients were Pennsylvanians. *Ken Turner Collection.*

ABOVE AND LEFT

Kearny Medal The Kearny Medal—named for General Philip Kearny, killed at Chantilly on September 1, 1862—was awarded to officers of the 1st Division, 3rd Army Corps, Army of the Potomac, who had "honorably served in battle." Kearny Medals were issued to 317 officers in the division; this one was bestowed upon Major James Ryan of the 63rd Pennsylvania Infantry. *Ken Turner Collection.*

Wearing his Kearny Medal Captain Samuel Craig of the 105th Pennsylvania Infantry wearing his Kearny Medal. *Ken Turner Collection.*

AFTERMATH

ABOVE

"French Mary" Marie Tepe of the 114th Pennsylvania Infantry was one of two women to receive the Kearny Cross, awarded for bravery. "French Mary" is seen here with the cross pinned to her shell jacket. In her role as vivandiere, Tepe provided soldiers with refreshment on the battlefield, and cared for the ill and wounded in camp. She served in 13 battles, and was the only woman who served at the battle of Gettysburg. At Chancellorsville, it was noted that her skirts "were riddled by bullets," and she was struck by enemy fire at the Battle of Fredericksburg. *Ken Turner Collection.*

LEFT

Captain Knox Captain Kilburn Knox of Lawrenceville was awarded this rare 17th Army Corps Medal of Honor while serving on the staff of General James McPherson. After the war, Knox would be called as a witness in the trial of Lincoln assassination conspirator, Michael O'Laughlin. *Both Ken Turner Collection.*

CHAPTER 5

ABOVE

Unlikely Fame Private Jacob Soles, a member of Thompson's Battery, Independent Pennsylvania Light Artillery, was 19 when he and three friends sat down in Ford's Theater just 15 feet from the president. Moments later, the four soldiers and two guards carried the dying president across the street. The veteran would sustain an injury after the war when he lost an eye in a coal mining accident. After retiring to Turtle Creek, Allegheny County, Soles would recount the story when asked but was humble about his connection to the world-changing event. He was an active member of The Grand Army of the Republic (GAR), a fraternal organization of Union Army veterans. Soles died at age 90 in 1936, the last of the six who bore the wounded president.
Soldiers and Sailors Memorial Hall and Museum Trust.

LEFT

Lincoln Life Mask Cast by noted sculptor Clark Mills and his son Theodore in February 1865, this plaster life mask captured Lincoln as he appeared two months before his assassination. When compared to a pre-war life mask, this likeness shows the great physical toll the Civil War had on the president. Clark Mills also made masks of Robert E. Lee and other notables. Theodore later worked as an exhibit preparator at Pittsburgh's Carnegie Museum.
Courtesy of the Carnegie Museum of Natural History.

LINCOLN ASSASSINATION

On April 14, 1865, President Lincoln was shot by John Wilkes Booth at Washington, D.C.'s Ford's Theater. The president was carried across the street to the Peterson boarding house by six soldiers—five of them from Pennsylvania. Jacob Soles, John Corey, John Weaver, Jacob Griffiths, and Bill Sample carefully bore the wounded president up the steep steps of the row house and into a bedroom on the first floor. They "reverently placed the body of Mr. Lincoln sideways on the bed, since the bed was too short," reported Dr. Charles Leale, one of the attending physicians. Their grim duty done, the soldiers melted back into the crowd gathering outside the house to await news of the president's condition.

CHAPTER 5

OPPOSITE

Lincoln Funeral Train The body of the slain president was conveyed by rail from the District of Columbia to Springfield, Illinois, for burial. As the funeral train traveled west, stops were made in cities Lincoln had visited while traveling to his 1861 inauguration. Shown here is the funeral train in Harrisburg (above) and the catafalque in Philadelphia.

(Above) Pennsylvania State Archives, MG-218 GPC, Military, Civil War.

(Below) Ken Turner collection.

ABOVE

Conspiracy Commission A military commission of "nine competent military officers" was established by presidential order on May 1, 1865, to hear evidence against the seven men and one woman charged with conspiring to murder President Lincoln. All were found guilty; four were sentenced to hang. One of the nine officers (here with three special judge advocates) is Brevet Brigadier General James A. Ekin of Pittsburgh, fourth from left.

Ken Turner Collection.

ABOVE

Trial by Military Commission Brevet Brigadier James A. Ekin of Pennsylvania was one of nine officers on the military commission which tried the defendants of President Lincoln's assassination. In agreement with his fellow commission members, Ekin found all eight conspirators guilty. *Ken Turner Collection.*

LEFT

Hartranft and Staff Brevet Major General John F. Hartranft of Pennsylvania, seated center first row, is flanked on his left by Lieutenant Colonel William H.H. McCall of the 200th Pennsylvania, and on his right by Colonel Levi A. Dodd of the 210th Pennsylvania. Hartranft later served as state governor, but in 1865 was commander of the Old Capitol prison and special provost marshal general of the commission trying the conspirators. On July 7, he led the four sentenced to die to the gallows and read them their last rites.
Library of Congress, cwpb-04199.

"In accordance with the directions of the President of the United States, the foregoing sentences in the cases of David E. Herold, G.A. Atzerodt, Lewis Payne, and Mary E. Surratt, will be duly executed at the Military Prison near the Washington Arsenal...Brevet Major General John F. Hartranft, USV, Commandant of the Military Prison is charged with the execution of this order."

The Execution of the Conspirators With this directive, issued by General Winfield Scott Hancock, three men and one woman, the first female to be executed by the U.S., were hanged on July 7, 1865. *Library of Congress, cwpb-04228.*

Fraternity Among Veterans

After fighting to preserve their nation, Union soldiers returned home to rebuild personal lives. Although gratified to be far from the horrors of the battlefield, many missed the bond formed among soldiers who had shared the rigors of military life. Several fraternal organizations emerged to unite veterans and extend relationships forged in battle. The Grand Army of the Republic (GAR) established military-style chapters or "posts" in nearly every community, named in honor of national heroes or fallen local commanders. With "Charity, Loyalty and Fraternity" as its motto, members, who called themselves "Comrades," brought aid to disabled and unemployed veterans as well as to war widows and orphans. National and state-level meetings called "encampments" were held annually, bringing together thousands of posts across the country.

ABOVE
Sergeant at Arms GAR members, like this unidentified man, wore uniforms styled similarly to those worn during the war and assumed leadership roles within the post according to military rank. Meetings followed a prescribed fraternal ritual, which included specific duties for the Sergeant at Arms, seated near the door.
Kraus/Messick Collection.

RIGHT
Robert Brush Post 190 member Robert Brush, a veteran of Pennsylvania regiments 136th and 212th, wears the Membership Badge of the GAR on his uniform.
Soldiers and Sailors Memorial Hall and Museum Trust.

CHAPTER 5

BELOW
The Old Canteen Valued for the life-sustaining water it held, the canteen became a symbol of survival in the war. This photograph of a "bullseye" canteen, taken in New Castle, appeared along with a poem "My Old Canteen" in an 1889 veterans' publication.
Andrew Carnegie Free Library, Carnegie, Pa.

Pennsylvania's first post, the General George G. Meade Post Number 1 in Philadelphia, was chartered in 1866. By the turn of the century, the commonwealth counted 619 posts, with more than 43,000 members.

ABOVE
Espy Post 153, Carnegie In 1861, budding industrialist Andrew Carnegie helped organize the U.S. Military Telegraph Corps. Three decades later, the town of Mansfield, Allegheny County (south of Pittsburgh), changed its name to Carnegie in return for the steel captain's gift of building a high school and library/music hall. In this 1903 photo, members of Carnegie GAR (Captain Thomas Espy Post 153) pose in front of the Carnegie Free Library on Decoration/Memorial Day. The holiday originated as a way to honor Civil War veterans.

In 1906, Post 153 veterans secured a second floor room for their meeting hall and filled it with artifacts. The restored room is the only GAR post in Pennsylvania remaining in its original location with all its original contents. Of note in the photograph are the African American veterans whose membership was welcomed in Post 153. *Carnegie Library, Carnegie, Pa.*

AFTERMATH

ABOVE
"Men who for truth and honor's sake stand just and suffer long" Even though its national platform claimed the GAR to be color-blind, black veterans were more likely to join "colored" posts; by 1886, Pennsylvania hosted 15. This 1927 view from an unknown location in the Monongahela Valley south of Pittsburgh celebrates the 63rd anniversary of Company F, 32nd United States Colored Troops with an elaborate diorama that includes land and sea battles.
Ken Turner Collection.

The evocative verse is from Ralph Waldo Emerson's *A Nation's Strength:*
Not gold but only men can make, A people great and strong;
Men who for truth and honor's sake, Stand fast and suffer long.
Brave men who work while others sleep, Who dare while others fly...
They build a nation's pillars deep, And lift them to the sky.

LEFT
James Montgomery James E. Montgomery, from Donora, Washington County, enlisted in Company F of the 32nd U.S. Colored Troops. *Ken Turner Collection.*

CHAPTER 5

LEFT
Without the Use of his Legs Reclaiming former lives wasn't easy, and was particularly difficult for the disabled. A worn sign on the side of this veteran's dogcart in Scranton reads "Can't Walk— Licensed Peddler."
Kraus/Messick Collection.

RIGHT
Widows and Orphans
"To care for him who shall have borne the battle and for his widow and his orphan." These words, taken from Lincoln's second inaugural address, helped awaken the social conscience of the nation and became the mission of the GAR.
Kraus/Messick Collection.

"To care for him who shall have borne the battle and for his widow and his orphan."

~Abraham Lincoln

GAR National Commander, 1936 In 1936, William Ruhe, National Commander of the GAR (center, wearing the GAR badge), visited Carlisle, Pennsylvania. Ruhe had served with the 4th Pennsylvania Cavalry for five months in 1865. By this time—71 years after the war ended—he presided over a quickly shrinking organization. *Soldiers and Sailors Memorial Hall and Museum Trust.*

Medals of the Grand Army of the Republic

Service medals were rarely given and rarely worn during the war; however, afterward, veterans often decorated their GAR uniforms with commemorative and membership badges. Every convention or "encampment," whether on a national or state level, offered attendees specially designed medals to mark the occasion.

ABOVE LEFT

POW Medal The Union Ex-Prisoners of War Organization was established under the umbrella of the GAR. Robert A.A. Patterson's Pennsylvania Survivor ribbon features a bar for each prison in which he was held. Along with most of his regiment, the 103rd Pennsylvania, Patterson was captured at Plymouth, North Carolina.
Kraus/Messick Collection.

ABOVE RIGHT

Membership Badge Early versions of the GAR membership badge, which resembled the Congressional Medal of Honor, were produced from recycled bronze, melted from captured Confederate cannon. *Dave Aeberli.*

LEFT

Honoring the Dead The annual practice of decorating soldiers' graves evolved into Memorial Day, the national holiday for honoring our war dead. In this 1891 photo, George B. Forsythe visits the grave of two Washington County soldiers from the 100th Pennsylvania who were killed in 1863 at Fort Sanders, Tennessee.
Kraus/Messick Collection.

AFTERMATH

BATTLEFIELD AS MONUMENT

In the late 1880s, veterans eager to have their service commemorated at Gettysburg began planning and erecting monuments. On September 11 and 12, 1889, with thousands of Keystone State veterans in attendance, "Pennsylvania Day" was held to dedicate dozens of regimental monuments. In 1895, the battlefield became a National Park—today the most visited Civil War site in the National Park system, with the monuments helping to tell the story of the battle.

ABOVE LEFT

Honoring a Noble Woman Among the first volunteers to aid Union soldiers passing through Philadelphia was Anna M. Ross, matron of the hospital in the Cooper Refreshment Saloon. Working tirelessly, she dressed wounds, prepared fresh clothing, and helped raise money for a home for disabled soldiers. Ross became ill from exhaustion, passing away in December 1863. After the war, GAR Post 94 remembered the devoted nurse by naming their organization after her—the only woman to receive the honor. *Kraus/Messick Collection.*

ABOVE RIGHT

Woman's FCL Medal FCL—Fraternity, Charity, Loyalty, virtues of the GAR—extended to the WRC, the Women's Relief Corps. *Kraus/Messick Collection.*

LEFT

The Lion of the Round Top Photographed during his last trip to Gettysburg in May 1913, Joshua Chamberlain (left), hero of Little Round Top, poses in front of the Pennsylvania Monument with Charles McKenna of the 155th Pennsylvania. Chamberlain was too ill to attend the 50th reunion held only a few months later. He would pass away in February 1914 from complications of a devastating wound received at Petersburg in 1864. *Soldiers and Sailors Memorial Hall and Museum Trust.*

CHAPTER 5

The Women's Relief Corps

The Women's Relief Corps, an off-shoot of the GAR, raised money, contributed aid, and prepared meals for special functions. Formal acceptance came in 1881, when the WRC became The Ladies of the GAR, an authorized auxiliary organization.

Several Generations Three veterans of Alexander Hays Post 3 pose with descending generations of relatives in this front porch photo from 1920. Second from the left is Mrs. Anna Sharp McDowell, who in 1901 was voted an honorary member of GAR's Post 3. Anna's "faithful and valuable services" in Post 3's choir led to the rare acknowledgement.
Soldiers and Sailors Memorial Hall and Museum Trust.

AFTERMATH

"WE HAVE FOUND ONE ANOTHER AGAIN AS BROTHERS AND COMRADES IN ARMS, ENEMIES NO LONGER, GENEROUS FRIENDS RATHER, OUR BATTLES LONG PAST, THE QUARREL FORGOTTEN, EXCEPT THAT WE SHALL NOT FORGET THE SPLENDID VALOR, THE MANLY DEVOTION OF THE MEN ARRANGED AGAINST ONE ANOTHER, NOW GRASPING HANDS AND SMILING INTO EACH OTHER'S EYES."

~ President Woodrow Wilson to the assembly on July 4, 1913

Though he vowed, "we shall not forget the splendid valor," President Wilson and much of the country forgot the root cause of the war and ignored the racial divide that still existed. Tens of thousands of African American Union veterans who likewise fought as "comrades in arms" were not present at the reunion except as manual laborers.

CHAPTER 5

1913: 50TH ANNIVERSARY

In 1913, the federal government invited all honorably discharged Union and Confederate veterans to Gettysburg for the 50th anniversary of the battle. The 53,407 attending made it the largest-ever Civil War reunion; the 280-acre encampment held 48 miles of streets, 173 kitchens, and thousands of tents. Earlier gatherings had been rife with sectional tensions, but by 1913, the root causes of the war had been supplanted by the shared experience and a nostalgia for a simpler past of honor and duty. Reconciliation between North and South trumped inclusion of African Americans or even any mention of the nation's racial policy failures.

OPPOSITE
No Longer Enemies Standing before the High Water Mark monument on the Gettysburg battlefield during the 50th anniversary observance, Confederate and Union veterans clasp hands in a symbolic gesture of reconciliation.
Soldiers and Sailors Memorial Hall and Museum Trust.

BELOW
Reunion snapshot Members of the GAR Post 169 in Mercer were photographed at the 50th reunion by Frank France, a traveling photographer from Washington County. France donated 400 of his glass plate negatives, including 20 taken at the 50th Gettysburg reunion, to Meadowcroft Rockshelter and Historic Village, a prehistoric archaeological site and rural museum founded by his friend Albert Miller.
Meadowcroft Rockshelter and Historic Village, France Coll., F7, B6.

Old Defenders Veterans of the 72nd Pennsylvania, "Baxter's Fire Zouaves," gather in front of the stone wall they defended, 50 years after the Battle of Gettysburg. This image was incorrectly identified by the photographer.
Library of Congress, ggbain-13844.

AFTERMATH

ABOVE
Gettysburg Battlefield Guards Posing against a background of oak trees, these six Gettysburg Battlefield Guards helped enforce park regulations. The four center guards are Civil War veterans, as illustrated by the GAR membership badges pinned to their coats. Ironically, two of them, William Spangler and William Lady of Adams County, were not present at the battle; they were serving with the 165th Pennsylvania in Virginia.
Soldiers and Sailors Memorial Hall and Museum Trust.

LEFT
Family Heirloom Margaret Hewitt's family treasures the medal her great-great-grandfather received at the 75th reunion, when he was 92. Eli L. Haynes, from Livingston, New York, served with the 58th Regiment, New York Infantry National Guard, D Company in 1864. These GAR medals were numbered on the back—Eli's is number 138. Attendants who traveled to Gettysburg with each veteran received a coordinating medal. *Margaret Hewitt.*

CHAPTER 5

1938: 75th Anniversary

In 1938, the nation once again honored the surviving soldiers and the town at the center of the Civil War's most famous battle. The 75th anniversary brought 1,845 white-whiskered veterans from the former Union and Confederate armies.

ABOVE

Anniversary Commemorative The U.S. Mint struck 50,000 commemorative silver half dollar coins for the Gettysburg anniversary. James Power Sankey of Crafton, who joined the 100th Pennsylvania at age 16, served as the model for the coin's profile of a Union soldier. He lived to be one of Allegheny County's last surviving Civil War veterans.

Kraus/Messick Collection.

LEFT

Official Emblem The official emblem of the 75th reunion of the Battle of Gettysburg, held July 1–3, 1938.

From Pennsylvania at Gettysburg, 1939, *Kraus/Messick Collection.*

AFTERMATH

Shake hands For years after the war, the GAR and its southern counterpart, the UCV (United Confederate Veterans) preached reconciliation. In reality, both sides harbored ill-feelings that prevented them from holding joint reunions. After the 50th anniversary at Gettysburg, it would be another 25 years before the former enemies would meet again in peace. Here they shake hands at the Bloody Angle on July 3, 1938. *Special Collections / Musselman Library, Gettysburg College, Gettysburg, Pa., GCW_R_Ph_0053.*

CHAPTER 5

Farewell An elderly veteran waves good-bye as he departs the 75th anniversary commemoration.
Special Collections / Musselman Library, Gettysburg College, Gettysburg, Pa., GCW_R_Ph_0168.

"From these honored dead we take increased devotion to that cause for which they here gave the last full measure of devotion."

~ Abraham Lincoln at Gettysburg, November 1863

BIBLIOGRAPHY

Annotated Catalogue of Relics in Memorial Room, Capt. Thomas Espy Post No. 153 Library Building, Carnegie, Penna. N.p., 1911.

Armor, William C. *Lives of the Governors of Pennsylvania.* Philadelphia: Jms K. Simon, 1873.

Ayers, Edward L. *In the Presence of Mine Enemies, The Civil War in the Heartland of America 1859–1863.* New York: W.W. Norton, 2003.

Bates, Samuel P. *A Brief History of the One Hundredth Regiment (Roundheads).* New Castle, Pa.: W. B. Thomas, 1884.

Bates, Samuel P. *History of Pennsylvania Volunteers, 1861–65.* Five volumes. Harrisburg: Singerly, State Printer, 1869–71.

———. *Martial Deeds of Pennsylvania.* Philadelphia: T.H. Davis, 1876.

Bazelon, Bruce S. *Pennsylvania's Industry During the Civil War.* Unpublished Draft 2-A, 2009.

———, ed. *Swords From The Public Collections In The Commonwealth Of Pennsylvania.* Lincoln, R.I.: Andrew Mowbray, n.d.

Beyer, W.F., and O.F. Keydel. *Deeds of Valor, How America's Heroes Won the Medal of Honor.* Detroit: Perrien-Keydel, 1907.

Bixley, Lawrence G. "Gettysburg Mystery Photo: A 2nd Look." *Military Images,* 4 (1), (July-August 1982): 24-25.

Blackett, R.J.M., ed. *Thomas Morris Chester, Black Civil War Correspondent, His Dispatches from the Virginia Front.* Baton Rouge: Louisiana State Univ. Press, 1989.

Blair, William A., ed. *A Politician Goes To War: The Civil War Letters of John White Geary.* Univ. Park: Penn State Univ. Press, 1995.

Blair, William, and William Pencak. *Making and Remaking Pennsylvania's Civil War.* Univ. Park: Penn State Univ. Press, 2001.

Blight, David W. *Race and Reunion: The Civil War in American Memory.* Cambridge, Mass, Belknap Press of Harvard University Press, 2002.

Blockson, Charles. *African Americans in Pennsylvania, Above Ground and Underground, An Illustrated Guide.* Harrisburg: BB Books, 2001.

Boatner, Mark M. III. *The Civil War Dictionary (Revised Edition).* New York: David McKay, 1988.

Boucher, John N. [Newton], and John W. [Woolf] Jordan. *A Century and a Half of Pittsburgh and Her People.* New York: Lewis Pub. Co., 1908.

Brady, James P. *Hurrah for the Artillery: Knaps' Independent Battery E, Pennsylvania Light Artillery.* Gettysburg: Thomas Publications, 1992.

Brandt, Nat, and Yanna Kroyt Brandt. *In the Shadow of the Civil War: Passmore Williamson and the Rescue of Jane Johnson.* Columbia: Univ. of South Carolina Press, 2007.

Brown, Jack R. and, Roger D. Hunt. *Brevet Brigadier Generals In Blue.* Gaithersburg, Md.: Olde Soldier Books, 1990.

Brown, Henry Box. *Narrative of the Life of Henry Box Brown.* Manchester, England: Lee & Glynn, 1851.

Brown, Kent Masterson. *Retreat from Gettysburg: Lee, Logistics, & the Pennsylvania Campaign.* Chapel Hill: Univ. of North Carolina Press, 2005.

Brown, J. Willard. *The Signal Corps in the War of the Rebellion.* 1896. Reprint, Baltimore: Butternut and Blue, 1996.

Busey, John W., and David C. Martin. *Regimental Strengths and Losses at Gettysburg.* Hightstown, N.J.: Longstreet House, 1986.

Busey, John W. *These Honored Dead, The Union Casualties at Gettysburg.* Hightstown, N.J.: Longstreet House, 1988.

Cavada, Frederick. *Libby Life.* Philadelphia: Lippincott, 1865.

Chamberlin, Thomas. *History of the 150th Regiment Pennsylvania Volunteers.* Philadelphia: McManus, 1905.

Cogar, William B. *Dictionary of Admirals of the U.S. Navy, Volume 1 1862–1900.* Annapolis: Naval Institute Press, 1989.

Colman, Penny. *Corpses, Coffins, and Crypts.* New York: Henry Holt, 1997.

Commemorative Biographical Record of Central Pennsylvania. Chicago: J.H. Beers, 1898.

Cubbison, Shirley, and Cindy Stouffer. *A Colonel, A Flag, And A Dog.* Gettysburg: Thomas Publications, 1998.

Davis, William C., ed. *The Confederate General,* 6 vols. Harrisburg: National Historical Society, 1991.

Darrah, William Culp. *Cartes de Visite in Nineteenth Century Photography.* Gettysburg: W.C. Darrah, 1981.

Detzer, David. *Donnybrook, The Battle of Bull Run, 1861.* Orlando: Harcourt, 2004.

Doster, William E. A. *A Brief History of the 4th Pennsylvania Veterans' Cavalry.* 1891. Reprint, Hightstown, N.J: Longstreet House, 1997.

Dorwart, Jeffrey M. *The Philadelphia Navy Yard: From the Birth of the US Navy to the Nuclear Age.* Philadelphia: Univ. of Pennsylvania, 2001.

Drago, Harry Sinclair, *Canal Days in Pennsylvania.* New York: Bramhall House, 1972.

Dreese, Michael A. *Torn Families: Death and Kinship at the Battle of Gettysburg.* Jefferson, N.C.: McFarland, 2002.

Dyer, Frederick H. *A Compendium of the War of the Rebellion,* 3 vols. 1908. Reprint, New York: Thomas Yoseloff, 1959.

Eberly, Robert E. *Bouquets from the Cannons Mouth-Soldiering with the 8th Pennsylvania Reserves.* Shippensburg, Pa.: White Mane, 2005.

Editors of Time-Life Books. *Echoes of Glory: Arms And Equipment Of The Union.* Alexandria: Time-Life Books, 1991.

Faust, Drew G. *This Republic of Suffering: Death and the American Civil War.* New York: Vintage Books, 2008.

Faust, Patricia L., ed. *Historical Times Encyclopedia of the Civil War.* New York: Harper & Row, 1986.

Field, Ron, and Robin Smith. *Uniforms of the Civil War: An Illustrated Guide.* Guilford, Conn.: Lyons Press, 2005.

Fleming, George Thornton ed., *Life and Letters of Alexander Hays.* Pittsburgh: Gilbert Adams Hays, 1919.

Fortier, John. *15th Virginia Cavalry.* Lynchburg: H.E. Howard, 1993.

BIBLIOGRAPHY

Fox, Arthur B., *Our Honored Dead: Allegheny County, Pennsylvania in the American Civil War.* Chicora, Pa.: Mechling Bookbindery, 2008.

———. *Pittsburgh During the American Civil War, 1860–1865.* Chicora, Pa.: Mechling Bookbindery, 2002.

———. "Pittsburgh Builds a 'Brown Water Navy' for the Civil War." *Western Pennsylvania History*, Summer 2011, 48–60.

Fox, William F. *Regimental Losses In The American Civil War.* Albany: Joseph McDonough, 1898.

Frassanito, William A. *Gettysburg, A Journey in Time.* New York: Charles Scribner's Sons, 1975.

Geary, Mary DeForest. *John White Geary: A Giant in Those Days.* Brunswick, Ga.: 1980.

Gibbs, Joseph. *Three Years in the Bloody Eleventh.* Univ. Park: Penn State Univ. Press, 2002.

Gibbons, Tony. *Warships and Naval Battles of the Civil War.* New York: Gallery Books, 1989.

Gladstone, William. "Gettysburg Mystery Photo." *Military Images*, 3 (5), (March-April 1982): 16-19.

———. *United States Colored Troops 1863–1867.* Gettysburg: Thomas Publications, 1990.

Gottfried, Bradley P. *Brigades of Gettysburg: The Union and Confederate Brigades at the Battle of Gettysburg.* Cambridge, Mass.: Da Capo Press, 2002.

Hackenburg, Randy. *Pennsylvania in the War with Mexico.* Shippensburg, Pa.: White Mane Publishing, 1992.

Hagerty, Edward J. *Collis' Zouaves: The 114th Pennsylvania in the Civil War.* Baton Rouge: LSU Press, 1997.

Harper, Douglas R. *"If Thee Must Fight" A Civil War History of Chester County, Pennsylvania.* West Chester: Chester County Historical Society, 1990.

Hasseltine, William B. *Lincoln and the War Governors.* New York: Alfred A. Knopf, 1955.

Hays, Gilbert A. *Under the Red Patch; Story of the Sixty Third Regiment Pennsylvania Volunteers, 1861–1865.* Pittsburgh: Press of Market Review, 1908.

Heitman, Francis B. *Historical Register and Dictionary of the United States Army 1789–1903.* 1903. Reprint, Gaithersburg, Md.: Olde Soldier Books, 1988.

Hertzog, Kate, *More Than Petticoats: Remarkable Pennsylvania Women.* Augusta, Ga.: Two Dot Books, 2007.

Hitchcock, Frederick L. *War from the Inside: Story of the 132nd PA Volunteers.* Philadelphia: J.B. Lippincott, 1904.

Hoch, Bradley, R. *The Lincoln Trail in Pennsylvania: A History and Guide.* Univ. Park: Penn State Univ. Press, 2001.

Hoptak, John David. *First in Defense of the Union: The Civil War History of the First Defenders.* Author House, 2004.

Hunt, Roger. *Colonels in Blue: Union Army Colonels of the Civil War, the Mid-Atlantic States: Pennsylvania, New Jersey, Maryland, Delaware, and the District of Columbia.* Mechanicsburg, Pa.: Stackpole Books, 2007.

Huntington, Tom. *Pennsylvania Civil War Trails.* Mechanicsburg, Pa.: Stackpole Books, 2007.

Jezierski, John Vincent. *Enterprising Images: The Goodridge Brothers, African American Photographers, 1847–1922.* Detroit: Wayne State Univ. Press, 2000.

Judson, Amos M. *History Of The Eighty-Third Regiment Pennsylvania Volunteers 1861–1865.* Erie: B.F.H. Lynn, 1865.

Karle, Ted. "More Photographs of the U.S. Steamer Michigan," Military Images 30 (3), November-December 2008: 38–40

Kelsey, Charles C. *To the Knife: Biography of Major Peter Keenan, 8th PA Cavalry.* Ann Arbor: Kelsey, Cushing-Malloy, 1964.

Kirstein, Lincoln. *Lay This Laurel.* New York: Eakins Press, 1973.

Korngold, Ralph. *Thaddeus Stevens, A Being Darkly Wise and Rudely Great.* New York: Harcourt, Brace, 1955.

Ladd, David L., and Audrey J. Ladd, eds. *The Bachelder Papers: Gettysburg in Their Own Words, Volume I.* Dayton: Morningside House, 1995.

Lane, Roger. *William Dorsey's Philadelphia and Ours: On the Past and Future of the Black City in America.* New York: Oxford Univ. Press. 1991.

Lang, Scott. *The 123rd Pennsylvania at Marye's Heights— The Forgotten Charge.* Shippensburg, Pa.: White Mane, 2002.

Langellier, John P. *Army Blue, The Uniform of Uncle Sam's Regulars 1848-1873.* Atglen, Pa.: Schiffer Military History, 1998.

Long, E.B. *The Civil War Day by Day, An Almanac 1861-1865.* Garden City, New York: Doubleday, 1971.

Mahood, Wayne. *Alexander "Fighting Elleck" Hays, The Life of a Civil War General, From West Point to the Wilderness,* Jefferson, N.C.: McFarland, 2005.

Martin, David G. *Gettysburg July 1.* Conshohocken, Pa.: Combined Books, 1995.

Matthews, Richard E. *The 149th Pennsylvania Volunteer Infantry Unit in the Civil War.* Jefferson, N.C.: McFarland, 1994.

McClure, A.K. *Abraham Lincoln and Men of War-Times.* Philadelphia: Times Publishing Company, 1892.

McGuinn, William, and Bruce Bazelon. *American Military Buttons Makers and Dealers: Their Backmarks and Dates.* Chelsea, Mich.: Book Crafters, 1984

McPherson, James M. *The Negro's Civil War,* New York: Vintage Books, 1993.

Military Images, 30 (3), November–December 2008: 29.

Military Images, 4 (1), July–August 1982: 16–23.

Military Images, 29 (1), July–August 2007: 26.

Military Images, 30 (2), September–October 2008: 39.

Military Images, 18 (3), "Uncommon Cavalrymen," November–December 1996: 25-26

Military Images, 30 (3), November–December 2008: 29.

Miller, William J. *The Training of an Army, Camp Curtin and the North's Civil War.* Shippensburg, Pa.: White Mane Publishing, 1990.

Mingus, Scott L., Sr., and James McClure. *Civil War Voices from York County PA.* Orrtana: Colecraft Industries, 2011.

BIBLIOGRAPHY

Morgan, Michael. "Breakout from Rat Hell." *Civil War Times*, October 1999

Muffly, J.W., ed. *The Story of Our Regiment, A History Of The 148th Pennsylvania Volunteers*. Des Moines: Kenyon Printing, 1904.

Nachtigall, Herman. *History of the 75th Regiment, Pennsylvania Volunteers*. North Riverside, Ill.: W.P. Printers, 1987.

Necciai, Terry. "The Monongahela Black Community." *Southwestern Pennsylvania*, 1984 (4): 47-50.

Nevin, James, and William B. Styple. *What Death More Glorious: A Biography of General Strong Vincent*. Kearny, N.J.: Belle Grove Publishing, 1997.

Newland, Samuel J. *The Pennsylvania Militia; Defending the Commonwealth and the Nation, 1669–1870*. Annville: Commonwealth of Pennsylvania, Department of Veterans Affairs, 2002.

Nichols, Edward J. *Toward Gettysburg, A Biography of General John F. Reynolds*.1958. Reprint, Gaithersburg, Md.: Olde Soldier Books, 1987.

Nicholson, John P., ed. *Pennsylvania at Gettysburg*. Volumes I and II. Harrisburg: Wm. Stanley Ray, State Printer, 1904.

Norton, Oliver Wilcox. *Attack and Defense of Little Round Top, Gettysburg July 2, 1863*. 1913. Reprint, Dayton, Oh: Morningside House, 1983.

Obreiter, John. *Seventy-Seventh Pennsylvania at Shiloh, History Of The Regiment*. Harrisburg: Harrisburg Publishing Co., 1908.

Pemberton, John C. *Pemberton, Defender of Vicksburg*. Chapel Hill: Univ. of North Carolina Press, 1970.

Penn, William. *No Cross, No Crown*. Edited by Ronal Sellack Richmond, Ind.: Friends United Press, 2007.

Pfanz, Harry. *Gettysburg, The Second Day*. Chapel Hill: Univ. of North Carolina Press, 1987.

Pfister, Harold Francis. *Facing the Light: Historic American Portrait Daguerreotypes*. Washington D.C.: National Portrait Gallery, 1978.

Polcino, Christine Ann. "Biography of H.H. Garnet" in *Cultural Heritage Map of Penna. Writers* (Fall 2004) Univ. Park: Penn State Univ., 2004.

Phillips, Stanley. *Civil War Corps Badges and Other Related Awards, Badges, Medals of the Period*. Marceline, Mo.: 1982.

Price, Isaiah. *History of the 97th Pennsylvania Vol. Infantry During the War of the Rebellion 1861–5*. Philadelphia: 1875.

Ragan, Diane. *Grand Army of the Republic, Personal War Sketches of the African American Members of Col. Robert G. Shaw Post 206, Pittsburgh*. McMurray, Pa.: Printers USA, 2003.

Raus, Edmund J, Jr. *A Generation on the March, The Union Army at Gettysburg*. Lynchburg, Va.: H.E. Howard, 1987.

Reports of the Pennsylvania National Guard, Pennsylvania Adjutant General Reports, Citations and Commissions, 1870-1880, books 1-2. State of Pennsylvania Publishing Co., c. 1880.

Riley, Michael A. *"For God's Sake, Forward!" General John F. Reynolds, USA*. Gettysburg: Farnsworth House, 1995.

Ripley, Warren. *Artillery and Ammunition of the Civil War*. N.Y.: Promontory Press, 1970.

Rollin, Frank A. *Life and Public Service of Martin R. Delany*. 1883. Reprint, N.Y.: Thomson Gale, 1969.

Rollins, Richard. *The Damned Red Flags of the Rebellion*. Redondo Beach, Calif.: Rank and File Publications, 1997.

Rollins, Richard, and Dave Shultz. *Guide to Pennsylvania Troops at Gettysburg*. Redondo Beach, Calif.: Rank and File Publications, 1998.

Rose, Thomas E., "Libby Tunnel," *National Tribune*, May 1885.

Roy, Paul L. *Pennsylvania at Gettysburg, The Seventy-Fifth Anniversary of the Battle of Gettysburg*. Gettysburg: Times & News Publishing, 1939.

Robert M. Sandow, *Deserter Country: Civil War Opposition in the Pennsylvania Appalachians*. New York: Fordham Univ. Press, 2009.

Sauers, Richard A. *Advance The Colors!: Pennsylvania Civil War Battle Flags,* two Volumes. Harrisburg: Capitol Preservation Committee, 1987, 1991.

Sauers, Richard A. *Guide to Civil War Philadelphia*. Cambridge, Mass.: Da Capo Press, 2003.

Sauers, Richard A., and PeterTomasak. *Ricketts' Battery: A History of Battery F, 1st PA Lt. Artillery*. Luzerne, Pa.: Luzerne National. Bank, 2001.

Saylor, Richard C. *Soldiers to Governors: Pennsylvania's Civil War Veterans Who Became State Leaders*. Harrisburg: Pennsylvania Historical and Museum Commission, 2010.

Schneller, Robert J., Jr. *A Quest for Glory, A Biography of Rear Admiral John A. Dahlgren*. Annapolis, Md.: Naval Institute Press, 1996.

Schroeder, Patrick A. *Pennsylvania Bucktails, A Photographic Album of the 42nd, 149th & 150th Pennsylvania Regiments*. Daleville, Va.: Schroeder Publications, 2001.

Scott, Donald, Jr. *Camp William Penn*. Charleston, S.C.: Arcadia, 2008.

Scott, Kate M. *History Of The One Hundred And Fifth Regiment Of Pennsylvania Volunteers*. Philadelphia: New-World Publishing Company, 1877.

Sears, Stephen. *Controversies and Commanders: Dispatches from the Army of the Potomac*. New York: Houghton Mifflin, 2001.

Silverstone, Paul H. *Civil War Navies, 1855-1883*. Annapolis, Md.: Naval Institute Press, 2001.

Slaughter, Thomas P. *Bloody Dawn, The Christiana Riot and Racial Violence in the Antebellum North*. New York: Oxford Univ. Press, 1991.

Smith, Derek. *The Gallant Dead, Union & Confederate Generals Killed in the Civil War*. Mechanicsburg, Pa.: Stackpole Books, 2005.

Smith, Myron J., Jr. *Tinclads in the Civil War: Union Light-Draught Gunboat Operations on Western Waters 1862-1865*. Jefferson, N.C.: McFarland, 2010.

Smith, Myron J., Jr. *The Timberclads in the Civil War: The Lexington, Conestoga, and Tyler on the Western Waters*. Jefferson, N.C.: McFarland, 2008.

BIBLIOGRAPHY

Smith, Timothy H. *John Burns "The Hero of Gettysburg."* Gettysburg: Thomas Publications, 2000.

Speer, Lonnie R. *Portals To Hell, Military Prisons of the Civil War.* Mechanicsburg, Pa.: Stackpole Books, 1997

Spiller, Roger J., ed. *Dictionary Of American Military Biography.* 3 volumes. Westport, Conn.: Greenwood Press, 1984.

Still, William. *The Underground Railroad.* Philadelphia: Porter & Coates, 1872.

Stille, Charles. *History of the United States Sanitary Commission.* Philadelphia: J.B. Lippincott & Co., 1866.

Strong, Michael J. *Keystone Confederate: The Life and Times of Gen. Johnson Kelly Duncan CSA.* York, Pa.: Historical Society of York County, 1994.

Sullivan, David M. *The United States Marine Corps in the Civil War—The First Year.* Shippensburg, Pa.: White Mane Publishing Company, 1997.

Sutton, Robert K. ed., *Rally on the High Ground: The National Park Service Symposium on the Civil War.* Eastern National, 2001.

Taylor, John M. *While Cannons Roared: The Civil War Behind The Lines.* Washington, D.C.: Brassey's, 1997.

Taylor, F.H. *Philadelphia in the Civil War 1861–1865.* Philadelphia: Rudolf Blakenburg, 1913.

Thompson, Heber S. *The First Defenders.* Pottsville, Pa.: Miners Journal Press, 1910.

Tinckom, Harry Marlin. *John White Geary: Soldier-Statesman.* Philadelphia: Univ. of Pennsylvania Press, 1940.

Todd, Frederick P. *American Military Equipage 1851–1872.* New York: Charles Scribner's Sons, 1980.

Torrance, Eli. "The Pennsylvania Reserves," in *Glimpses of the Nation's Struggle, Third Series–Papers read before the Minnesota Commandery of MOLLUS, 1889-92,* edited by Chaplain E.D. Neill, DD, 57. New York: D.D. Merrill, 1893.

Tucker, Spencer. *Arming The Fleet, U.S. Navy Ordnance in the Muzzle-Loading Era.* Annapolis, Md.: Naval Institute Press, 1989.

Under the Maltese Cross: Antietam to Appomattox Campaigns—155th Pennsylvania Regiment. Pittsburgh: 155th Regimental Association, 1910.

United States Of America's Congressional Medal Of Honor Recipients and their Official Citations. Columbia Heights, Minn.: Highland House II, 1994.

U.S. War Department. *The War of the Rebellion: A Compilation of the Official Records of the Union and Confederate Armies,* 128 vols. Washington, D.C.: U.S. Government Printing Office, 1880-1901.

Valuska, David L., and Christian B. Keller, *Damn Dutch: Pennsylvania Germans at Gettysburg.* Mechanicsburg, Pa.: Stackpole Books, 2004.

Warner, Ezra J. *Generals in Blue.* Baton Rouge: LSU Press, 1964.

——— *Generals in Gray.* Baton Rouge: LSU Press, 1959.

Waskie, Anthony. *Philadelphia in the Civil War: Arsenal of the Union.* Charleston, S.C.: History Press, 2011.

Weigley, Russell F., ed. *Philadelphia: A 300-Year History.* New York: W.W. Norton, 1982.

Welsh, Jack D., M.D. *Medical Histories of Union Generals.* Kent, Ohio.: Kent State Univ. Press, 1996.

Wheelan, Joseph. *Libby Prison Breakout: The Daring Escape from the Notorious Civil War Prison.* New York: Public Affairs, 2010.

Wiggins, Sarah Woolfolk. *The Journals of Josiah Gorgas 1857–1878.* Birmingham, Ala.: Univ. of Alabama Press, 1995.

Wilson, Joseph T. *The Black Phalanx: African-American Soldiers in the War of Independence, War of 1812, and Civil War.* 1888. Reprint, New York: DaCapo Press, 1994.

——— *Union Army Uniforms at Gettysburg.* Gettysburg: Thomas Publications, 1998.

Winey, Michael J. "Pennsylvanians in Gray, Early Civil War Uniforms in the Keystone State," *Military Images* 4 (1), July-August 1982: 16-23.

Wudarczyk, James. *Pittsburgh's Forgotten Allegheny Arsenal.* Apollo, Pa.: Clossen Press, 1997.

LEFT

Military Co-workers Clerks at the headquarters of the Pennsylvania Reserves in Culpeper, Virginia, September 17, 1863. Most of the men were from Lancaster County. *Ken Turner Collection.*

About Pennsylvania Civil War 150

Pennsylvania Civil War 150 is the state's official commemoration of the 150th anniversary of the Civil War, 2011-2015. The PACW150 Committee, convened by the Pennsylvania Historical and Museum Commission (PHMC), is an alliance of history, heritage, arts, and cultural organizations from across the state. PACW150's mission is to leverage the strengths of these institutions and bring high-quality programming to the commonwealth's commemoration of the American Civil War. PA Civil War 150 includes a wide array of statewide initiatives and facilitates numerous activities and events at the regional and local levels.

FUNDING PROVIDED BY
Philadelphia Industrial Development Corporation
Pennsylvania Department of Community and Economic Development
National Endowment for the Humanities
Institute of Museum and Library Services

Programs

Many programs are being presented around the state during the 4-year commemoration. Above, United States Colored Troop reenactors gather on the steps of the Messiah Lutheran Church on November 5, 2010, to commemorate the 150th anniversary of the Civil War and to recognize the Pennsylvania Grand Review in Harrisburg on November 14, 1865. Regiments from Pennsylvania, North Carolina, New York, Virginia, New Jersey, Ohio, Massachusetts, Rhode Island, Tennessee, and South Carolina participated in the event.

Online & Events

The official PACW150 web site is filled with in-depth information about the war. It also includes an interactive map, an online store, helpful tips on planning a visit to Pennsylvania, and a calendar of events listing dozens of programs from lectures to reenactments. Visit www.pacivilwar150.com

Publications

The Heinz History Center is coordinating the publication of two books and media initiatives to further reveal an accurate and engaging account of the commonwealth's Civil War story. Plans include the publication of this book *The Civil War in Pennsylvania: A Photographic History* in 2012, and *The Civil War in Pennsylvania: The African American Experience* in 2013. In addition, a collaborative magazine project will bring together content from the Heinz Center's *Western Pennsylvania History*, the PHMC's *Pennsylvania Heritage*, and the Historical Society of Pennsylvania's *Pennsylvania Legacies* in 2013.

About Pennsylvania Civil War 150

Exhibits

The Pennsylvania Civil War Road Show, a multi-dimensional traveling exhibition experience based in an expandable 53-foot tractor-trailer, traveled across the state during the summers of 2011 and 2012. The Road Show engaged local communities and connected them with the history of their Civil War experience, from the battlefield to the home front. Through interactive exhibits and activities, joined by engaging programs and performances at each host community, the Road Show introduced the compelling stories of the Civil War to more than 110,000 visitors. Components of the Road Show have been installed at The State Museum in Harrisburg where they can be enjoyed year round.

The Heinz History Center and PACW150 have collaborated to develop an exhibit that will travel to more than 50 venues across the state. *The Civil War in Pennsylvania* is a 500-square-foot exhibit featuring 3-D "life figures" of Martin Delany, Strong Vincent, Tillie Pierce, a young woman at the Allegheny Arsenal, and even Dog Jack. Museum cases allow host sites to display their own Civil War artifacts.

History Center visitors can explore *The Civil War in Pennsylvania,* including many images drawn from this book, in 2013. This major exhibition will highlight Pennsylvanians' roles on the battlefield and the home front. To learn about additional History Center exhibits, publications, and programs related to PACW150, visit www.heinzhistorycenter.org/civil war.

Digital

The People's Contest: A Civil War Era Digital Archiving Project is a collaboration of the Richards Civil War Era Center, The Pennsylvania State University Libraries, Senator John Heinz History Center, the Historical Society of Pennsylvania, and the Pennsylvania Historical and Museum Commission. Part of a series of initiatives to commemorate the Civil War sesquicentennial, the project aims to advance scholarship on one of the least understood aspects of the Civil War: the experiences of the Northern home front during that conflict. For this project, that era begins in 1851 with Pennsylvanians' resistance to the Fugitive Slave Act and ends in 1874 with the revision of the state constitution.

ABOUT PENNSYLVANIA CIVIL WAR 150

PENNSYLVANIA CIVIL WAR (PACW150) STEERING COMMITTEE

Karen Dougherty Buchholz, Committee Chair and PHMC Member, V.P. of Administration, Comcast Corporation

Bill Blair, Director, Richards Center for Civil War Era Studies, Penn State University

Alice Lubrecht, Director, Bureau of State Library, Pennsylvania Department of Education

Andrew E. Masich PHMC Chair, President and CEO, Heinz History Center

John Meko, Director, Foundations of the Union League

J. Mickey Rowley, President, Pennsylvania Heritage Foundation

Kim Sajet, President and CEO, Historical Society of Pennsylvania

John Seitter, PA Civil War 150 project manager

Sandra Smith, Director of Education and Visitor Services, Senator John Heinz History Center

James M. Vaughan, Executive Director, PHMC

Laurie Zierer, Interim Director, Pennsylvania Humanities Council

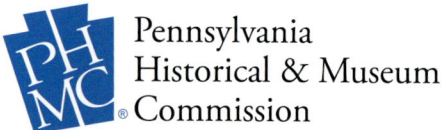

Andrew E. Masich, *Chairman*
John A. Barbour
Karen Dougherty Buchholz
Susan M. Corbett
Jim Ferlo, Senator
William V. Lewis, Jr.
Robert Matzie, *Representative*
Ann M. Moran
Scott A. Petri, *Representative*
Fredrick C. Powell
Richard M. Sand
Joseph B. Scarnati III, Senator
Jean Craige Pepper Victor
Ronald J. Tomalis, *ex officio, Secretary of Education*

The Pennsylvania Heritage Foundation™ is a non-profit organization supporting the Pennsylvania Historical and Museum Commission (PHMC), the official state agency charged with preserving and interpreting the commonwealth's heritage and culture.

www.paheritage.org

Pennsylvania Heritage Federation Board

J. Mickey Rowley, President
Ann Moran, Vice President
James M. Vaughan, Secretary
Anne J. Yellott, Treasurer
William Alexander
Gene Barr
Karen Dougherty Buchholz
Barbara Chaffee
Glenn N. Holliman
Franklin L. Kury, Esq.
William V. Lewis, Jr.
Andrew E. Masich, ex officio

PACW150 PUBLICATIONS COMMITTEE

Andrew E. Masich, Chairman, Pennsylvania Historical and Museum Commission (PHMC), President and Chief Executive Offcer of the Senator John Heinz History Center (HHC)

Rick Beard, Senior Advisor, PACW150

Karen Dougherty Buchholz, Chair, PACW150

James M. Vaughan, Executive Director, PHMC and Co-chair, PACW150

Brian Butko, Director of Publications, HHC

Michael J. O'Malley III, Editor, *Pennsylvania Heritage*, PHMC

Howard M. Pollman, Chief of External Affairs, PHMC

Kim Sajet, President and CEO, HSP; Chair, Civil War History Consortium

John R. Seitter, Project Manager, PACW150

Sandra Smith, Director of Education and Visitor Services, HHC

THE KEN TURNER COLLECTION

This book would not be possible without the many private collectors who have generously aided the PACW150 effort. Ken Turner has been collecting Civil War artifacts for more than 40 years. A boyhood interest in the war and the knowledge that his ancestors served in Pennsylvania regiments in the Union army inspired Ken to study the conflict. A native Pennsylvanian, Ken's collecting naturally gravitated toward the Keystone State's fighting men: "These people are real to me. I want to bring them back to life. I want to tell their stories so they're not forgotten."

Ken's Civil War photographs lend a face to stories of duty and heroism performed by the more than 300,000 Pennsylvanians who fought in defense of the Union. Many of his thousands of images are one-of-a-kind, lending added importance to their preservation. His Civil War material, one of the finest private collections in the world, is also rich in recruiting broadsides, uniforms, inscribed swords, diaries, manuscripts, and corps badges. More than 400 of his rare images and artifacts are featured in this publication.

"I love studying the Civil War and American history and am proud of the significant role Pennsylvanians played in making this a great country," says Ken. "I hope *The Civil War in Pennsylvania: A Photographic History* will foster a better understanding of the crucial role the Keystone State played in the events of 150 years ago."

ABOVE

Brady's Company K, 1862 Captain Evans R. Brady of Punxsutawney, Jefferson County, and his Company K of the 11th Pennsylvania Reserves (40th Pennsylvania Infantry) relax in front of their tent, 1862. During the Peninsula Campaign that spring, the 11th PRVC moved by boat down the Virginia coastline in an attempt to capture Richmond. They were only a few miles from the Confederate capital before being stopped. Brady was captured and exchanged, returning to command only to be killed at the battle of South Mountain that September. *Ken Turner Collection.*

LEFT

Gilded Stars Standing in front of a painted backdrop a self-assured soldier displays his sword and photograph case for a portrait. Gold paint, applied over selected parts of the image by the photographer, enhance the composition. *Ken Turner Collection.*

Acknowledgments

The authors are pleased to acknowledge the assistance and support of family, friends, colleagues, and repositories of historical treasures from across the Commonwealth of Pennsylvania.

Leading the list are Andy Masich and Brian Butko of the Heinz History Center, both of whom listened to our outlandish idea and then made it possible to produce this tribute to the people of Civil War-era Pennsylvania. Andy facilitated our needs and kept the project alive when funds and the anniversary were both far off. Brian worked endless double-shifts to conceptualize the project, organize and edit the content, track down stray images and information, and bring out the best in every image. He worked many of those long hours sending the final pieces of this intricate puzzle to designer Pammy Pieretti, who likewise took a mountain of text and images and made them look engaging and downright lovely to look at! We would also like to thank Dr. Edward L. Ayers, president of the University of Richmond, for his elegantly penned Foreword, which lends much to this volume; Galen L. Schroeder, Dakota Indexing, for his thorough work; and Kelly Anderson Gregg for fact-checking and proofreading. Special thanks to Robert B. Uhler, a graduate of the U.S. Military Academy at West Point and a member of the Smithsonian's National Museum of American History board, whose support and encouragement helped make this book possible.

Our proofreaders were invaluable and saved us great embarrassment from errors of thought and type; they include Michael O'Malley and Howard M. Pollman, PHMC; William Blair, director of the Richards Civil War Era Center at the Pennsylvania State University and editor of The Journal of the Civil War Era; Rick Beard, Senior Adviser, PACW150 and Pennsylvania Heritage Foundation; Margaret Hewitt; Linda A. Ries, head of the Arrangement and Description Section, State Archives, PHMC; and Karen Fisher Younger.

Heinz History Center staff who helped with proofing and fact-finding include Jennifer Kissel, Lauren Uhl, Elizabeth Simpson, Regina Brinza, and Sandra Smith.

Helpful colleagues include historian Nicholas Ciotola, curator of Cultural History, New Jersey State Museum; historian David Halaas; journalist and author Donald Scott; Carolyn Sautter, director of Special Collections & College Archives, Musselman Library, Gettysburg College; and Brenda Wetzel, collections management, PHMC. Much of the artifact photography is by Richard Stoner.

Thanks are also due the following individuals and institutions that contributed photographs or artifacts from their collections for inclusion in this volume:

Private Collections: David Aeberli, Sue Boardman, John L. Carnprobst, Ron Field, John Ford, Margaret Hewitt, Higby Family Descendents, Bill Jacobsen, Ted Karle, Patrick Knierman, Tom Molocea, Rich Moore, Mike Murphy, Descendents of Gertrude Virginia Sharp Myer, Ronn Palm, Betty G. Y. Shields, Karl Sundstrom, Dean Thomas, Karen S. Urbanek, David Wynn Vaughan, and Louis E. Wagner,

Institutions: Bryn Mawr University, Chester County Historical Society, Espy Post Carnegie Free Library, Gettysburg College, Historical Society of Pennsylvania, Historical Society of Western Pennsylvania, Library Company of Philadelphia, Library of Congress, Monroe County Historical Association, Pennsylvania State Archives, Soldiers & Sailors Memorial Hall and Museum Trust, State Museum of Pennsylvania, The Eden Historical Museum, United States Army Military History Institute, University of Pittsburgh, York County Heritage Trust.

ABOVE
Useful to Our Country In 1864, the William Penn Hose Company in Philadelphia purchased a new Amoskeag Steam Engine from Manchester, New Hampshire. The fire company's motto was "Like William Penn, We Will Be Useful to Our Country." More than 11,000 firemen went to the war; many from the William Penn firehouse joined the 72nd Pennsylvania, Baxter's Fire Zouaves. The station was in the Kensington neighborhood at 1129 Frankford Avenue near Girard. *Ken Turner Collection.*

Michael Kraus Foremost thanks to Cheryl Messick-Kraus, wife, friend, and fellow collector with whom I've shared many wonderful years raising a family and building a collection of 19th century photos. Bountiful thanks to my children Dylan and Madison Kraus for putting up with an eccentric father. Thanks as well to my long-time friend Davis Alexander whose help and guidance through compiling and editing of this book was appreciated beyond words. Reflective thanks go to Charles S. King, my mentor, who guided a young student to develop an interest in history for life. Finally special thanks to my life-long comrades in Company "I" 116th Pennsylvania Volunteer Infantry and especially David Kincaid whose Civil War Irish music helped inspire me through the process.

David Neville First and foremost I thank my late parents, Bernard and Evelyn Neville, who inspired my love of history. A debt of gratitude is owed to Irene Miller, my aunt, who passed away at age 94 shortly before this volume went to press, and to my "pards" Doug Richardson and the late Keith Ayers for decades of friendship. A special thank you is extended to my in-laws, Bob and Gina Ladefian, and the extended Ladefian family. Most importantly, thanks to my lovely wife Teresa and step-daughter Jessica, whom I love more than words can say. Your love and support has sustained me throughout the entire project.

Ken Turner Special thanks to my wife and best friend Pam Turner for putting up with this all these years, my son Kasey Turner and his wife Erica Ambrogio Turner, and my other best friend, Aragon the Canine Companion for Independence Facility Dog (he helps people in need and also helped me). Also deserving of special thanks: Cody Magill, Jack Turner, Carole Starz my aunt and our portrait photographer, my friend Tim Brookes, my guide Bruce Bazelon of the PHMC (retired), Kim Sajet, director of the Historical Society of Pennsylvania, Dr. Daniel Rolph, Roger Hunt, and the late Irv Rider.

INDEX

Page numbers followed by suffix "t" are references to the book text. All other page numbers refer to sketches, maps, photos, and photo captions. Abbreviation CSA stands for Confederate States of America.

about the authors, 301, 303. *See also back cover*
African Americans. *See also* racial discrimination
    Distinguished Colored Men (lithograph), 31
    freedman portrait, unknown subject, 28
    Freedman's Bureau, 214
    Fugitive Slave Act of 1850, 26, 38
    Glenalvin Goodridge (photographer), 57
    Henry (janitor), 30
    women as domestic help, 30
African Americans, soldiers. *See also* U.S. Colored Troops
    commissioned as officers, 214
    exclusion from Gettysburg 50th anniversary, 7, 287t
    GAR membership, 279, 280
    Hannibal Guards (militia), 139
    leadership by whites, 37
    Medal of Honor recipients, 210, 263, 266–67
    military service, 21t, 210t–11t
    Nick Biddle (former slave), 52
    recruitment, 10, 143t, 208
    service in Revolutionary War, 29, 211t
    unidentified soldiers, 214, 301. *See also front/back covers*
    U.S. Navy enlistment, 121t
Alabama, 51, 196, 209t
Aldred, Joseph (lieutenant), 203
Allegheny Arsenal (Pittsburgh), 109t, 112, 112–13
Allegheny County
    population of 1860, 25
    surviving war veterans, 291
    war dead, 249
    Western Penitentiary, 182
Allegheny River, 18
Altoona, PA, 242
American Revolutionary War, 13t, 29, 63, 211t
Ames, Adelbert (general), 256
Andersonville National Military Park Cemetery (GA), 249
animals
    as casualties of war, 162
    cavalry horse, 73
    dogs as mascots and companions, 76, 77, 79
    horses and mules, 21
Anti-Slavery Society, 26, 35, 212
Archambault, Joseph, 93

Arlington National Cemetery, 110
Armistead, Lewis (CSA general), 176, 179
Army of the Potomac
    appointment of Grant as commander, 209t
    arrival at Gettysburg, 156t
    command offered to Reynolds, 156
    insignia and badges, 200–207
    last soldier killed, 257
    McClellan as commander, 130, 228
    replacement of Burnside with Hooker, 144
    replacement of Hooker with Meade, 147t, 155
Army soldiers. *See* African Americans, soldiers; Union Army
artillery. *See also* weapons and ammunition
    3-inch ordnance rifle (cannon), 54
    Dahlgren rifle, 124
    Frankford Arsenal fuses, 115
    manufacture at Schuylkill Arsenal, 108
    Rodman Gun (cannon), 111. *See also back cover flap*
    uniforms and insignia, 71, 72
artillery units. *See also* military units, Pennsylvania; Pennsylvania militia
    Battery A, 2nd U.S. Artillery, 54
    Battery F, Pennsylvania Independent Artillery, 71
    1st Pennsylvania Light Artillery (Cooper's Battery), 132, 165, 240
    1st Regimental Pennsylvania Artillery, 306
    2nd Pennsylvania Heavy Artillery, 81
    3rd Pennsylvania Heavy Artillery, 72, 260
    6th Pennsylvania Heavy Artillery, 3, 103, 247, 259
    9th Massachusetts (Bigelow's) Battery, 162
    28th Pennsylvania (Knaps' Battery), 174, 199. *See also back cover*
    Pennsylvania Independent Light Artillery, 145
    Pennsylvania Reserves, 54, 66
    Ringgold Light Artillery (Reading), 11, 53t
    Washington Artillery (Pottsville), 53
Asher, Jeremiah (chaplain), 211
Aspinwall, PA, 18
Asylum for Persons Deprived of the Use of Their Reason (mental hospital), 22
Attack and Defense of Little Round Top (Norton), 170
Avery, Robert (lt. colonel), 244

Baily, Silar (general), 67
Baker, Joseph F. (lieutenant), 121
Baldwin Locomotive Works, 24
Ball, Norman (soldier), 257
Ballier, John F. (colonel), 45
Baltimore, MD, 52
Barker, William Wardle (captain), 196
Barndollar, Jacob (soldier), 137
Barr, Alexander Campbell, 71

Barringer, Rufus (general), 259
Bartley, Rueben (lieutenant), 237
battle flags, 106–08, 130, 142, 180, 264
battles. *See also* military actions
Battle of Antietam (MD), 9, 70, 106, 127t, 130, 134, 135, 136
Battle of Bull Run (VA), 66, 120, 128
Battle of Carlisle (PA), 153
Battle of Cedar Mountain (VA), 174
Battle of Chancellorsville (VA), 68, 143t, 144, 145, 146, 149, 155, 174
Battle of Chantilly (VA), 96
Battle of Charles City Cross Roads (VA), 66, 132, 268
Battle of Chickamauga (GA), 195
Battle of Cold Harbor (VA), 74, 209t, 248
Battle of Deep Bottom (VA), 245
Battle of Fair Oaks (VA), 77, 127t, 128
Battle of Falling Waters (VA), 53
Battle of Falls Church (VA), 238
Battle of Five Forks (VA), 251t
Battle of Fredericksburg (VA), 69, 96, 106, 136, 137, 138, 143t, 145, 147
Battle of Gaines' Mill (VA), 52, 67, 127t, 145
Battle of Gettysburg (PA). *See also* Gettysburg, PA
    50th anniversary (1913), 7, 286–89
    75th anniversary (1938), 291–93
    100th anniversary (1963), 7
    arrival of troops in area, 147t
    bird's-eye view map. *See front inside cover*
    casualties, 156t, 163–71, 175t, 176, 191
    casualty count, 11
    diary account of battle, 89
    exhumation and reburial of bodies, 8
    fallen soldiers, 8, 158. *See also back inside cover*
    insignia and badges, 201–07
    women in battle, 270
Battle of Gettysburg, military actions
    actions on Day 1, 156t
    actions on Day 2, 162t
    actions on Day 3, 175t
    battlefield map. *See front cover*
    Bloody Angle, 175, 201, 202, 292
    Cemetery Hill/Cemetery Ridge, 156t, 165, 177
    Copse of Trees, 175, 176
    Culp's Hill, 174
    Devil's Den, 189
    Little Round Top, 169, 170, 172–73, 285
    Pickett's Charge, 142, 175t, 177, 201
    Seminary Ridge, 181
    Stoney Hill, 168
    Tostle Farm, 162, 204
    Wheatfield, 166, 168
Battle of Hatcher's Run (VA), 79
Battle of Honey Hill (SC), 214
Battle of Jackson (MS), 106

INDEX

Battle of Pocotaligo (SC), 138
Battle of Ringgold (GA), 244
Battle of Second Bull Run (VA), 93
Battle of Spotsylvania (VA), 67, 209t, 239
Battle of Stones River (TN), 127t, 140, 143t, 197
Battle of the Wilderness (VA), 62, 67, 106, 142, 209t, 236, 238
Battle of Todd's Tavern (VA), 231
Battle of Vicksburg (MS), 106, 143t, 146t, 147t
Battle of Waterloo, 93
battlefield monuments. *See* war memorials
battlefield photography
    Alexander Gardner, 8
    Bergstresser Brothers. *See front cover flap*
    Frank France, 287
    Frederick Gutekunst, 58
    Glenalvin Goodridge, 57
    Joseph Saxton, 56t
    Matthew Brady, 9, 60, 65, 161, 181, 192, 240
    Peter Weaver, 189
    Robert Cornelius, 56, 56t
    Robert M. Cargo, 23, 183
    Timothy O'Sullivan, 158
Battles, Seven Days (VA), 106, 108
Beal, William, Jr. (officer), 45
Beaver, James A. (lt. colonel), 241
Beaver County, 28, 67, 168, 244
Bergstresser Brothers, photography studio. *See front cover flap*
Berks County, 11, 68
Berlin, John H. (soldier), 261
Biddle, Nick (former slave), 52
Bingham, Henry Harrison (officer), 179
Bird, Phineas (soldier), 194
Birney, David (general), 269
The Birth of a Nation (film, 1915), 7
Blair County, PA, 240
Blanchard, Henry (sergeant), 108
Bohlen, Henry (general), 91
Bonaparte, Napoleon, 93
Booth, John Wilkes, 271t
Bowser, David (artist), 210
Brady, Evans R. (captain), 301
Brady, Hugh H. (general), 260
Brady, Lemuel (army enlistee), 62
Brady, Mathew (photographer), 9, 60, 65, 161, 181, 192, 240
Bragg, Braxton (CSA general), 195
bridges. *See* transportation
Brown, Henry ("Box"), 29
Brown, Henry D. (lieutenant), 182
Brown, John (abolitionist), 32
Brown, Joseph (officer), 65
Browne, Robert Audley (chaplain), 96

Brush, Robert (GAR veteran), 278
Bryan, Abraham (freedman), 184
Buchanan, James (15th president), 40, 108
Buckner, Simon Bolivar (CSA general), 66
Burchfield, Eva Marie Nourse, 171
Burchfield, James Penrose (surgeon), 170, 171
Burns, John (civilian), 161
Burnside, Ambrose (general), 144
Burr, Richard (doctor), 185t, 186
Butler, James (corporal), 205

Caitlin, William (soldier), 215
Caldwell, William (soldier), 247
Cameron, James (colonel), 129
Cameron, Simon (secretary of war), 41
Camp, March and Battlefield (Stewart), 97
The Camp Kettle (unit newsletter), 82
Camp Lafayette, 306
camp life
    activities away from battle, 76t
    activities when in battle, 79t
    camp possessions and furniture, 77
    diversions from boredom, 83, 86
    letter writing and stationery, 55t, 83–85
    sutler supplies and token, 81
    tents and shelters, 78
    unit newsletters, 82
    Volunteer Refreshment Saloons, 80
Camp Wilkins (PA), 52
Camp William Penn, 175
Camp William Penn (PA), 208, 210–12
Camp Wright (PA), 52
Cargo, Robert M. (photographer), 23, 183
Carlisle, PA
    Dickinson College, 30
    fall to Confederate forces, 147t, 153
    market day scene, 22
    U.S. Army War College, 50
Carnegie, Andrew, 279
Casey, Silas, 81
Catto, Octavius (activist), 37
Cavada, Adolpho Fernandaz, 89
Cavada, Frederico, 89
Census of 1860, 25
Chadds Ford, PA, 306
Chamberlain, Joshua (veteran), 285
Chambersburg, PA, 32, 147t, 243
charity/charitable organizations
    Christian Commission, 224–27
    Refreshment Saloons, 80
    Sanitary Fairs, 209t, 216–20
    Women's Relief Corps, 284
Charleston, SC, 7, 124, 214, 249
Cheltenham, PA, 212
Cheney, Nathan (soldier), 73

Chester, PA/Chester County, 79, 120, 126, 185t, 207, 221, 256
Chestnut Street (Philadelphia), 37
children. *See also* families
    buglers and drummer boys, 98–99
    industry - child labor, 23
    memorializing infant death, 16
    "oil dippers," 20
    portraiture, 57, 58
    support of war effort, 10
Childs, James (colonel), 135
Christiana, PA, 38
churches. See religion and churches
The Civil War in Pennsylvania: The African American Experience (Heinz History Center), 298
The Civil War in Pennsylvania (traveling exhibit), 299
Civil War reenactments, 298
Clark, John B. (colonel), 68
Clarke, Robert (militia officer), 54
Clinton County. *See front cover flap*
clothing. *See* uniforms and clothing
coal industry, canal transport, 12
Cobham, George A. (colonel), 241
Collins, Charles R. (CSA colonel), 231
Collins, Napoleon (commander), 126
Colored Youth Institute (Philadelphia), 37
Confederate Army. *See also* military units, Confederate
    burial of dead soldiers, 8
    invasion of the North, 143t, 146t
    Pennsylvania men in service of, 231–35
    surrender at Appomattox, 251t
Conway, Hugh H. (soldier), 260
Cooke, Jay and Jay, Jr., 228
Corey, John (soldier), 271t
Corman, Alfred (sergeant), 256
Cornelius, Robert (photographer), 56, 56t
Corrie, William (soldier), 146. *See also front cover*
Cousin, Stanton (doctor), 246
Covode, George Hay (colonel), 238
Covode, John (politician), 41t
Cowan, Edgar (politician), 41t
Craft, Ellen and William (slaves), 31
Craig, Calvin (colonel), 245
Craig, Samuel (captain), 269
Crawford, Samuel (general), 166
Crawford County, 32, 73
Crimean War, 91, 95
Crippen, Benjamin (sergeant), 159
Crotzer, Henry W. (captain), 87
Crumleigh, James (bugler), 99
CSS *Florida*, 126
Cuba/Cuban immigrants, 88–89

— 305 —

INDEX

Cummins, Robert (colonel), 158
Curry, William E. (captain), 182
Curtin, Andrew Gregg (the "Great War Governor"), 41t, 42, 66, 135, 151, 250
Curvin, William (veteran volunteer), 230

Dahlgren, John A. (admiral), 11, 124–25
Dahlgren, Ulric (colonel), 239
Dandy, G. B. (general), 260
Danforth, Henry W. (lieutenant), 132
Dauphin County, 25, 232
Davis, Charles C. (major), 265
Davis, Edward M., 212
Davis, Jefferson (Confederate president), 260
Davis, Richard P. (captain), 204
Davis, William Watts Hart, 133
De Korponay, Gabriel (colonel), 90
deaths and casualties. *See also* hospitals and medical care; war memorials
 African American soldiers, 209t, 212
 Battle of Gettysburg, 156t, 163–71, 175t, 176, 191
 civilians, 179
 embalming and undertaking, 185t, 186–87
 Pennsylvania soldiers/units, 22t, 147t, 202, 255t
 prisoners of war, 248t
Delany, Martin (abolitionist), 39, 299
Delaware County, 306
Derickson (captain), 87
DeVore, William (embalmer), 185t
Dickey, James (private), 168
Dickinson, Anna (social advocate), 229

Dickinson College (Carlisle), 30
Distinguished Colored Men (lithograph), 31
Dodd, Levi A. (colonel), 274–75
Dog "Jack," 76, 299
Dog "Sallie," 79
Dorrington, Frank (soldier), 254. *See also front cover*
Douglass, Frederick (abolitionist), 31, 32, 39
Drake, Edwin, 19
Drayton, Percival (USN lieutenant), 233, 235
Drayton, Thomas (CSA general), 233, 235
drums/drummer boys, 3, 43, 98–99
Duquesne Grays (militia), 45

Eagleson, Andrew (lieutenant), 134
Early, Jubal (CSA general), 151
Eastman, Frank M. (corporal), 244
Edwards, Herbert (soldier), 95
Ekin, James A. (general), 273, 275
Elliot, Fergus (sergeant), 243
Emancipation Proclamation
 document, 141
 eligibility for military service, 210t
 enactment, 143t
 Pennsylvania support of, 41t
Emerson, Ralph Waldo, 280
equipment and supplies. *See also* home front support; uniforms and clothing
 backpack and blanket roll, 73
 canteens, 109, 279
 complete infantry kit, 68
 Confederate Army, 232
 "Cracker Line" initiative, 196
 knapsack, 49

 mess kit, 80
 pontoons, 116–17
 Sanitary Fairs, 209t
 sutler card and token, 81
 tents and shelters, 78
Erie, PA/Erie County, 25, 52, 121, 122, 169
Erie Extension Canal near Sharon, PA, 12
Everett, Edward, 193
Evergreen Cemetery, Gettysburg, 164–65. *See also front cover*
Everhard, William (soldier), 74
Ewell (CSA general), 147t

families. *See also* children; women
 burial of dead soldiers, 187
 dealing with infant death, 16
 lifestyle and activities, 16, 58
 slave escapes to the North, 29, 31, 36, 39
Faust, Alonzo (soldier), 107
50th Anniversary of the Civil War (1913), 7, 286–89
firemen/fire-fighting equipment, 65, 76
Fitch, Charles P. (soldier), 226
flags. *See* battle flags
Floyd, John B. (secretary of war), 109
Forbes, Edwin, 175
Forsythe, George (veteran), 283. *See also back cover*
Fort Ethan Allen (VA), 259
Fort Fisher (NC), 251t, 253, 256, 258
Fort Monroe (VA), 260
Fort Pitt Foundry (PA)
 5.1-inch Dahlgren rifle, 124
 Rodman Gun (cannon), 108
Fort Sanders (TN), 283
Fort Stedman (VA), 251t
Fort Sumter (SC), 21t, 51t, 124
Fort Wagner (SC), 212
Foster, Stephen (songwriter), 99
Fox, Chalkey (soldier), 201
France, Frank (photographer), 287
France/French immigrants, 91, 93, 121, 262
Frankford, PA/Frankford Arsenal, 22, 109t, 115
Franklin County, 32, 166
Franklin, PA, 142
Franklin, William B. (general), 147

LEFT

Camp Lafayette Men of the 1st Regiment Pennsylvania Artillery, Philadelphia Home Guard, relax at Camp Lafayette, Chadds Ford, Delaware County, in July 1861. The pastoral atmosphere of the camp during the first month of the war reveals little of hardships to come. *Ken Turner Collection.*

INDEX

Freedman's Bureau, 214
Frick, Jacob G. (colonel), 148, 149
Fugitive Slave Act of 1850, 26, 38
Fullerton, James (sergeant), 132
Fullerton, John (soldier), 202

Gad (African-born slave), 211
Gamble, John N. (soldier), 238
Gardner, Alexander (photographer), 8
Gardner, James A. (lieutenant), 240
Gardner's Photographic Sketch Book of the War (Gardner), 158
Garnet, Henry Highland (abolitionist), 31
Garretson, Isaac. *See back cover*
Garrison, William Lloyd (journalist), 39
Geary, Edward (lieutenant), 199
Geary, John White (general, governor), 174, 198, 207t
Geety, John (lieutenant), 138
Gerard, Joseph (captain), 77
Gerker, Frederick (adjutant), 201
Germantown, PA, 29, 226
Germany/German immigrants, 21t, 91, 249
Gettysburg, PA. *See also* Battle of Gettysburg
    battlefield commemoration, 285t
    battlefield guards, 290
    Evergreen Cemetery, 164–65. *See also front cover*
    Lutheran Theological Seminary, 156
    Soldiers National Cemetery, 8, 161, 193
Gettysburg Address, 11, 161, 193
Gillen, William (soldier), 207
Glory (movie), 212
Goodman, Joseph (captain), 244
Goodridge, Glenalvin (photographer), 57
Gordon, John B. (general), 148
Gorgas, Josiah (CSA officer), 232
Gorsuch, Edward (slave owner), 38
Gosline, John (colonel), 74, 145
Graeff, Rudolph M. (soldier), 204
Grand Army of the Republic (GAR), 271
    African American membership, 279–80
    caring for the disabled, 281
    chartering of posts, 278t–79t
    honorary membership, 284
    medals and badges, 283–84
    reconciliation with UCV, 292
    shrinking membership, 282
    Women's Relief Corps, 284
Grant, Ulysses S. (general), 209t, 251t
Great Central Fair, Philadelphia, 216t, 222–23
Great Lakes, U.S. naval presence, 122
"Great Train Raid of 1861," 234
Green (captain), 244
Greencastle, PA, 147t

Greene County, 168
Griffin, Charles (general), 253
Griffiths, Jacob (soldier), 271t
Grow, Galusha (politician), 41t
Gutekunst, Frederick (photographer), 58
Guy, Frank (soldier), 107

Haller, Granville (major), 149
Hampton, Robert (captain), 145
Hancock, Winfield Scott (general), 177, 179, 201, 245, 250, 276
Hanover, PA/Hanover Bridge, 147t, 152
Harper's Ferry, VA, 32, 33
Harper's Weekly, 33, 113
Harris, John (colonel), 120
Harrisburg, PA
    Confederate threat to, 150
    Lincoln funeral train, 272
    population of 1860, 25
    threat from Confederate forces, 147t, 148
Hartranft, John F. (general), 274–75
"A Harvest of Death" (O'Sullivan), 158
Harwood, Andrew A. (commodore), 123
Hathaway, Leland (lieutenant), 182
Haupt, Herman (general), 116–18
Hawkins, Thomas R. (sergeant), 210, 267
Haynes, Eli L. (veteran), 290
Hays, Alexander (general), 142, 180
Hays, Will (lieutenant), 182, 183
health. *See* hospitals and medical care
Hennon, Joseph W. (soldier), 70
Henry, Alexander (mayor), 150
Henry, George W. (soldier), 203
Hewitt, Margaret, 290
Higby, Charles (private), 263
Hill, A. P. (general), 158
Hilton, Leroy (soldier), 212
Hoffman, Jeremiah (lieutenant), 159
Holtzman [Hausmen], John (corporal), 158
home front support. *See also* equipment and supplies
    Philadelphia Great Central Fair, 222–23
    Pittsburgh Sanitary Fair, 216–20
    Sanitary Fairs, 209t, 216t
    U.S. Christian Commission, 224–27
    Volunteer Refreshment Saloons, 80
Hooker, Joseph (general), 144, 147t, 155
horses. *See* animals
hospitals and medical care
    battlefield hospitals, 96t, 158, 159, 163, 170
    Camp Letterman Military Hospital, 189
    Citizen's Volunteer Hospital, 185
    construction of military hospitals, 185t
    Episcopal Hospital (Philadelphia), 187, 190, 191
    mental hospitals, 22

Housum, Peter (lt. colonel), 140
Howell, Horatio S. (chaplain), 96t
Hugh, William (slave owner), 34
Hungary/Hungarian immigrants, 90
Huntington County, 232
Huston, Josiah (soldier), 261

"Illustrations of Camp Life" (Brady photo series), 65
immigrants, 89t
insignia and badges. *See also* medals and decorations
    artillery, 72
    color bearers (battle flag), 108
    memento of Appomattox, 261
    "Red Heart Corps Badge," 261
    regimental and corps, 200–207, 244, 258
    uniform buttons, 73
    U.S. Christian Commission, 225
    U.S. Marine Corps, 120
    Zouave D'Afrique, 162
Internet, PACW150 information, 298
Ireland/Irish immigrants, 21t, 88–89, 90
Irish Ripple, PA, 70
iron industry, child labor, 23

"Jack" (dog, mascot), 76, 299
Jackson, Thomas J. "Stonewall" (CSA general), 51, 53, 144, 234
Jann, Charles U. (soldier), 206
Jarrett, Phaon (militia colonel), 53
Jenkins, Albert (general), 147t
Jennings, William W. W. (colonel), 151
Jim Crow era, 7
Johnson, Jane (slave), 26
Johnston, Joseph (general), 251t

Kaufman, Casper (soldier), 205
Kearny, Philip (general), 269
Keasey, Hiram (bugler), 105
Kelly, Alexander (sergeant), 266
The Ken Turner Collection, 9, 301
Kiddoo, Joseph Barr (general), 214
Killian, Phillip (soldier), 262
Kilpatrick, Judson (general), 239
Knap, Joseph M. (captain), 174, 214
Knox, Kilburn (captain), 270
Knoxville, TN. *See back cover flap*
Koltes, John (colonel), 93

Ladies of the GAR (formerly Women's Relief Corps), 284
Lady, William (veteran), 290
Lancaster, PA, 15, 41t, 65, 101, 128, 148, 156t

INDEX

Landis, Benjamin (soldier), 72
Laughlin, George (officer), 253
Lawrenceville, PA, 270
Lawson, John (seaman), 263
Leale, Charles (doctor), 271t
Lee, Robert E. (CSA general), 146t, 175t, 234, 271
Lemmon, Thomas (army enlistee), 62
Lenni-Lanape people (Delaware Indians), 14
Lewis, Marcus (sailor), 121
Lewistown, PA, 53
The Liberator (newspaper), 39
Lincoln, Abraham
  arrival of militia in Washington, 52
  assassination and the aftermath, 271t–77
  call of militia to federal service, 51t
  as Commander-in-Chief, 156
  election of 1864, 130, 228–29
  Emancipation Proclamation, 41t, 141, 143t, 210t
  National Cemetery dedication (Gettysburg Address), 11, 161, 193, 293
  nomination for president, 41
  portraiture, 192
  presidential guard, 87
  trial of conspirators, 270
  use of colored troops, 39, 213
  war service with a stand-in, 237
livestock. *See* animals
Longstreet, James (CSA general), 162t, 175t, 179, 194t, 199
Louis, Daguerre (inventor), 56t
Lucas, William (private), 62

MacConnell, Charles C. (captain), 231
Mahler, Francis (colonel), 160
Mansfield, PA, 279
Manual for the Militia, 46
maps
  Battle of Chancellorsville, 144
  Battle of Gettysburg. *See front inside cover*
Maratta, Caleb (soldier), 247
Maryland campaigns, 206
Mason, William (daguerreotypist), 14
Mason-Dixon line, 9
Massachusetts, 121t, 210t–11t
Matthews, Ezra (captain), 165
May, Robert (soldier), 254. *See also front cover*
McCabe, James (sergeant), 259
McCall, William H. H. (lt. colonel), 274–75
McCandless, William (captain), 259
McCarty, James (sergeant), 258
McCausland, John (CSA general), 243
McClellan, George Brinton (general), 131, 228

McClintock Riots of 1847, 22
McClurg, William (soldier), 67
McComb, William (CSA colonel), 235
McDowell, Anna Sharp (GAR honorary member), 285
McFall, George F. (general), 66
McKeesport, PA, 238
McKenna, Charles (veteran), 285
McLane, John White (militia colonel), 52
McNeil, Hugh Watson (colonel), 133
McPherson, James (general), 270
Meade, George Gordon (general), 147t, 155, 250
Meadowcroft Rockshelter and Historic Village, 287
Meadville, PA, 32
Mechanicsburg, PA, 147t
medals and decorations. *See also* insignia and badges; war memorials
  Gettysburg Battlefield 75th anniversary, 290–91
  Grand Army of the Republic, 283–84
  Kearney Cross/Kearney Medal, 269–70
  Medal of Honor, 149, 179, 256, 263t–68
  recognition of women, 285
  17th Army Corps Medal of Honor, 270
Meigs, John R. (lieutenant), 110
Meigs, Montgomery C. (general), 110
Mercer, PA/Mercer County, 17, 48, 128, 168, 234, 287
Mexican-American War (1846-48), 43–45, 91, 128
military actions. *See also* Battles
  Appomattox Campaign, 251t
  Atlanta Campaign, 209t, 229, 243
  burning of Columbia-Wrightsville Bridge, 148, 149
  Chattanooga Campaign, 197–99
  Lookout Mountain, 197
  Pennsylvania militia, 51
  Red River Campaign (LA), 252
  Shenandoah Valley, 248
  siege of Petersburg, 209t, 240, 251t
  siege of Vicksburg, 106, 143t, 146t, 147t
  Western Theater, 194t, 195–96
military chaplains, 96–97
military units, Confederate. *See also* Confederate Army
  2nd Florida Cavalry, 232
  2nd Kentucky Cavalry, 182
  7th Kentucky Cavalry, 182
  8th Kentucky Cavalry, 182
  15th Virginia Cavalry, 231
  26th Tennessee, 139
  Kentucky Mounted Rifles, 182
military units, other States
  1st New York Cavalry, 147t
  2nd District of Columbia Volunteers, 237
  2nd Wisconsin, 128
  10th Vermont Infantry, 226

  54th Massachusetts, 210t, 212
  55th Massachusetts, 210t
  58th Regiment, NY Infantry National Guard, 290
  79th New York (The Highlanders), 128
  102nd New York, 244
military units, Pennsylvania. *See also* artillery units; Pennsylvania militia
  battle flags, 106–08
  1st Corps, 160, 201
  2nd Corps, 201–02
  3rd Corps, 202, 238
  5th Corps, 202–04
  6th Corps, 205
  9th Corps, 206
  11th Corps, 160, 206
  12th Corps, 206, 207t
  1st Division (Sarsfield Rifles), 45, 260
  1st Pennsylvania Cavalry, 246, 264
  1st Pennsylvania Reserves, 166, 245
  2nd Pennsylvania Cavalry, 73, 92–93, 94
  2nd Pennsylvania Infantry, 241
  4th Pennsylvania Cavalry, 50, 135
  4th Pennsylvania Cavalry (militia), 249, 282
  5th Pennsylvania Volunteer Reserves Corps, 136
  6th Pennsylvania Cavalry ("Rush's Lancers"), 63–64
  6th Pennsylvania Heavy Artillery, 3
  7th Pennsylvania Cavalry, 265
  8th Pennsylvania Cavalry, 146. *See also front cover*
  8th Pennsylvania Reserves, 134
  8th Pennsylvania Volunteer Reserve Corps, 4, 67
  9th Pennsylvania Cavalry, 99, 256
  9th Pennsylvania Reserves, 108
  9th Pennsylvania Volunteer Reserve Corps, 67
  10th Pennsylvania Infantry, 214
  10th Pennsylvania Reserves, 130
  11th Pennsylvania Reserves, 301
  11th Pennsylvania Volunteer Infantry, 53, 79
  12th Pennsylvania Volunteer Infantry, 45, 50, 135
  13th Pennsylvania Reserves (1st Rifles/Bucktails), 133
  14th Pennsylvania Cavalry, 268
  15th Pennsylvania (Anderson's) Cavalry, 72, 255
  16th Pennsylvania Cavalry, 257
  17th Pennsylvania Cavalry (Sheridan's Scouts), 248, 259
  17th Pennsylvania Infantry, 52
  18th Division, 43
  21st Pennsylvania Cavalry, 105
  23rd Pennsylvania, 74, 77
  25th Pennsylvania Infantry, 133, 135
  28th Pennsylvania, 62
  29th Pennsylvania, 207
  31st Pennsylvania, 204

INDEX

33rd Independent Pennsylvania Infantry, 71
40th Pennsylvania Infantry, 301
45th Pennsylvania Infantry, 241
46th Pennsylvania Volunteers, 98, 230
47th Pennsylvania, 138
48th Pennsylvania, 80
51st Pennsylvania, 68, 106
52nd Pennsylvania, 262
56th Pennsylvania Infantry, 95, 108, 156t, 230
61st Pennsylvania Infantry, 62, 77, 128, 205, 267
62nd Pennsylvania, 65, 75, 167, 189, 203
63rd Pennsylvania Infantry, 238, 269
69th Pennsylvania (Irish Brigade), 89, 175t, 176
71st Pennsylvania, 175t, 202
72nd Pennsylvania ("Baxter's Fire Zouaves"), 65, 175t, 185t, 202, 288–89, 303
73rd Pennsylvania Infantry, 93, 206
74th Pennsylvania Regiment (German), 89t
75th Pennsylvania Volunteer Infantry, 91, 160
77th Pennsylvania Infantry, 140, 195, 262
78th Pennsylvania Volunteer Infantry, 139, 197
79th Pennsylvania, 107
82nd Pennsylvania, 205
83rd Pennsylvania Volunteer Infantry, 52, 75, 106, 170, 236, 249
87th Pennsylvania, 207
88th Pennsylvania, 201, 211
90th Pennsylvania ("National Guards"), 201
95th Pennsylvania (Zouaves), 74, 145
97th Pennsylvania, 256, 258
98th Pennsylvania Volunteer Infantry, 45
99th Pennsylvania Infantry, 253
100th Pennsylvania Volunteer Infantry, 61
100th Regiment ("Roundheads"), 82, 194, 239, 283, 291. *See also back cover flap*
101st Pennsylvania, 103
102nd Pennsylvania Infantry, 76, 97, 236, 244
103rd Pennsylvania, 283
104th Pennsylvania Volunteer Infantry, 130, 133
105th Pennsylvania Infantry, 269
106th Pennsylvania, 100, 175t, 201
107th Pennsylvania, 201
109th Pennsylvania, 243
110th Pennsylvania Infantry, 240
111th Pennsylvania, 107, 241
114th Pennsylvania Infantry, 101, 270
118th Pennsylvania, 204
123rd Regiment of Pennsylvania Volunteers, 68, 237
128th Pennsylvania, 68
129th Pennsylvania, 149
130th Pennsylvania Volunteers, 138
131st Pennsylvania Regiment, 96
132nd Pennsylvania, 136
133rd Pennsylvania Volunteers, 137
134th Pennsylvania Volunteer Infantry, 60, 69, 204
137th Pennsylvania, 214
140th Pennsylvania, 163, 168
142nd Pennsylvania, 158, 159
143rd Pennsylvania, 159
147th Pennsylvania Infantry, 244
148th Pennsylvania, 241
149th Pennsylvania Bucktails, 98, 157, 254. *See also front cover*
150th Pennsylvania Bucktails, 87, 157, 158, 161
155th Pennsylvania, 246, 254
165th Pennsylvania, 290
193rd Pennsylvania, 104–05
200th Pennsylvania, 275
203rd Pennsylvania Infantry, 253
208th Pennsylvania Infantry, 96
210th Pennsylvania Infantry, 265, 275
Philadelphia Brigade, 175t, 201, 202
Philadelphia Horse Troop (militia), 63
Saeger's Regiment, 75
military units, Union forces. *See* Union Army
militia. *See also* Pennsylvania militia
  mobilization for federal service, 51t
  relationship to Union Army, 62t
Miller, Albert, 287
Miller, James (sergeant), 132
Mills, Clark and Theodore (sculptors), 271
Mississippi River, 15
Momyer, Joshua (soldier), 254. *See also front cover*
Monongahela City/Valley/River, 15, 23, 214, 216, 280
Montgomery, James E. (soldier), 280
Montgomery, William (soldier), 257
Montgomery County, 248
Moody, William (lt. colonel), 236
Moore, John W. (colonel), 130, 253
Moore, Reese (soldier), 72
Morgan, John Hunt (CSA colonel), 182t
Morton, John (soldier), 107
Mott, Lucretia (abolitionist), 212
music/musicians
  buglers, 99
  cavalry bugle, 105
  drummer boys, 98–99
  fife/fifers, 103, 189
  Octarara Coronet Band (Lancaster), 101
  "Old Iron City" fiddle, 104–05
  patriotic song sheets, 85, 102
  regimental bands, 100
  use in military life, 99t
"My Old Canteen" (poem), 279
Myers, P. and Martin, Jr., 23
The Mystery (newspaper), 39

"A Nation's Strength" (Emerson), 280
Native Americans (Lenni-Lanape people), 14t
Negley, James (general), 43, 195, 196
Neill, Albert B. (soldier), 175
New Castle, PA, 279
New Orleans (steamboat), 15
New York, 10, 121t, 290
New York Times, 9
Nicholson, John E. (sailor), 121
Norris and Sons Locomotive Works, 24
The North Star (newspaper), 39
Norton, Oliver Wilcox (soldier), 170

Oakford, Richard (colonel), 136
Obrien, Edward (colonel), 69
Ocker, Jonathan (drummer boy), 98
Octarara Coronet Band (Lancaster), 101
Ohio River, 15
oil industry, 19, 20
O'Kane, Dennis (colonel), 176
O'Laughlin, Michael (assassination conspirator), 270
Oldham, Robert (soldier), 146. *See also front cover*
100th Anniversary of the Civil War (1963), 7
150th Anniversary of the Civil War, 2011-2015, 7, 298
Orr, Robert L. (major), 267
O'Sullivan, Timothy (photographer), 158

PACW150 Committee, 298, 300
Parker, William (freedman), 38
Patterson, Francis E. (militia colonel), 52
Patterson, John (colonel), 236
Patterson, Robert A. A. (POW), 283
Patterson, Robert Emmett (colonel), 51, 88
Pemberton, John C. (CSA general), 231
Pendleton, George (vice-presidential candidate), 228
Penn, William, 14
"Penn's Woods," 13t
Pennsylvania
  answering the call to war, 9–10, 13, 43t, 53t, 55t, 66, 68
  battlefield monuments, 285t
  Beaver as governor, 241
  Camp William Penn, 208, 211–13, 214
  Census of 1860, 25
  Confederate incursions, 9–10, 143t, 243
  Curtin as governor, 41t, 42, 66, 135, 151, 250
  Geary as governor, 174
  Medal of Honor recipients, 263t
  Navy and Marine enlistments, 121t
  recruitment of colored regiments, 143t
  recruitment of colored soldiers and sailors, 208–10

INDEX

slaves/slavery, 25t, 29–30t
support of American Revolution, 13t
support of emancipation, 41
war deaths, 13, 13t, 22t, 147t, 156t, 175t, 255t
Pennsylvania Anti-Slavery Society, 26
Pennsylvania Civil War 150 Committee, 298, 300
Pennsylvania Civil War Road Show, 299
Pennsylvania Colored Troops, 210. *See also* African Americans, soldiers
Pennsylvania Episcopal Church, 187, 190, 191
Pennsylvania Heritage Foundation, 300
Pennsylvania Historical and Museum Commission (PHMC), 298, 300
Pennsylvania militia. *See also* artillery units; military units, Pennsylvania
   3rd Regiment Reserve Brigade. *See back cover flap*
   21st Pennsylvania, 45
   26th Pennsylvania Emergency Militia, 151, 203
   27th Pennsylvania Emergency Militia, 148, 149
   Allen Rifles (Allentown), 53t
   Duquesne Grays, 45
   Emergency Militia, 147t, 148, 149, 151
   Erie Regiment, 52
   "First Defenders," 11, 52, 53t
   Gray Reserves, 48
   Hannibal Guards, 139
   Logan Guards (Lewistown), 53t
   Mercer Blues, 48
   Militia of 1862, 135
   National Light Infantry (Pottsville), 53t
   Pumpkintown White Coats, 48
   Sarsfield Rifles (Philadelphia), 45
   Scott Legion (Philadelphia), 44
   uniforms and clothing, 70t
   Wayne Guards, 49
Pennsylvania Monument (Gettysburg), 285
Pennsylvania National Guard, 214
Pennsylvania Railroad, Locomotive No. 146, 24
Pennsylvania Veteran Volunteers, 230
Pennypacker, Galusha (colonel), 256, 258
The People's Contest: A Civil War Era Digital Archiving Project, 299
Petersburg, siege of, 209t, 240, 251t
Pettigrew, J. Johnston (CSA general), 180
Pettit, Frederick (soldier), 239
Philadelphia
   Citizen's Volunteer Hospital, 185
   Colored Youth Institute, 37
   Confederate threat to, 148, 150, 154
   Girard House, 114
   Great Central Fair, 216t, 222–23
   Lincoln funeral train, 272
   population of 1860, 25
   return of the battle flags, 250

Shiloh Baptist Church, 211
shipbuilding industry, 121t
steam locomotive manufacture, 24, 252
street scene (Chestnut Street), 14, 37
U.S. Christian Commission, 224–27
Volunteer Refreshment Saloons, 80
William Penn Hose Company, 303
Philadelphia Brigade, 175t, 201, 202
Phillips, David (soldier), 254. *See also front cover*
Phillips, Shadrack (soldier), 254. *See also front cover*
Phoenixville, PA, 54
photography. *See also* battlefield photography
   ambrotype process, 57-58
   battlefield use, 58t
   daguerreotype process, 56t
   importance as a communications tool, 10
   wet-plate process, 60t
Pierce, Tillie, 299
Pittsburgh
   abolition movement, 29
   military hospital, 185t
   population of 1860, 25
   Sanitary Fair, 216–20
   shipbuilding industry, 121t
   Sligo Iron Works, 23
   steamboat construction and river traffic, 15
Pittsburgh Sunday Visiter, 29
Pleasanton, A. J. (general), 146, 150
Porter, David Dixon (admiral), 126, 251t, 258
Portersville, PA, 237
Potter, Alonzo (reverend), 187
Potter County, 25
Powell, James (missionary), 226
prisoners of war
   Battle of Antietam, 136
   Battle of Gettysburg, 181
   Christian Commission and, 225t
   escape from Libby Prison, 195, 249
   GAR medals, 283
   incarceration in Pennsylvania, 182
   Kilpatrick-Dahlgren expedition, 237, 239
   prisoner exchanges, 66, 248t
   treatment of, 183
prisons
   Andersonville (GA), 248t, 249
   Florence, SC, 249
   Libby Prison (Richmond), 66, 195, 249
   Ohio State Prison, 188
   Western Penitentiary (Allegheny County), 188, 189
Probasco, James (private), 71
Prussia/Prussian immigrants, 94
Purcell, Hiram W. (sergeant), 130
Pyle, Enoch (private), 262

Quakers (Religious Society of Friends), 14, 22

racial discrimination, 7. *See also* African Americans
   exclusion from anniversary celebrations, 7, 287t
   exclusion from officer ranks, 37
   exclusion from Pittsburgh Sanitary Fair, 221
   soldier treatment and pay, 211
railroads. *See* transportation
Randolph, W. A. (musician), 103
Raub, Jacob F. (doctor), 265
Read, Louis Wentag (doctor), 245
Reading, PA, 11, 148
reenactments, 298
religion and churches
   Episcopal Hospital (Philadelphia), 190, 191
   military chaplains, 96–97, 211
   U.S. Christian Commission, 224–27
Religious Society of Friends. *See* Quakers
Renovo, PA. *See front cover flap*
Reynolds, John F. (general), 147, 156, 201
Richards Civil War Era Center, 299
Richmond, VA
   failure to capture, 130
   Kilpatrick-Dahlgren expedition, 237, 239
   Libby Prison, 66, 195, 237, 249
   surrender of, 251t, 260
Ricketts, Bruce (lieutenant), 165
right to vote, 37, 228, 229
Rihl, William (corporal), 147t
Rippey, Oliver Hazzard (colonel), 128
Roberts, Richard P. (colonel), 162
Robinson, Samuel (soldier), 255
Rodman, Thomas Jackson (major), 111
Rogers, Alexander (sergeant), 106
Rogers, John D. (captain), 202
Root, George F. (songwriter), 99
Rose, Thomas (colonel), 195
Ross, Anna M. (nurse), 285
Rothrock, Ustick (bugler), 254. *See also front cover*
Ruhe, William (veteran), 282
Rush, Richard (colonel), 63–64
Ryan, James (major), 269

Saeger, Charles (sergeant major), 75
"Sallie" (dog, mascot), 79
Sample, Bill (soldier), 271t
Sanders, Charles W. (chaplain), 96
Sanitary Fair, Pittsburgh, 216–20
Sankey, James Power (soldier), 291
Saxton, Joseph (photographer), 56t
Saxton, Rufus (Union general), 36

RIGHT

Tinclad on Patrol Seventy-six small river steamers were converted for use as light-draft gunboats along the Mississippi River and its tributaries. Not as large or heavily armored as the better-known "ironclads," these "tinclads" could move more rapidly to patrol waterways. The Argosy, built in Monongahela, Washington County, in 1862 as a commercial vessel, was acquired by the U.S. Navy in 1863 and fitted for service with cannon and iron plate armor.
Ken Turner Collection.

Schall, Edwin (officer), 248
Schimmelfennig, Alexander (general), 160
Schoonmaker, James M. (colonel), 268
Schuylkill Arsenal (Philadelphia), 109t, 115
Schuylkill Haven, PA, 21
Scott, George Washington (CSA lt. colonel), 232
Scott, John (US congressman), 232
Scott, Winfield (general), 44
secession of southern states, 40
Secrist, Asbury (soldier), 255
Seeman, Daniel (drummer boy), 99
Seidentopf, Conrad (sergeant), 94
Sewickley, PA, 214
Shafer, Jacob (lieutenant), 204
Shambaugh, Charles (corporal), 268
Sharp, Thomas Robinson (CSA captain), 234
Shelow, John W. (private), 240
Shenkel, Jacob (soldier), 188–89
Sheridan, Phillip (general), 248, 259
Sherman, William T. (general), 209t, 251t
Shields, David (lieutenant), 142
Shields, William (soldier), 142
Shippensburg, PA, 147t
Sickles, Daniel (general), 162
Sirwell, William (colonel), 139
slaves/slavery
   abolition movement, 29–30t
   Act of Gradual Abolition (1780), 25
   Carlisle riot of 1847, 22
   Christiana riot of 1851, 38
   documented escapes, 29, 31
   Emancipation Proclamation, 41t, 141, 143t, 210t
   forgotten as cause of war, 7, 286
   Fugitive Slave Act of 1850, 26
   Underground Railroad, 34–36
Slemmons, Joseph (private), 61
Sligo Iron Works (Lyon, Shorb & Company, Pittsburgh), 23
Small, Cassandra, 151

Smith, William F. (general), 147
Smyth, Thomas A. (general), 90
Soldiers National Cemetery, 8
Soles, Jacob (private), 271
Solfield, Alfred (captain), 157
Spangler, William (veteran), 290
Spence, Matthew (soldier), 74
Spera, Weidner (major), 248
Stanton, Edwin Lamson, 42
Stanton, Edwin M. (Secretary of War), 213
Stanton, Edwin McMasters (secretary of war), 39, 42
Staples, John Summerfield (soldier), 237
steamboats. *See* transportation
Stevens, Thaddeus (politician), 41t
Stewart, Alexander (chaplain), 97
Stewart, Henry (army enlistee), 62
Still, William (Father of the Underground Railroad), 34–35
Stoddard, Robert (soldier), 260
street scenes, cities and towns
   Carlisle, PA, 22, 153
   Chestnut Street (Philadelphia), 14, 37
   Harrisburg, PA, 272
   Mercer, PA, 17
   Philadelphia, 44, 80, 114
   Pittsburgh, 220
   Washington, DC, 219, 224–25
Stroudsburg, PA, 237
Stuart, J. E. B. (CSA general), 51, 53, 147t, 153
supplies. *See* equipment and supplies
Susquehanna River, 147t, 148
Sweitzer, J. Bowman (colonel), 65
Swisshelm, Jane Grey Cannon (abolitionist), 29
System of Infantry Tactics (Casey), 81

Templeton, Aaron. *See* back cover
Tennessee
   Battle of Stones River, 127t, 140, 143t, 197
   Chattanooga Campaign, 197–99

   military actions, 209t
Tepe, Marie ("French Mary"), 270
Thomas, Hampton (lt. colonel), 264
Thompson, James (private), 201
Thorn, Peter and Elizabeth, 165
Titusville, PA, 19
Torrance, Eli (chaplain), 67
Town, Gustavus (colonel), 145
transportation
   burning the Columbia-Wrightsville Bridge, 148
   Confederate military railroad, 234
   conversion of river steamers to gunboats, 311
   Erie Extension Canal, 12
   Hanover bridge, 152
   Lincoln funeral train, 272
   steam locomotive manufacture, 24, 252
   steamboat construction and river traffic, 15, 252
   U.S. Military Railroad (USMRR), 116–18, 152-53
Trimble, Isaac Ridgeway (CSA general), 180
Tschudy, Martin (lt. colonel), 176
Tubman, Harriet (nee Araminta Ross), 36
Tucker, Andrew G. (adjutant), 159
Tudhope, James (private), 167
Turner, T. P. (CSA major), 237
Turtle Creek, PA, 271

Underground Railroad, 10, 26, 34, 36
The Underground Railroad (Still), 34–35
uniforms and clothing. *See also* equipment and supplies
   cavalry short coat, 73
   Chasseur au Pied uniform, 75
   Chasseur de Vincennes uniform, 167
   early militia uniforms, 44–45, 61, 70–75
   frock coat, 62, 72
   Grand Army of the Republic (GAR), 278
   kepi (cap), 258
   manufacture, 109t, 114–15
   musician's frock coat, 103

INDEX

prisoners of war, 183
"Quaker Hat," 52
short shell coat, 71, 72
swallowtail coatee, 48–49
uniform buttons, 73
Zouave fez and uniforms, 74, 246
Union Army. *See also* Army of the Potomac; artillery units; U.S. Colored Troops
    army structure and components, 62t
    creation of Medal of Honor, 263t
    draftees and hired substitutes, 237
    insignia and badges, 200–207
    First Army Corps, 93, 156t, 160, 201t
    Second Army Corps, 90, 177, 180, 201t
    Third Army Corps, 163, 202t, 238, 269
    Fifth Army Corps, 96, 155, 202t, 253
    Sixth Army Corps, 147, 205t
    Ninth Army Corps, 96, 194t, 251t
    Eleventh Army Corps, 156t, 160, 206t
    Twelfth Army Corps, 174, 198, 207t
    Fourteenth Army Corps, 195, 197
    Seventeenth Army Corps, 270
    Twentieth Army Corps, 241
    Twenty-fourth Army Corps (Red Heart Corps), 258, 260–61
    2nd U.S. Artillery, 54
    Veteran Reserve Corps, 230t
Union Ex-Prisoners of War Organization, 283
Union Refreshment Saloon, Philadelphia, 80
United Confederate Veterans (UCV), 292
Unversagt, William (soldier), 249
U.S. Army. *See* Union Army
U.S. Army Corps of Engineers, 110
U.S. Army War College, 50
U.S. Christian Commission, 224–27
U.S. Colored Troops. *See also* African Americans, soldiers
    creation of U.S. Colored Troops, 133
    6th U.S. Colored Troops, 210, 211, 266–67
    11th U.S. Colored Troops, 212
    22nd U.S. Colored Troops, 214
    25th U.S. Colored Troops, 208
    32nd U.S. Colored Troops, 214, 280
    104th U.S. Colored Troops, 39
U.S. Constitution, 15th amendment, 37
U.S. Marine Corps (USMC), 120t
U.S. Military Railroad (USMRR), 116–18, 152–53
U.S. Military Telegraph Corps, 279
U.S. National Park Service, 284t
U.S. Navy (USN), 121t, 209, 252, 263t, 311
U.S. Sanitary Commission, 209t, 216–20
USS *Argosy* (river gunboat), 311
USS *Cricket* No. 6 (steamboat), 253
USS *Hartford*, 263
USS *Michigan*, 121, 122
USS *Pawnee*, 124
USS *Silver Lake*, 121
USS *Vandalia*, 126
USS *Wolverine*, 122

Van Lew, Elizabeth (Union spy), 239
Vera, J. Adams (captain), 60
Vicksburg, siege of, 106, 143t, 146t, 147t
Victoria, TX, 262
View along the Allegheny River Near Aspinwall, Pa. (Wall, 1867), 18
Vincent, Blanche Strong (child), 169
Vincent, Elizabeth Carter (wife), 169
Vincent, Strong (colonel), 169, 170, 299
Volunteer Army, 62t
vote/voting rights, 37, 228, 229

Wade, Mary Virginia ("Jennie"), 178
Wagner, Louis (colonel), 211
Wales/Welsh immigrants, 95
Wallace, Maggie (from New Castle). *See front cover*
William Penn Hose Company, 303
Walworth, James (soldier), 74
Wampum Belt of Peace (1682), 14
war memorials. *See also* medals and decorations
    69th Pennsylvania (Irish Brigade), 176
    100th Regiment ("Roundheads"), 283. *See also back cover flap*
    143rd Pennsylvania, 159
    GAR remembrances, 283
    Gettysburg battlefield commemoration, 285t
    honoring the dog "Sallie," 79
    Pennsylvania Monument (Gettysburg), 285
Ward, Eliab (doctor), 80
Warfield, Carneal (CSA lieutenant), 183
Warren, Gouverneur (CSA general), 240
Warren, PA/Warren County, 133, 241
Washington County, 168, 214, 252, 283, 287
Watson, John (soldier), 230
Waynesburg, PA, 67
weapons and ammunition. *See also* artillery
    Allegheny Arsenal (Pittsburgh), 109t, 112–13
    breech-loading carbine, 63
    Brown's Pike, 32
    cavalry lances, 63
    Enfield rifle, 260
    flintlock musket, 46, 61
    Haupt's torpedo (explosives), 119
    M1842 musket, 71
    marksmanship medal, 48
    presentation swords, 86–87, 180
    Sharps rifles. *See back cover flap*
    swords, sabers and pistols, 62, 72–73, 136, 169
Weaver, John (soldier), 271t
Weaver, Peter (photographer), 189
Weaver, Samuel, 8
Webb, Alexander (general), 175t
Wentz, Frank, H. (sergeant), 201
West Chester Military Academy, 216
Westmoreland County, 48, 79, 207
Wheeler, John Hill (slave owner), 26
Whiskey Rebellion of 1795, 51t
White, Adison (soldier), 194
White, Elijah V. (colonel), 150
White, Plympton A. (lieutenant), 249
White Hall, PA, 185t
Wilcox, Strong Vincent (child), 170
Wilcox, Vincent (lt. colonel), 136
William Penn Hose Company (Philadelphia), 303
William Wilson & Sons, 263t
Williamson, Passmore (abolitionist), 27
Wilmot, David (politician), 41t
Wilson, Ashton (child), 198
Wilson, Henry W. (officer), 198
Wilson, Woodrow (president), 7, 286
Wilson family (Mary E., Sue, and Henry), 58
Wister, Langhorne (colonel), 157
women. *See also* families
    abolition and women's rights, 29, 212, 229
    cartridge rollers, 112–13
    casualties of war, 179
    clothing of the day, 21
    domestic and artistic endeavors, 16
    escape from slavery, 36
    GAR membership, 284
    hospital care providers, 191
    Lincoln assassination, 276
    mental illness, 22
    support of war effort, 10, 53, 216t, 219, 221, 222, 242
    war service, 239, 270, 285
    war-industry employment, 109t, 114
Women's Relief Corps (GAR), 284
Woodward, Orpheus S. (colonel), 236
Wren, James (militia captain), 52
Wrightsville, PA, 147t, 148

Yoder, Seneca (soldier), 68
York, PA, 147, 148, 151, 185t
Young, Samuel Baldwin Marks (soldier), 50
Young Men's Christian Association (YMCA), 225t

Zeilin, Jacob (colonel), 120
Zentmyer, David (adjutant), 136
Zentmyer, Frank (captain), 136
Zinn, Henry (colonel), 138
Zook, Samuel Kosciuszko (officer), 163